D1612661

TESTIMONIALS

"Thank you for writing *The Big Solution*. Thank you for being a deep thinker. Thank you for having the vision and the thinking we need. I am a big fan of engineering things. The thinking to solve the major issues by some of the brightest people I know—at Google and Apple—they all want to solve these world problems. Bringing this level of thinking to the larger issues, thank you for doing that."

—Jack Canfield
author of Chicken Soup for the Soul, *which has sold hundreds of millions of copies*

"Finally—a book for those of us seeking to understand the world of finance and how to better our current situation but lacking a degree in economics. *The Big Solution*'s faux round-table style is clear, informative, and actually fun to read. I now understand how banks affect everything and how a revamped strategy could work more to our collective advantage. Jensen is an engaging voice and a great teacher, especially for those of us who felt these financial concepts were 'above' us."

—Alycia Ripley
Penguin Publishing Group author

"The world needs more provocative free thinkers. Jarl Jensen obliges—a sincere effort to better the world!"

—Simon Nynens
CEO at NJII and Harvard Business School alum

"*The Big Solution* is an invitation to understand how the economy works by looking at nature. It teaches in conversational style the physical basis of economic concepts (wealth, loans, debt, banking) and focuses on money and how we can change the flow of money for the benefit of all of us. Key is the idea that when banks loan out money, they are loaning out work that someone did and someone else will do. Banks are enabling work creation. I recommend *The Big Solution* very highly because it puts the science in economics."

—Adrian Bejan
J. A. Jones distinguished professor. He is quoted in the book, but most importantly he has been writing papers about a very similar topic. In his book Freedom and Evolution: Hierarchy in Nature, Society and Science, *and his research article,* "Energy Theory of Periodic Economic Growth," *very similar perspectives are deployed.*

"Jensen has written a comprehensive tale of how the financial system centered around the banking system has failed to create a sustainable society where everybody has a chance to aspire to a productive and meaningful life. Instead we have created a system where the rich get richer and the poor can't possibly catch up. He offers a comprehensive way out to an exciting society where everyone has the opportunity to live a fulfilling life."

—Richard Cassata
Wall Street bond insurance expert

"*The Big Solution*, the Wolfe Trilogy Book 3, makes it clear that

'There's something very wrong with this country.'

"Author Jarl Jensen has the courage to place before the public a novel that is not only searingly written as a story, but also points out the flaws in our current society. Jarl is an inventor of multiple patented medical devices, and as a successful businessman and executive for several companies, he now turns his creativity to writing this astonishingly fine book of ideas that could change our world. *The Big Solution* is the third volume of the Wolfe Trilogy and carries the hottest sparks!

"To understand Jarl's stance, the trilogy should be consumed in toto. Before this Book 3 opens, he has stated, 'A master storyteller is able to tell a story to an elephant loaded with new ideas and change the beliefs and abilities of the elephant. Educated and wiser, the elephant can now simply stand up and break its rope. This is such a story. It is a story for you; it is a story for humanity; it is a story that will break our collective rope so we can stand up and be free.'

"Keenly aware that the best way is to point out our flaws and focus on repair, Jarl continues to tell a story that underlines all of his concepts. Jarl's synopsis is a fine road map to continue his bristling series: 'Justin Wolfe and his crew have to overcome academia's fake science, polarized political beliefs, an entrenched financial system, and the assertion that growth is progress. To make things appealing and interesting, the heroes don't just put together a bunch of footnotes, charts, and economic papers—they set out to solve the problems of the world in simple language using anecdotes and analogies that anyone can understand. Justin, Evan, Connie, and Laz all take turns making their unique points of view known, debating the pros and cons, all while bringing their colorful personalities into the mix, creating a hilarious atmosphere, and delivering a big solution.' A quote from Justin Wolfe: 'Our world is remarkably automated. Resources remain in abundant supply. Life should be so simple. So prosperous. And yet the vast majority of people still aren't making a decent living. America's promise of equal opportunity, a sustainable future, and liberty for all has become a distant memory. But I, Justin Wolfe, have a plan to finally change the dynamics that have been holding this country and the world back. Imagine a simple idea that could change the world forever. An idea that will deliver us from this economic train wreck and prevent further hardships from falling on the shoulders of future generations. Shouldn't we get started?'

"Jarl Jensen, through the voice of his titular Justin Wolfe, bangs the drum for waking up and paying attention to our world as we find it and, in doing so, revs up the changes that MUST happen! Rarely has an author demonstrated that an exceptional story can become a viable and nearly irresistible force for change! Highly recommended."

—Grady Harp
Top 10 Amazon reviewer

"I've known Jarl a long time. He's always been laser focused on things he wishes to accomplish. So it's no surprise that he is a master storyteller, an excellent writer, and a top idea man as we push through the twenty-first century. *The Big Solution* is a must-read."

—John Linholm
author of The Last of the Third

"Have you ever wondered what the purpose of life is? You certainly know that your decisions create your life experience. Yet, there are things outside of your control that are part of the society you live in, right? Are there societal systems that are in the way of your happiness?

"In Jensen's book, he explains what is not quite right in society and what you can do about it. Once you see society's weaknesses and they are revealed, you will be delighted to find there are massive opportunities waiting for you. Imagine awakening to your life purpose and reigniting entrepreneurship and knowing you can build the world you want to live in!

"Truly, you and I get to make the rules for how society functions. Everything we do must put people first so that the path for humanity is a sustainable, prosperous, and peaceful one!"

—Terri Levine
PhD and chief heart-repreneur, business strategist, best-selling author of dozens of titles, and keynote speaker

"Without a doubt, this is Jarl Jensen's best book. A brilliant and timeless look at global economics and what is needed for changing things for the better. Jensen puts things in such a way that the reader doesn't need an economics degree to absorb and understand how the banks, not politics, control our lives, and what can be done going forward. I loved the book and your style."

—Louis Romano
successful author of many crime books

"Amazing book with horrible revelations. I had nightmares and woke up with sweat on my forehead. But unfortunately it was not just a dream. The book describes our reality. I started reading the book with an open mind. Along the way I put on my tinfoil hat as I thought of conspiracy theories. But as I continued reading and gnawed my way through the book, I put my hat aside and realized, clearly, this is not a conspiracy theory! This isn't even a twisted fantasy. This is the truth. And I probably will not survive to see the solution. But I have children and grandchildren. So let's get started."

—Lars Berndorff
Danish citizen and rock star

"*The Big Solution* exposes the universal inefficiencies of banking and a debt-driven world. You will walk away from this book with an entirely refreshing perspective of money and how we can transition to an economy that works for rich and poor."

—Bruce Debon
managing director at Diversified Security Solutions, Inc.

"*The Big Solution* is the third installment of the Wolfe Trilogy, a series of books authored by Jarl Jensen dealing with the world economy, using microeconomics to explain his theories. Like his prior efforts, this work criticizes the reliance of the modern world economy on debt and its dependency on banks. In all of his work, Jensen uses his education and experience as an engineer to give a fresh look at economic reality.

"*The Big Solution* reintroduces the reader to theories raised in his prior works but also touches upon the social premises raised in *Walden* by Henry Thoreau, *Walden Two* by B. F. Skinner, and to a degree by George Orwell in *Animal Farm* and *1984*.

"In creating folksy story lines, Jensen exposes the flaws in our economic system and opines that the track we are on will lead into the abyss. He asserts that by creating more and more debt in order to 'grow' the economy, we will ultimately be consumed by it.

"Placing the reader alternately in a commune or the natural environment of the 'woodsperson,' Jensen demonstrates how man has emerged from a self-sufficient society to one totally dependent on others to achieve 'success.' Moneylenders act as the pied pipers for generation after generation of humans seeking wealth and prosperity, leading, however, to a never-ending accumulation of personal, corporate, and government debt.

"Jensen does not directly blame banks or government for the precarious financial condition in which we find ourselves. He does, however, blame the system that he calls 'Bankism.' To support his "Ticking Time Bomb" prophecy, Jensen provides historical examples of the failure of Bankism. In the twentieth century, the Great Depression and a series of twenty-first-century recessions produced great human duress as well as financial collapse for many long-standing businesses. In each case, there was a government bailout of banks or reorganization of the 'system.' There are older historical events that demonstrate the boom-and-bust nature of Bankism (e.g., the Hudson Bay bubble and the Tulip bubble in Holland). These 'busts' are the inevitable results of a flawed system.

"Fortunately, Jensen has advanced a solution to this conundrum. Science! He posits that the measure of the economy is not the health of the banking system but the 'measure of desirable human outcomes.'

"This theory pervades *The Big Solution*. It is thought-provoking and provides a road map away from the pathway Bankism has created. Give it a read; you will be pleasantly surprised."

—Alfred F. Maurice
top-rated attorney selected to the NJ Super Lawyers

"People situated on the 'poor' end of the economic spectrum are burdened with a set of socioeconomic and psychological problems that differ from those plaguing people on the 'rich' end. These disparities have been part of every type of economic system since bartering; however, none of these has provided an all-encompassing solution including our overriding human nature and/or cultural behaviors. That being said, given that the course of human existence has vaulted humanity forward on many issues such as world hunger, poverty, and access to information, we must confront the shortcomings of the economic systems we have installed in order to improve our lot and avoid upheaval.

"In *The Big Solution*, Jarl Jensen has clearly identified the players on today's national and global chessboard, crediting them with both the beneficial and harmful influences they are causing. Instead of tossing the baby out with the bath water, Jensen proposes a logical step forward to retain the former while catalyzing elimination of the latter. His breakthrough is to call the baby by its name (Bankism) and to show how it shackles both capitalistic and socialistic/communistic societies. He builds a farsighted economic model that values incentives and competition while prioritizing individual and global well-being.

"Jensen's thesis is laid out in a narrative form that is as relatable to the uninformed reader as it is to the schooled economist. It is highly recommended that voters as well as policy makers expose themselves to its pages in order that the next chapter in human history will exclude disruptions such as economic turbulence, climate deterioration, or wars. Although it has been foretold that we would have to toil for our daily bread, it was not stated that our work would be undervalued. Having eaten from the Tree of Knowledge, perhaps we should also taste of the Tree of Life."

—Dr. Moshe Davidovitch
DDS, MMSc, and Harvard Medical School alum

"*The Big Solution* exposes the universal inefficiencies of banking and a debt-driven world. You will walk away from this book with an entirely refreshing perspective of money and how we can transition to an economy that works for rich and poor."

—Bruce Debon

managing director at Diversified Security Solutions, Inc.

"Without giving away the entire plan, *The Big Solution* is a worthy attempt—perhaps one of the best attempts I've read to date—at providing the base blueprints for a more equitable future in America (and ostensibly the world) where hard work and entrepreneurialism is indeed rewarded, but where it does not wind up in the hands of those who simply shift money and debt around without producing some sort of measurable product. Also inherent in the plan is a way to ensure that nobody goes hungry, gets sick, or loses a home simply because of being trapped beneath a wealth-disparity-imposed pile of debt. Implementation would also not require a Robin Hood–style robbery of the rich to prop up the poor. Lastly, the Big Solution would begin to pave the way for addressing global climate issues in a manner where remediation would be profitable and able to unite the world as a truly global economy. Sound too lofty to work? Good, then you're just like me—a healthy skeptic who welcomes the question marks that pop up over my head as I read.

"To help with the necessary role of devil's advocates, Jarl employs conversations between people who are basically characterizations of differing schools of thought—financially, socially, and politically. I use the plural here because there are many divergent viewpoints regarding not only the Big Solution itself, but how we got to the place where it became necessary to develop such an enterprising new idea, and everyone's perspective must be taken into account when proposing something as preposterous as a one-size-fits-all solution. The banter feels unscripted and jovial (if not meandering at times); however, it does indeed help to pro-actively address the many 'buts' that inevitably crop up and would invariably bring the reading experience to a halt if not addressed in situ.

"Of course (and not specifically covered in the book, but alluded to toward the end), implementing any sort of plan of this magnitude would require cementing a few bedrock pillars to accomplish. First is education, which would open people's minds to the idea that change coming in the form of a seismic shift doesn't necessarily have to be painful despite the learning curve. However, in the age of 'fake news' and unchecked internet propaganda, solid education cemented through logic and critical thinking is a tough sell for people who live in a world of cognitive dissonance where it's a badge of honor to refuse to accept that something they believe might actually be wrong, despite evidence to the contrary.

"Second would be bold, progressive leadership in politics, and I use this term without any political party connotation. These leaders would need to be stalwart visionaries who are willing to do what's right for the good of the country—and mankind as a whole—despite possible negative consequences on his or her reelection bids or ill feelings from political party members. Unfortunately, we're in extremely short supply of these at present on both sides of the aisle, and creating an environment where these sorts of legislators can flourish would require many of them voting against their own personal best interests.

"Last would be colossal infrastructure improvements and advances, which would be necessary to enable everyone to participate in a meaningful way, with enough security in place to ensure against bad operatives. Remember—not everyone in this country's got a computer, or a bank card, or even a bank account. Of course, executing this step is inextricably linked to the first two points above.

"The one thing this book does not definitively address, however—and would probably take a new book to even begin to tackle—is the innate human lust for power, driven by the allure of political might and irrational religious zealotry, that will still exist and inevitably creep into the system on some level even when everyone's financially sound. On the other hand, will the innate structure of the Big Solution give enough power to those who adopt it to effectively render these sorts of bad actors irrelevant on the world stage?

"In conclusion, is *The Big Solution* a one-shot panacea for the world's financial ailments? Certainly not. But it's loaded with good, sound ideas that are worthy of consideration, well developed and thoughtfully assembled. Reading it also gave me a distinct feeling of hope for the future—that there are people out there who are actually working hard not just for themselves, but for a world that their children and grandchildren may inherit with pride. As with any massive undertaking, it's all got to start with moving that first shovel of dirt, and if there is one country in this world that desperately needs to start leading the global community again by example and striding toward a brighter future for all, it's the United States of America. Do we have the courage to attempt it?"

—Eric Pseia
business operations manager

THE
BIG
SOLUTION

JARL JENSEN

THE
BIG
SOLUTION

DEACTIVATING THE TICKING TIMEBOMB OF TODAY'S ECONOMY

ForbesBooks

Copyright © 2021 by Jarl Jensen

All rights reserved. No part of this book may be used or reproduced in any manner whatsoever without prior written consent of the author, except as provided by the United States of America copyright law.

Published by ForbesBooks, Charleston, South Carolina.
Member of Advantage Media Group.

ForbesBooks is a registered trademark, and the ForbesBooks colophon is a trademark of Forbes Media, LLC.

Printed in the United States of America.

10 9 8 7 6 5 4 3 2 1

ISBN: 978-1-950863-89-1
LCCN: 2021908332

Cover design by David Taylor.
Layout design by Mary Hamilton.

This custom publication is intended to provide accurate information and the opinions of the author in regard to the subject matter covered. It is sold with the understanding that the publisher, Advantage|ForbesBooks, is not engaged in rendering legal, financial, or professional services of any kind. If legal advice or other expert assistance is required, the reader is advised to seek the services of a competent professional.

Advantage Media Group is proud to be a part of the Tree Neutral® program. Tree Neutral offsets the number of trees consumed in the production and printing of this book by taking proactive steps such as planting trees in direct proportion to the number of trees used to print books. To learn more about Tree Neutral, please visit **www.treeneutral.com**.

Since 1917, Forbes has remained steadfast in its mission to serve as the defining voice of entrepreneurial capitalism. ForbesBooks, launched in 2016 through a partnership with Advantage Media Group, furthers that aim by helping business and thought leaders bring their stories, passion, and knowledge to the forefront in custom books. Opinions expressed by ForbesBooks authors are their own. To be considered for publication, please visit **www.forbesbooks.com**.

This book was written with the best of intentions for my wife, Susan, the future for my kids, Grace, Hugh, and Finn, and the future for all of us. The world is in crisis, but there is a solution that nobody is talking about. Debt is running amok on global, national, corporate, and personal levels. Governing has become impossible, as spending has to be rationalized for even the most basic human purposes. Corporations have to lay off staff to compete in a global economy. People have to cut back their spending to pay for school debt, mortgages, and credit card bills. Trade used to build peace, but now we talk about trade wars. The United States has been in one war or another with no end in sight. Something is fundamentally wrong with the system, and this book exposes the reader to both the problem and the solution.

CONTENTS

INTRODUCTION

*Storytelling is the very soul of humankind
made plain for all to experience.*

—JOHN APPIUS QUILL, Quoteslyfe.com

They say that every person tells a story about himself to himself. What story is humanity collectively telling itself? People's entire lives are built by their personal story. In this same way, humanity's collective story has built our world.

For example, an elephant can be controlled by a thin rope because the story it tells itself is that it can't break it. It tells this story because, when the elephant was a baby, that same rope kept it from getting up and running around. Does humanity have such a rope on itself? It does, but it's more like a noose, and it keeps getting tighter every year. Time is running out for humanity, and you, the reader.

Time is running out for humanity, and you, the reader.

Storytelling is the most powerful way to put ideas into the world.

—ROBERT MCKEE

A master storyteller is able to tell a story to an elephant loaded with new ideas and change the beliefs and abilities of the elephant. Educated and wiser, the elephant can now simply stand up and break its rope. This is such a story. It is a story for you; it is a story for humanity; it is a story that will break our collective rope so we can stand up and be free.

CHAPTER ONE

A LIFE IN THE WOODS

There is something wrong with our world, something
fundamentally and basically wrong.

—MARTIN LUTHER KING JR., Rediscovering Lost Values

Picture yourself as a woodsperson. You can drop yourself into any era you like, but imagine you have a little property somewhere in the woods where woodspeople typically reside.

There's a little shack. Or, hey, maybe a fine upscale cabin—this is your fantasy, not mine. Either way, there's a clearing with enough sunlight to allow you to grow crops, maybe a greenhouse, and definitely an outhouse.

You and your woods-spouse and woods-children have fashioned an elaborate rig that allows you to harvest rainwater as it trickles down through the forest canopy high above. So you have plenty of drinking water for you, your pets, and your livestock.

Yes, in this fantasy, you raise your own animals. Feel free to choose any animals you like. I'm fond of chickens for their general utility as food producers and being food themselves. Plus, they're hilarious, the way they run around pecking at things and squawking.

What water you don't drink, you feed into your remarkably sophisticated channel irrigation system, which keeps your crops thriving. And in fact, your elaborate rig is so effective that, unlike some outdoorsy types, you're always well showered.

You've got a barn where you can do your hide tanning and fish skinning and carcass cleaning, just like any other self-respecting member of your trade. Speaking of which, you've compiled a proper arsenal of the things you need in order to fish and hunt game.

Given that I am a tech billionaire and NFL franchise owner who is nothing even remotely similar to a woodsman, I have exhausted my knowledge of what other things a woods-family might have to keep themselves going. Furs come to mind. You probably have lots of furs.

In any case, here we have a picture of what you might call an ideal life and what my writing collaborator, Evan White, would certainly call a natural life. Either way, as long as you're okay with the draftiness of the cabin and the spiders the size of small puppies, you want for nothing. Sure, you have to work for what you need, but at least you can rest easy. And my guess is, after the days you have, you sleep amazingly well. You can rest easy because you know that if you ever need something, you can always go out and get it.

Entertainment? The world is your entertainment. You share an uncommon bond with your family. Plus, someone you love probably plays the guitar or banjo.

Speaking of love, it's all around you.

A sense of self? You're a woodsperson, for goodness' sake! You're amazing!

Food? Well, you had that nice harvest and did all that canning, jarring, and storing, or you could go out and kill something.

Water? You had to put a lot of work into setting up a system to capture rainwater for drinking, washing, and irrigation, but now that the work is done, everything you need literally falls from the sky. And because of that free-flowing water, everything else you need in life is accessible.

This, my friends, is an example of a natural economy, where you can simply live in the woods, and the water and sunlight provided by nature are simply there. And because they're there, you can grow crops and make a life for yourself.

Of course, we know that this is not the case for our current lives. We have to have money to make ends meet, to pay our rent or mortgage, our food bills, our car lease, and so on. Natural life in the modern world isn't possible because living in the modern world takes money, and money doesn't behave like sunlight or rain. Natural life for people in the United States is no longer possible.

Unfortunately, the modern economy creates something far different from a natural life. In the modern economy, you either have to borrow from a bank or earn money that someone else owes to a bank. And not everyone's ability to borrow or earn is equal. Your drinking and farming water isn't appearing naturally like rain. In fact, in the real world, water costs money. As for collecting rain from the street gutters, good luck with that.

Bottom line: it used to be that survival was a matter of access to water, personal resourcefulness, and a willingness to work hard for what you needed. Now we need money. In the United States of America, you can't do anything you need to do unless you have access to money.

This might be a good point to address a counterargument I'm anticipating from my more discerning readers like you. You might say, "Wait a minute, J-Dub. Didn't you just say that I could have a good life in the woods, and all I need is water? I mean, what's preventing me from just unplugging from the grid and going out to be a woodsperson?"

Good point, my more discerning reader. I wish you well. Just know that it'll be a ton of work to set all that up. Also, you're almost certain to have to pay property taxes, so you'll still need a means to earn money. The government doesn't let you pay in furs or chicken eggs, no matter how much you may want to. Maybe you could sell those furs or eggs in person. This will necessitate transportation to a physical location, both of which tend to cost money. Or maybe you could sell them online, which would require an internet connection and online presence, both of which cost money. Also, to help make for a better life at the shack, you might want to buy some fertilizer. Or a water filter. Or maybe some medicine. The list goes on …

Point is, you'll need money, no matter how woodsy you get. You might be saying, "Well, obviously we're not cavemen anymore, so a natural life isn't possible." If you're saying this, then you're missing the point. Here's the point: why is it that with all the technology and other advancements that show up with each new day, life doesn't seem any easier? We have access to smartphones and same-day delivery; we have self-driving cars and robots to do certain jobs; we have crafted this whole world around the notion of ease of access and convenience.

And as a final point of explanation about my woodsman story— or what some might call overexplanation (hey, I do like to get my point across, especially when it has implications for the whole book)—life today is all about extremes. For instance, one person can find himself starving and homeless in a back alley of a restaurant that serves steak dinners for $150 to hundreds of patrons every day, all of whom care nothing about the poor person just a few feet away. Contrast this to the woodsman, who seems far more likely to take care of his neighbor who fell upon misfortune. After all, it makes sense to do unto your neighbors as you would like them to do unto you. The woodsman could make up the additional food by hunting a little more and sowing a few more seeds. If he needs more room to house his neighbor, he just gathers the materials and builds. Maybe the neighbor can sleep in the barn until the extra bedroom is finished.

In any case, he also helps his neighbor restore his lot from the misfortune. And in the end, they're both better off, because if misfortune ever came the woodsman's way, his neighbor would be there for him, ready to repay the favor. In essence, while it might look noble and selfless, it was actually entirely selfish behavior that led the woodsman to take care of his neighbor. Contrast this with the homeless person behind the restaurant. Any effort to help the person is purely benevolent. Expecting the help to be returned someday is wishful thinking.

All told, a natural life leads to abundance, while the modern world has ingrained a sense of perpetual scarcity. This book explores why, gets to the root cause, and then provides a solution—or a Big Solution, as it were.

Anyway, I'm getting slightly ahead of myself. Let's back up and address that first question: why doesn't life seem any easier than it was out there as a woodsman in nature?

There's Something Very Wrong with This Country

Yes, I'm aware that writing about how there's something very wrong with this country makes me sound like a younger and slightly less handsome Bernie Sanders. So let's all take a moment to reflect on the surreal nature of a billionaire drawing comparisons between himself and Bernie Sanders in section number two of his book. It's a strange position to find oneself in. But here we are.

Before I write anything else, let me just differentiate myself from Senator Sanders by making this solemn promise: I'm going to bend into a pretzel to avoid any prolonged ranting in the pages of this book. Yes, there's something very wrong with this country—and I believe it's all connected to a singular (albeit shiftily complicated) culprit—but just because there's something very wrong, that doesn't mean you need another egghead yelling at you about it.

Evan says that any good book should present its thesis up front. Okay, fine, Evan. Let's do that. But to do that, I'm first going to have to tell you what my thesis isn't. This is true because every time I try to explain my Big Solution to people, they think I'm talking about socialism or basic income or just generally handing out free money with no rules or strings attached.

So, here's what my Big Solution isn't: it's not socialism. It's not basic income. It's not an attempt to save capitalism. It's not even particularly similar to any of those things when you get to the bottom of it. But it is an attempt to save all of us from the doom and gloom that we are heading toward.

The Big Solution is also not a rehashing of an old idea. Old ideas like basic income, socialism, communism, and a host of other "isms"—even traditional capitalism—absolutely do not work. This is, after all, why my writing partners and I sat down to write this thing; all these "isms" have had their decades and centuries to prove themselves, and I'm sorry to say, all these "isms" have failed spectacularly. So it's time for a new economic system. Bonus points: the new system we'll be presenting in this book doesn't even end in "ism"!

To help accentuate the matter, I'm just going to set this in its own bolded paragraph:

This Big Solution is a brand-new idea. While you may be tempted to draw comparisons to other ideas, this Big Solution is completely distinct and independent from any other economic way of thought. It is new. Completely.

Okay, now here's what this book is: it is a presentation of a new way to think about money and how money should work in a functional economy and society.

Here's how new this idea is: neither the anti-socialist nor the anti-capitalist camps are espousing anything like it currently, and what's more, once we have laid out the fundamentals, both camps will actually be in favor of these ideas. What? How is that possible? In this day and age of argumentative politics? Get out!

No, it's true. This book is pro capitalism in the sense that it believes that private, for-profit ownership of produc-

> **Now here's what this book is: it is a presentation of a new way to think about money and how money should work in a functional economy and society.**

tion is humanity's best chance. Are you listening, fiscal conservatives? Because there's this: Ayn Rand was right; we need to defend the producers. But don't worry, lefties—she's only right as long as there is a healthy dose of competition between those producers, including competing for employees.

Okay, now it's your turn, Bernie Bros. This book is also very much about social justice and guaranteed liberty, and it puts people first. In other words, the Big Solution recognizes the importance of a social fabric that takes care of everyone. I daresay, card-carrying socialists, democratic socialists, and social-focused Democrats, this Big Solution is bound to turn you into capitalist pigs. Put a more direct way, whichever camp you belong to, you'll soon see that the system in place gives very few and mostly poor choices on how to run our governments.

How can there be a better option that is capitalistic and small government, and eliminates the need for social safety nets? Well, shoot, read the rest of this book.

Meantime, let's all embrace the idea that this isn't another book trying to divide us politically. This book seeks consensus. And the best way to get consensus is to destroy the arguments of both parties and unite them in a singular pursuit, which in a nutshell is to replace the way we currently think about and use money (which forces people into a life of dependence on government safety nets) into a new and better way to think about it, one that promotes a more natural system that allows for dignity, liberty, and growth.

Okay, actually, I can't wait. I have to give up a couple of nuggets about why the extreme left and extreme right will get along so well on this idea: we're going to eliminate the need for safety nets. When you have no safety nets, the government will be small. Now don't get too up in arms, socialists, social democrats, and progressives, because it's going to become clear (and really quickly) that people are better at taking care of themselves than the government is at taking care of them.

People are better at taking care of themselves than the government is at taking care of them.

Progressives, let's not forget the 1970s, with its inflation, high-priced unions, and government-run utilities. If this is what you want back, or if this is what you think will return America to its place as an economic world leader, then the Big Solution will bring you a new way to look at things. We don't need to bring back the 90 percent tax rate to ensure that everyone can lead a comfortable life. The math doesn't add up anyhow.

Conservatives, you guys believe that capital markets are the most efficient use of labor. And you know what? This is true! When it comes to increasing productivity, capital markets will always do a better job than the government can. But! Capital markets do not pursue the common good; rather, they pursue the desires of the capital owners. Because of the advancement of technology, capital markets are no longer about labor. This forces governments to use massive resources for safety nets. It is the ultimate cause of big government (and the ultimate cause of indebted servitude, like so many people are facing in Japan). Capital markets driven by bank-issued debt have the nasty habit of yielding the deployment of anti-labor technologies and policies. This leads to a distorted distribution of wealth and big government. The Big Solution, meanwhile, offers a more efficient use of capital and a new way to guarantee the liberty of people.

Let's remember that capitalism sprang to life out of aristocracy and slavery, and to this day it squeezes the working man until he can barely survive. In fact, people are dying from poverty in very big, scary numbers every day. And if you don't see the wealth gap and shrinking middle class as capitalism's return to aristocratic times, then you aren't paying attention.

Okay, everyone intrigued?

No? All right, then what if I told you that the Big Solution solves almost every problem the world currently faces? That's right; after we explain this new way to think about money, this book will address the host of problems in this country—all those things that are fundamentally and basically wrong (big hat tip to Dr. King)—strip those problems down, and show how the mechanics of the existing national or global economy aren't a side effect of those problems, but rather the root cause of those problems.

Once we've got that pinned down, we'll present the Big Solution, a sweeping change that doesn't simply fix all these problems but does so in a way that benefits everyone from the very poor to the very rich.

Next, the big question: what are you, the discerning reader, personally going to get out of this thing?

Great question. This book will help you see the United States, the economy, the manner in which countries interact with each other, and even your own life in a new and different way.

Once you are able to see the world in this new and different way, you will be better equipped to diagnose the problems we're currently seeing. And as any good doctor will tell you, diagnosis is the quickest, most effective way to the cure.

Time for a Brand-New Start

In this day and age of polarized belief systems and wariness of expertise, I worry that one group of people or another will write me off as too biased to be trusted.

Rightfully so. I'm a somewhat polarizing figure in some people's minds. And anyway, everyone is biased in some way. Everyone has their opinions, even if they aren't rule-bending tech billionaires. And thanks in part to social media and in part to the general shouty-ness of cable news, most people aren't shy about applying those opinions and writing off any others that don't jive with them.

Just like the Big Solution has something that both conservatives and progressives will love, I also want to make sure that this book itself doesn't get qualified as progressive or conservative or anywhere between. I want to write a book for everyone, because the Big Solution is for everyone, no matter who they are, where they come from, or what god or political party they pray to.

So, in an effort to avoid the natural bias that we're all subject to, I've decided to be something far less than the sole author of this book. Instead, I'm opening this bad boy up to other writers. Sometimes, those other writers will take whole sections all to themselves. Other times, we'll engage in conversation, as you'll see shortly.

The important thing to remember is that these other writers reside on different points of the political spectrum. This allows them to contribute an array of (often conflicting) opinions to the conversation. The goal will be not to shout at each other but to carefully and respectfully debate. If more than one opinion shows up on these pages, we'll be able to reconcile different viewpoints and, ideally, come to a consensus on what the Big Solution is, what it means, and what it can do for the world.

So let's meet the contributors. And let's do this in a round-table style, complete with speaker cues to identify each of our four speakers. I'll start.

Justin: I'm Justin Wolfe, inventor, CEO, and yacht owner. People have often described me as slightly left of center politically (probably because I've always been slightly left of center about everything). And that was certainly true in the past. But lately, I've seen some things, man, and those things make me identify as more of a revolutionist. In short, I believe that humanity has gone crazy, and anything short of a revolution will not suffice. Centrist compromise just will not fix crazy. And if a country and its citizens—including you, the reader—don't know where you are going but you are going so fast it could kill you, then you might just be crazy. It is insane to risk everything for the pursuit of aimless progress.

But the good news is that I am not talking about a bloody revolution; I am talking about a simple adjustment to how we think and what we believe about how this country and its economy should function.

Next, I've already mentioned Evan White. Everyone say hi to Evan. He's the guy over there in the corner, blushing and adjusting his glasses. Conveniently enough, he's apolitical. Although I do have to say he likes guns a whole lot more than I do.

Evan: Are you saying that gun ownership indicates a rightward lean?

Justin: Not at all. It was just the most visceral contrast between us that I could think of off the top of my head. Of course, we disagree on more than just guns. I, for one, am interested in politics.

Evan: It isn't that I'm not interested in politics. I just find straight economics more intriguing.

Justin: See? Apolitical. Which is a good thing. You're going to be the guy who keeps pulling the rest of us out of our political bubbles. You're our outside-the-box guy, both politically and in terms of your economic thinking.

Evan: I'm honestly flattered.

Justin: Tell our readers what else you bring to the table, Evan.

Evan: I'm a big fan of numbers and the stories they tell. I figure between your big-picture ideas, Justin, and my data and anecdotes, we should be able to speak directly to the largest percentage of Americans—those who try not to let their political affiliations get in the way of their perception of good solutions.

Justin: Amen, brother. So now that we've finished hugging it out, let's wander to one of the far reaches of the political spectrum. Please allow me to introduce my lovely girlfriend, Connie, who in no way landed this job because she's my lovely girlfriend.

Connie: Well, I should hope not.

Justin: Obviously not, Con. Nepotism doesn't apply if the person benefiting from it also happens to kick ass at what she does. I like your font, by the way. It's a good choice. Suits your vibrant personality.

Connie: You should know by now that flattery gets you nowhere with me.

Justin: This is true. Okay. You want honesty? You're here because many have called you a right-wing nutjob.

Connie: That's more like it. And I wear that label proudly, by the way.

Justin: You don't have to tell me that. I've seen you on TV, wearing it like a badge as you serve the president. Did I mention my girlfriend worked for a Republican president? Seems like a credential I should've mentioned. Anyway, she's good at what she does, and she's very much a conservative thinker. So she'll hold down the fort from the right side of the political spectrum.

On to the left side. Laz Hammond, where you at?

Laz: Yo, yo, yo. I'm here, boss.

Justin: Solid chime-in. Tell us a little about yourself.

Laz: I guess I'm the left-wing kook around here. I'm also a former homeless guy and current entrepreneur. Like Connie, you may have seen me hollering on a few talking-head shows recently. Some people agree with my opinions. Others don't.

Connie: I'm very much one of the others, incidentally.

Justin: Hey now, you two. Let's save it for the debate stage. Anyway, that's Laz. He's opinionated. Just don't ask him about the robot uprising and you should be fine.

Laz: You're joking, but the robot uprising is a genuine concern. Today's advanced AI is—

Justin: Okay, okay, iRobot. We'll get to that when we let you weigh in on automation later in the book.

Laz: Hold on to your socks.

So there's your cast of characters. They'll all be contributing quite a bit to this book as we move through the observations and principles to come. They're all brilliant in their own ways, and they are all more than qualified to hold up their portion of the political (or apolitical) spectrum. The poor saps don't know this yet, but even after all their hard work and strong contributions, it'll just be my name on the cover of this book. Ain't that just like life?

The World's a Mess. Why Should You Care?

I kicked this book off with an anecdote that gets to the general spirit of this whole discussion: my firm belief that this country is somehow broken. But just because I believe that this country is somehow broken, please don't mistake this book for another entry into the "Oh my God, the planet is crumbling, and we can only stop it if we all work together and recycle our plastic and ride our bikes to work" genre. The world doesn't need any more of that. The world doesn't need someone to list a bunch of data points that you can easily find and fact-check on the internet. The world doesn't need a million more footnotes about surveys and studies.

I'm writing this book to you. You. You, the person who is wondering why the world seems so off the rails; why work seems so much less rewarding than it used to be; why people can't seem to stop shouting at each other; why the rich are so much richer, the poor stay poor, and extreme poverty never goes away—and most importantly, I'm writing to you because you would actually like to know how to fix all this shit. And for that matter, you want to know why in the world there is no plan for a happy, sustainable future for us.

Because of my background, I recognize that there are millions of people out there who don't give a damn about some of the bigger-picture problems we're going to be discussing in this book. It's much harder to do anxiety cartwheels over global warming when you have to figure out how to pay for dinner for your family tonight in the midst of a life-upending pandemic and economic collapse. If that describes you, please don't stop reading, as this book is also for you. It shows how we can claw our way out of the present situation, where the vast majority of people struggle just to shelter and feed themselves.

For many people, life is already in tatters, so why should they care about everyone else's lives being ripped to shreds? I also recognize that there are more than a few Chicken Little haters out there who don't believe the sky is falling and do believe that the libs are overreacting. I totally get it. Totally.

So who's to blame, then?

This is a loaded question, because it will likely trigger some deeply ingrained belief of yours that will make you throw this book out the window. In order to change your beliefs about how the world works, your current beliefs are going to have to be challenged. I have named this type of emotional baggage "belief triggers," because once they are triggered, some people have a difficult time thinking outside the lines of their political affiliations. So let's take a deep breath and go with the flow. It's just a new way of looking at our world, and it will help solve a lot of problems.

Let's start with billionaires. There's this huge movement to blame guys like me for the economic problems in this country. Meanwhile, you might be thinking that you're more likely to make money working for a billionaire than taxing the hell out of one. And you, my friend, would be right. We should have coffee sometime and talk about it.

There's another movement blaming immigrants for job loss in this country (and elsewhere—this is not a uniquely American problem). Well, my friend, the will-they-or-won't-they question about whether immigrants are stealing American jobs is irrelevant. What's relevant is the artificial shortage of jobs and therefore money and resources that is created by the existing economic system in this country and elsewhere. Here's the thing: immigrants don't determine how many jobs are available; the banking system does that. And this banking system is screwing a minimum of ten million people out of jobs and lots more with low wages. Working migrants don't make it any better or worse to find work at a livable wage, but if you're turning in an application for a job at the same time, it sure doesn't seem that way.

Or maybe you want to blame China? Here's the thing: if manufacturing hadn't moved to China, then it would still be here in America, and what exactly do you think the Chinese would be doing instead? What makes you think that 1.5 billion people working to make inexpensive products for you and every American is a bad thing? The Chinese are literally working for slave wages for you, the American. They don't determine how many jobs and what the wages are for the jobs available here in America. Those things are determined by the American banking system.

Anyway, why worry about the geopolitical displacement of jobs and trade wars when you're trying to find yourself a decent job? It might interest you when I say that I believe climate change and job loss are connected to the same (incredibly solvable) problem, but mostly you just want to know how the Big Solution will make your day-to-day life better.

And why worry about how the stock market is through the roof, making the rich richer while the working class hasn't gotten a raise in decades? All that really matters is how hard it is to keep up with the cost of living. When you're stuck in an hourly job in a country that makes it impossible to get out of that hourly job, what do you care about market pressures? But more importantly, how can you call yourself free?

This all adds up to a huge part of the problem: we have to acknowledge that most people have resolved to just take care of themselves because that's all they can do. Life in this country has become so difficult that too many of us have given up on trying to fix it.

That's not good enough! Especially when all we need is a shift in perspective—a new understanding about how the economy and society work (and should work).

As it turns out, I have an idea. A Big Solution. Yes! That is where I came up with the title for this book!

Evan, as the chief economist at my recent failed farm experiment (reference to Book 2 of The Wolfe Trilogy), our outside-the-box thinker, and our apolitical weirdo, maybe now would be a good time to highlight the real problem with this country.

Any Fool Can Know

Hello. Evan White here. Happy to be called an apolitical weirdo.

Einstein once said, "Any fool can know. The point is to understand." I think what this means is that if I keep my anecdotes and economic explanations simple, then more people will have a much better chance of understanding the point. So my first promise is to keep things simple.

My other promise is to keep them natural. Economics is a challenging science to get a handle on. I studied the subject for eight years, and I still can't predict what will happen with the current US economy (although if you believe Justin, we can predict at least one thing: it's going to continue to suck for the middle, lower, and impoverished classes.)

The best way to understand how the economy works is to look at nature, as Justin kind of did at the start of this chapter with his woodsman anecdote. If I can quote Einstein again, he also said that imagination is the highest form of research. The best way to engage our imaginations is through analogies. So in the pages to come, I'll use stories to explain why human society works one way and why nature works a completely different way.

Anyway, for now, I'm supposed to be telling you the "real problem with this country." It's this: money. More specifically, the real problem with this country is that money is the centerpiece of everything. Life has become utterly transactional.

Let's go back to that woodsman scenario Justin started with. Where does this shack and the people who live in it get their water? They get it exclusively from the rain, the natural way. For anything in this residence to work, they need water. You might say that this shack situation absolutely depends on rain for its existence.

What happens if it stops raining? How many problems would this create?

Rain is what allows the family's crops to live and thrive—to say nothing of the livestock and of the family itself. This is just like what money does for people. If people run out of money, then just like crops/livestock/human beings running out of water, they can no longer thrive (or even afford to have a life).

If you haven't noticed, this applies to the US government as well. It is all out of money and heavily in debt. This leads to one crisis after another as monetary rationing dominates the political discourse.

And yes, this ties in to war, global warming, healthcare, and all our other problems. Money, as it turns out, is everything. The reason money is connected to all of our problems is very simple: money is necessary for all transactions between people, whether we're talking about governments, corporations, or individuals.

Does it not therefore make sense that the Big Solution is about money?

A Brighter Future

Yes, all of our problems can be traced back to money. That's the bad news. It's also the good news, because now that we have identified the problem, we can work toward a Big Solution that will solve them all in one fell swoop.

Think about a country without paved roads. If every car in America had to drive on gravel or dirt roads, people would skid into ditches and get flat tires all the time. This would cause delays that would impact productivity across the board. But if we paved these roads, then cars would stop wrecking so much and getting flats, and suddenly we've solved a massive number of problems.

Currently, we live in an unpaved country (metaphorically), a country terribly inefficient because of the way money is used and because of the economic rules that determine how money comes and goes. Your gut might be telling you that the people in charge—the academics, the economists, our leaders—would not allow the very rules that we have created for our own society to in fact undermine our past, present, and future. But as we'll see in the pages to come, your gut is misleading you.

When I think about the many ways the Big Solution can fix this country, I like to imagine a future that looks like so:

A future where technology increasingly contributes to the common good, both for poor people and rich people (and hey, how about all the people in between?).

A future where supermarkets aren't throwing out 60 percent of their produce while people just up the street from the supermarket go hungry.

A future where five million children don't die a poverty-related death on an annual basis.

A future where the bottom 25 percent of the population no longer has absolutely nothing in their savings—and instead, they have the means to continue saving as the years go by.

A future where savings accounts yield a handsome return and not the insulting near-zero interest rates of modern times.

A future free of never-ending war, terrorism, and mass shootings.

A future where the environment is no longer cast aside just so we can scrape to make the economy work.

A future where sustainability is possible for nature, humanity, and wildlife.

A future where jobs are not precious, but instead ubiquitous, and not thought of as a rare commodity and manipulated to control wages.

A future where politicians have more than just bad options/decisions to address.

The Big Solution

If we change how money flows into our reality, then we will fundamentally change reality.

Surprisingly, the biggest obstacle is not the government or bureaucracy. The problem is in what humanity collectively believes money to be. In order to solve the world's problems, we're going to have to dismantle our definition of "money" and how we believe it's supposed to work.

And as a gentle reminder, this still isn't Bernie Sanders shouting into the sky. No one here is a socialist. And we're not promoting that fluffy pipe dream known as basic income either. It's also not a fleecing of the rich. In fact, wealthy people will be free to actually earn wealth instead of just waiting for stock and asset prices to go up. The Big

Solution is something everyone can and will benefit from. The Big Solution is so much more.

In the pages to come, we'll be discussing something entirely different from an obscure social construct. What we're promoting fits nicely into everything humanity has built to date. The Big Solution is simply a set of new financial products with a new set of desired outcomes. It also does not require anyone to take risks or sacrifice what they own or earn. None of us has to change a thing, except our perspective of what money is and what it is supposed to do.

Let's get started.

CHAPTER TWO

THE VIEW FROM UP HERE IS GENUINELY TERRIBLE

We have come to a clear realization of the fact that true individual freedom cannot exist without economic security and independence. Necessitous men are not free men.

—**FRANKLIN DELANO ROOSEVELT**, speech of January 11, 1944

S ince I was a kid, I've had this dream about being on the International Space Station. I've always wanted to be up there with a high-powered telescope—and not even to look up at the stars, but instead to look down at Earth. Imagine being in a place where you can see anything on the entire planet at will.

Okay, so let's do that. Put yourself there. We're on the ISS, looking down at our own planet through a high-powered telescope. This is a special telescope, though, in that it doesn't just let us see what's happening but also understand what's happening. This telescope allows us to determine exactly what people are doing and, just as importantly, why they're doing these things. As a result, we can see any society we want and really get to the bottom of what makes it tick.

The first thing we'll notice, no matter where we look, is that this society is really, really interconnected. The whole world operates as a single unit now, even if it doesn't operate in any semblance of harmony.

Because of this interconnectedness, we encounter a series of unexpected questions. For instance, why are some of these people just sitting around doing nothing, even when they're young and full of vigor? Why are other people migrating thousands of miles just to work or survive? Why are soldiers fighting wars on the opposite side of the planet from the country they're supposedly defending? Why are people spending the best years of their lives getting an education, only to spend the second-best years of their lives slaving at a desk to pay off all that tuition debt, their mortgage, and their car loans and leases? Why are so many people spending the last years of their lives doing very little because they have no money to spend even though they worked for decades and decades to earn money?

The next thing we'll notice is that there's a ton of disparity between rich and poor—both in terms of countries and individuals. Some have, and some have not. Our telescope allows us to see and understand that this is because of money. It doesn't flow evenly between the countries and people. Some are able to collect quite a lot more, while some quite a bit less. Some are able to ship tons of paper money overseas, year after year, and receive goods and services in return. Some are left out of these transactions.

So, why is that? If we adjust the lens on our telescope slightly, we get the answer. It's not governments. It's not billionaires hoarding money. It's not even the gigantic megacorporations we're seeing all over the planet. It's this, and I quote:

> *We have in this country one of the most corrupt institutions the world has ever known. I refer to the Federal Reserve Board. This evil institution has impoverished the people of the United States and has practically bankrupted our government. It has done this through the corrupt practices of the moneyed vultures who control it.*[1]

This rather unsubtle quote is from Congressman Louis T. McFadden, spoken way back in 1932.

To simplify the above: it's banks. Now, don't get me wrong; I'm not here to take it to Congressman McFadden extremes and say that banks are evil organizations. I'm just saying that the rules they follow lead to some really unnatural disparities. They can't help it. Them's the rules.

Introducing a Brand-New "Ism"

Thanks for the space walk, Evan. Now, let's get started, and let's start at the top of the food chain.

What kind of "ism" does the United States subscribe to? Capitalism. Easy. How about China? Communism. Denmark? Socialism. How about Iran? Not really an "ism," necessarily, but you could describe it as a monarchy or, in some circles, a dictatorship. Pick any country in the world, and we can probably align their supposed economic system into one of these categories.

If you're a sharp-eyed reader—and I know you are—you'll have spotted that I used the word "supposed" in that last sentence. I used it

---

1   Congressman Louis T. McFadden, *Congressional Record,* June 10, 1932, http://www.afn.org/~govern/mcfadden_speech_1932.html.

because these are the terms we all lean on to describe a country's government, even if these words are related directly to their economies.

Let's quit beating around the bush, shall we? None of those so-called "isms" actually matter much in a world with a homogenous banking system. Because of a pair of agreements from back in the 1940s (agreements that we'll discuss in greater detail in a later chapter), and because of all the rules and regulations that resulted, the entire planet is run by a single "ism." I call it Bankism. The definition of this word is "a world run by and for the benefit of banks."

If you're from China, you might sit back and watch your country manipulate its currency and call itself communist, but because every activity your country's government commits to requires money, and because every shred of money in the world is loaned out from central banks, your country is in fact dictated by Bankism. The real ruling force, no matter where you are in the world, is banks.

It all hinges on the way the money flows through the global economy. Today's definition of currency is that it is the only asset that does not exist. It is, after all, only printed into existence whenever someone demonstrates a need to borrow it. In other words, there is no money currently in circulation that is not owed to a debt. No wonder private, corporate, and national debts are exploding! Under the current system, for every dollar of additional spending, a few dollars are borrowed.

Money makes the world go round, right? Well, that's because the root of all power is the money in our economic system. So … what happens if you give certain people all the leverage to control all the money? By default, they will control everything a government can or cannot do, which in turn puts them in control (whether directly or indirectly) of the levers of the law. But that's not the problem; it's merely a symptom.

Think about how the US, whose banks are very much in the driver's seat of this arrangement, runs its economic policy. When the economy starts drifting too far in one direction or the other, the Federal Reserve either raises or lowers interest rates in an effort to bring things under control.

Who benefits most from this interest rate manipulation, though? It's not you or me. It's not even the US government or any of its representatives. It's banks. Banks benefit the most. These interest rate moves are, in fact, designed to directly benefit commercial banks by stabilizing markets, inflation, and the availability of cash it uses to make loans (which in turn make those banks money, which they in turn lend out in the form of more loans).

Bankism controls the US economy. And since we live on a planet with a homogenous global banking system, this means that Bankism controls the global economy. The people who run the world aren't in the White House or the Kremlin or Zhongnanhai; they're in the Eccles Building in Washington, and they're on Wall Street.

Democratic socialism means that we must
create an economy that works for all.

—BERNIE SANDERS

The best trick to Bankism is how very subtle and unseen it is. Few people recognize how much impact banking policy has on their lives. We blame the governments and their leaders. We blame war and the unstable economy. But because everything in the world—and all the work that any of us do—turns on the loans banks choose or do not choose to give, banks sit on top of the world. So when Bernie Sanders says that an economy must work for all, he's not really paying attention. The economy must work so the banking system can survive. It has nothing to do with the welfare of anyone, and it certainly cannot "work for all."

Put another way, people on both sides of the political aisle, including Bernie Sanders, believe that the government controls the economy. This is a very important falsehood I need you, the reader, to understand and accept in order for the rest of this book to add up.

To begin, let's consider a question that has always puzzled me: how it is possible that, in the US, $1 trillion is owed to the Federal Reserve (this number does not include quantitative easing, by the way), with another $77 trillion owed to commercial banks or their financial products like mortgages and T-bills (and this is just a pre-COVID number!)? This is possible because, essentially, banks take money from the Fed and then loan it out over and over again. And they've done this at least seventy-seven times, if my math is correct; Evan, can you check and make sure my math is correct?

Evan: Yeah, that checks out.

Thank you, Evan. It looks the same in China too. They might be currency manipulators, but even though they seem to be breaking the rules, they're also kind of following them. Their money all flows by way of loans from central banks as well. Their communist-sponsored banks or government-owned banks make loans to local cities so they can build homes for all their people, using these massive loans to devalue their currency. If these loans don't work out, well, they just go into default. Put simply, their behavior looks different, but it's really all the same. They're every bit as debt driven as the US and every other country on the planet. They're still playing the Bankism game, just like the rest of us.

Not Exactly Free

It is time to wake up to the reality that all those best-laid plans from back in the 1940s have led to some seriously enormous unintended consequences. Namely, banks have taken over the world.

If you're American, then you're told you live in the Land of the Free, and yet, if you're like the overwhelming majority of people in this country, my guess is that you don't exactly feel free. You likely feel as if your hands are tied by your financial situation. It's that old adage that you're not truly free unless you're financially free.

Think about it. You're free to choose, but your choices are not that good. You can go to college and have tremendous debt before you start life, or you can choose not to go to college, leaving yourself to an array of extremely limited choices for a career. In other words, all through life, you have choices between bad and really bad. Sure, some people get lucky. Some people are born with a silver spoon in their mouths. Others somehow manage to strike it big as entrepreneurs. Some people win the lottery. But for most people, the majority of choices are really poor.

Today, there is an increasing number [of people] who can't see a fat man standing beside a thin one without automatically coming to the conclusion that the fat man got that way by taking advantage of the thin one. So they would seek the answer to all fifteen problems of human need through government ... Howard K. Smith of television fame has written, "The profit motive is outmoded. It must be replaced by the incentives of the welfare state." He says, "The distribution of goods must be effected by a planned economy."

**—RONALD REAGAN, "A Time for Choosing"
speech, Los Angeles, October 27, 1964**

I am throwing this timeless Reagan quote in here to prove that this is not some socialist propaganda. Let's just say it outright: the rich are not taking from the poor. Just because some kids are born into rich families does not mean that they are making tuition go through the roof. The banks are doing that, so let's leave the rich kids alone.

Back to old adages. Money is not the root of all evil. Bankism is the root of all evil.

You're probably thinking, *Bold claim, J-Dub*. You're right. It is bold. So I guess I should back that up, yeah?

Okay, cool. Let's have some story time again, shall we? Gather round on your carpet squares, children, for I have a story to share.

Let's imagine a little village in middle of nowhere America. Most people live in little huts or something—or perhaps they all live in those woodsperson shacks that have been all the rage so far in this book. The roads in this town are all glorified goat paths, and there's no public sewer or electricity. This is a straight-out-of-a-spaghetti-western village.

Now, let's imagine that in this random village in middle of nowhere America, a forward-thinking numbers guy (maybe we should just call him Evan White) came up with a brilliant idea. He was going to call this idea a bank.

This forward-thinking numbers guy saw a problem, you see. He saw that all these woodspeople were making money for their furs or whatever and were just sort of piling it up in their shacks. These villagers needed a safe place to keep their money. So in all his creative glory, the numbers guy invented the safe. He invited all the villagers to keep their money safe in the, well, safe.

All the villagers were like, "Well, that makes sense! The appeal of your product is right there in the name!"

So everyone in town deposited their money in the safe at the bank.

"All right," they said. "My money is safe now. I can go back out and earn some more."

Meanwhile, the banker turned around and said, "Hey, wait. It doesn't make any sense to leave all this beautiful money in the safe collecting dust. Why don't I take this money and loan it out to someone so they can do something to better their lives?" He probably tented his fingers together as he added, "And I'll collect a nice interest rate on the loan. How about ten percent?"

That first-ever person who took the first-ever loan decided not to use that money to buy any goods and instead used it to pay some skilled laborers to build him a house.

That first borrower was happy. "Now I've got this nice beautiful house," he said, and then he got back to work so he could pay off the loan.

Here's where the banker had himself a pleasant surprise. Where do you think all those skilled laborers took their money after the job was done and they'd been paid? Straight back to the bank and its nice safe safe. So here the banker realized that, hey, he could loan out money, make money on that loan, and then, lo and behold, the original money he loaned out came right back to him.

What a grand system! he thought.

But that night, he tossed and turned. Couldn't sleep. Just something he couldn't seem to get out of his mind. Then, he leaped up in bed, startling his poor wife from sleep.

"Hey!" the banker rather hollered. "I'm not just going to let all that beautiful money sit there collecting dust in the safe. I'm going to make another loan with it."

Fortunately for the banker, everyone in town was envious of the first borrower's fancy new house. So there was no shortage of people to loan money to. The loans started with all the skilled laborers who had built the first borrower's house. They'd seen the luxury firsthand, so now they wanted houses like that too. Word spread so quickly that soon everyone in the village was taking out a loan to upgrade their woodsy shacks into luxury homes.

Whew! Now everyone in the whole village had a new house. Now all the money had been loaned out, and everyone had a debt to pay. And, wow, all that money had returned to the bank, because all those builders had been earning it back and they needed a place to keep it safe.

The banker, though … now he's got troubles. He doesn't have anyone else to loan to. The system he created won't work properly if he doesn't have anyone else to loan to. That beautiful money will just sit there collecting dust. And if it just sits there collecting dust, there won't be any work for people to do, and if there's no work for people to do, those people won't be able to pay back their debts.

The banker just had to find someone else to loan to. Fortunately, his wife—who was herself a shrewd numbers woman, which was a truly foundational reason for why these two had such a famously lovely marriage—came up with an idea in no time. "You should approach all the small businesses in town and suggest they take out loans to improve their businesses and grow."

"That's brilliant, my dear wife!" the banker said. "I'll go out and do that right now."

So he did. And now, boom, he's making all these small business loans. One by one, the businesses in town started renovating their shops, marketing their services, and so on and so forth.

But hoo-boy, here we go again. Now all the businesses in town have loans and they need to work so hard to pay their bills that they can't afford to take out new loans. Now the banker is really in a pickle. He has to find more ways to loan money or the economy will slow down.

"What we need, my dear wife, is a true and genuine sucker," he said. The famously lovely couple shared a rare moment of awkward silence. But then it occurred to the banker that he knew just such a sucker.

The next day, he went down to the municipal building and pitched some of his ideas to the decision-makers in the local govern-ment. "Oh my gosh, you guys," the banker said. "All the people and businesses have borrowed money, and have you noticed how beautiful our little town is starting to look?"

"I have been noticing that," said one of the true and genuine suckers at the municipal building.

"Well, you know," the banker said out of the side of his mouth, "it seems to me there's something missing around here. You know what we should do?" He looked back over one shoulder and then the other for effect. "You should borrow some money from my bank so you can pave the goat paths into proper roads and maybe put in some sidewalks. How pretty would that be?"

It took all of five seconds for the true and genuine suckers at the municipal building to sign the paperwork, thereby saddling the town up to its eyeballs in debt.

This brilliant strategy kept the economy turning and growing, kept people in jobs, and kept the money the banker loaned out flowing right back into the bank, where he would loan it out again.

Uh-oh, though. Now the banker had loaned to all the people, all the business, and to the municipality. Now there's definitely no one else to loan to. Whatever was he to do?

The system doesn't work without loans! he thought. Loans build houses, grow businesses, create jobs, and pave roads. *What on earth will we do without loans?*

This was where the banker and his wife really put their heads together and got down into the weeds. They hatched a plan where they would lower the interest rates on loans, which compelled the people who originally borrowed money to refinance their home loans or take out home equity lines of credit for home improvement projects. These lower interest rates also made new loans more affordable for the businesses and municipalities.

And, for a while at least, the system kept turning and the economy kept growing. Almost without realizing it, that once idyllic little town had become a debt-driven, Bankism-owned economic quagmire.

This town, fictional though it may be, was not unique. It was just one of many, many towns that operated the same way.

The first moral of the story: modern life is driven by debt, and since banks are the peddlers of debt, banks therefore determine the activity and work we do.

> **Modern life is driven by debt, and since banks are the peddlers of debt, banks therefore determine the activity and work we do.**

And the second moral of the story: it has never been safe to put money in banks because banks lend it out again and again. Every time the economy suffers a financial shock, we receive more proof of how unsafe it is.

The third moral of the story: banks always run out of people who want to borrow money. In response, they keep coming up with new products to sell. But it's like a black hole; eventually, debt will just swallow up everything.

And the fourth moral of the story is that before banks, money had to be earned through work. When banks loan out money, they are essentially loaning out work that someone else did and someone else will do. They are creating work that otherwise would not have happened because there wasn't enough money. Banks essentially create more work.

If I could just overexplain this point about Bankism ...

Bankism causes the loss of an individual's freedom because the borrower is indebted, legally, which means that not making payments can put you in jail or out on the street. A community, municipality, or government loses its sovereignty or ability to make decisions for itself, as its decision-making must first consider its payment of debt. Just look at what happened to Greece during the Great Recession.

Forget the politicians. The politicians are put there to give you the idea you have freedom of choice. You don't. You have no choice.

—GEORGE CARLIN, *Life is Worth Losing,* **HBO, November 5, 2005**

A discerning reader like you might say that Bankism seems to be worth it—after all, look at the new houses, streets, and businesses. But discern a little deeper and you'll find that there is no choice once the Bankism quagmire has properly set its teeth into society. People are forced to take loans just to get by. And no, the guy who leased a BMW he couldn't afford is not who we are talking about. We are talking about people using credit cards to pay the rent and put food on the table.

Let's also recognize that the bank loan to the municipality is not free, and in order to pay back the debt, property taxes have to go up. This means a higher cost of living, and everyone in town having to work even harder. Here is where we find ourselves at the opposite end of the woodsperson spectrum, where an unfortunate neighbor loses everything and it simply isn't in the interest of the neighbors to take care of that person because to get back the house they lost and the wages they lost is just not possible. This is how a homeless, starving person winds up in an alley behind a restaurant full of patrons paying $150 for a dinner most likely paid for by credit card.

Since everyone is busy paying off their debts, taking care of all the unfortunate people is just not possible. That job is left to the government. And the only way the government can pay for taking care of these people is either through higher taxes or taking on further debt from banks. Well, taxpayers hate taxes because they already have enough bills as it is, and the rich who can afford high taxes already pay the vast majority of taxes and can easily claim they are not getting their money's worth. Meanwhile, banks love issuing debt, as that's how they make money. So debt winds up being the only option left to a politician who wants to be reelected, and this is not actually a choice at all. With Bankism, there is no choice.

Okay. Story time over! Pack up your carpet squares in a neat little pile in the corner, please. And while you're doing that, I should probably stand up and stretch my legs for a second and share an important caveat: I'm actually not blaming banks for their behavior here. They're just playing by the rules. And what reasonable business that plays by the rules would pass up the opportunity to completely control the market they find themselves in? I own a few businesses, and I can tell you truthfully that this is my goal in all of them. It's how a successful business works; you see an opportunity, and you capitalize on it.

No, the banks and their leaders themselves are not to blame. The system is to blame, and that system is Bankism. The system is all-pervasive. It impacts everything we discussed in chapter 1 and will continue to discuss in the chapters to come. It is the cause of the rise in cost of living while income and standards of living stagnate; it is the reason governments are so overwhelmed with debt; it is the reason our leaders seem to have no effect on things like global warming or even healthcare and its laundry list of issues, including cancer, diabetes, and obesity; and it is the reason we all feel so handcuffed in our daily lives.

Perhaps you're harboring the notion that Bankism is a factual reality and progress would not be possible without it. To you, I would point out that the first bank in the world was established in 1472, and it still exists today (like a vampire that drinks blood from its victims and never dies). So if banks are the source of all progress, are we to assume that mankind made no progress prior to 1472? Then, conversely, after 1472, did progress just completely explode? The answer to both questions is "Hell no." Prior to that first bank, we advanced from living in caves all the way to just about the halfway point of the Renaissance. And the modern-day acceleration of progress only started a hundred years ago, and it went slowly at first.

The Big Solution is really about this: debunking the belief that society has to be controlled by banks. And okay, fine. Bankism is in charge. It makes our lives a little worse, but so what? What's the worst that could happen?

Good questions, my friend. The worst that could happen is that the whole system could collapse. And let me assure you, it will eventually collapse, because a system based on debt is always (always, always) doomed to fail. Even worse is its persistence, because it is fundamentally flawed. In fact, if it failed and just went away, progress could be made. But without the awareness that comes with complete and total collapse, it would likely be replaced by a similar flawed and doomed construct. Actually, you know what? We've already seen this happen. Very recently, in fact. More than once, if the pandemic counts.

The first time it happened, you might remember it … what was it called again? It's right on the tip of my tongue. Something about Great Recession-y something or other.

I don't know. Maybe there's something about it in chapter 3 …

CHAPTER THREE

THE SUICIDE BANK

I'd throw dollars out of helicopters if I had to,
to stimulate the economy.

—BEN BERNANKE, chairman of the Federal Reserve, 2006-2014

Travel back in time with me to September 15, 2008. The world had just wrapped up a truly remarkable Olympics. The US was gearing up for an Obama v. McCain showdown in November. I'd recently sold a VR company I founded for just over a billion dollars. I'd just met my girlfriend, Connie, at a rave or something.

Connie: I have to interject here. First, I should point out that,somehow, twelve years later, I'm still just his girlfriend. More importantly, though, we met in the library at Columbia University; I was a grad student at the time. Justin, being much older than me and in town to give a guest lecture, played the charmingly lame hand where he pretended to have forgotten his reading glasses and asked, "Young lady, could you by chance help me find the economics section?" Of course I was in love. The fact that he was famous for being one of the world's youngest billionaires helped. But anyway, we met in a library. Justin Wolfe has never been to a rave in his life.

Justin: Thanks for that helpful interjection, my love.

Connie: Anytime. Here to help.

Justin: Anyway, back in 2008, I didn't yet even know Evan White because he was still in short pants.

Evan: Is this an ageist thing we're doing here? Because I have some thoughts on that …

Justin: If we're through with the interruptions, whatever was happening on the global stage, in the library at Columbia, or in Evan's boyhood wardrobe, the big thing everyone wanted to talk about was Lehman Brothers, and how well and truly screwed they'd gotten themselves. The Bear Stearns collapse had already been underway since March, and now suddenly this financial juggernaut was just closing up shop? Just like that? It was crazy. It was like a market-collapsing economic tsunami that started by taking out the US economy before washing quickly over the rest of the world.

Laz: Hold on, boss. We've gotta remember that this book is going to be timeless. It could be twenty-some years from now when this particular reader is holding the thing and reading what you just wrote. They'll be saying, "C'mon, man, it's been x number of years since the friggin' Great Recession, and I've read about a million different postmortems of that situation already. Why would I want to do that again?

Justin: Good point, Laz. And you are certainly well versed and well read, my friend from the distant future. Also, I love that you use the word *friggin'*, as it's one of my personal favorites.

Your point is well taken, Laz and my future reader. So let me make a promise here: I'm not going to do another postmortem on the Great Recession (or the GR, for short). Instead, I'm going to use the GR as a backdrop for a story about something that occurred to me on September 15, 2008. Is that fair?

You look skeptical, Connie.

Connie: …

Justin: Okay, I guess we'll see.

Jump (or Don't Jump) … It Doesn't Really Matter

So here's the story.

You probably won't even believe it because it all just sounds so cliché. I happened to be walking through the financial district on that awful day in September—and let me tell you, what a weird time and place that was to find oneself in. I was still kind of getting used to my actual billionaire status, so I had this bounce in my step that can only come from becoming rich so recently. The timing couldn't have been better for me, because I was suddenly in all cash right as the markets dived. This turned out to be a blessing, because talk about buying low!

Funny thing here is that the economic collapse wound up making cash incredibly valuable. It wasn't that stocks were cheap; it was that there wasn't enough money to go around, so everything became cheap compared to money. And it became cheap because of those weird rigors of the bank loan story I took us through in the previous chapter. There suddenly wasn't enough money in the economy, so how were these bankers supposed to keep making loans? The cash I had on hand was now just crazy, crazy valuable.

I'd also just met Connie. All was right with my world, is what I'm saying.

Connie: (eyeroll)

Anyway, since I was out wandering through the world and not paying attention to my brand-new iPhone 2, I hadn't yet heard the news about the collapse of Lehman Brothers. I found out about it by way of the hubbub I bumped into up the street. A crowd had gathered, and everyone was craning their necks and sighing with concern at something happening about twenty stories up.

There stood a man in a fine suit. Right there on the window ledge. From the look of things, he'd had to shatter the thing to get out there, because it wasn't the kind of window you could open. And, yep, after surveying the ground outside the building, I found the spot where his desk chair had shattered into scattered nuts and bolts and fiberglass matchsticks.

"Don't jump!" everyone was hollering.

Curious, I started asking around. The incredulous crowd filled me in on what had happened with Lehman Brothers, and what the early word suggested it signified. Here we were, staring at a full-blown economic collapse spurred on by the kinds of bad loans Bear Stearns and Lehman Brothers had been championing.

As it turned out, the man on the ledge, his tie flapping in the wind, his tortured screaming only just barely intelligible from twenty stories below, was a banker with Lehman Brothers. Apparently, he'd been in deep on subprime mortgages, and he was at that moment feeling like something similar to the Typhoid Mary of the coming recession—or, for a more modern reference, whoever the Typhoid Mary of COVID happened to be. China, I guess, if you subscribe to the television channel on which Connie most frequently appears. Dude was maybe going to be a pariah, is what I'm saying.

At first glance, his reaction might seem somewhat reasonable. Guy builds his whole career around his skill with numbers and finance. He goes to a great school and lands his dream job in NYC, massive salary all but assured. He proves himself the kind of whiz-kid financial guy that climbs ladders and invents whole new junk funds for the rickety Bankism economy to prop itself up on. He had to have been an incredibly loaded young man. Now, suddenly, the system collapses, and he finds himself buried under a junk fund avalanche of his own making. Everything he thought he stood for and worked for? Gone in the blink of an eye.

I can kind of understand why he tossed that chair through the window and why he stood there screaming about wanting to jump. It's tough to lose everything.

By the way, I'm going to withhold until the end of the chapter the truth about whether the guy jumped. My writing coach tells me this is called a cliffhanger. What matters at this moment is the epiphany I had while staring up at this extremely troubled banker.

Here's the epiphany: this banker guy only *thought* he'd lost everything. The truth is, there was something very wrong with this picture, the banker guy standing on the edge of death. That banker guy had no reason to jump. He would soon be just fine. The Fed would simply print more money, buy all the bank's bad loans, and everyone would move on.

You know who did have plenty of reasons to jump? All those people who lost their houses after the system collapsed. These were everyday people just trying to work and make a better life for themselves. Who could have blamed them for taking that too-good-to-be-true mortgage deal? I would've done the same thing. So would Connie have, no matter what she tells you.

Truth be told, in the debt-driven quagmire that is our reality, where savings accounts don't yield a return, mortgages are not just necessary for home ownership for most people; they are a good idea.

Connie: I absolutely would not have taken a too-good-to-be-true mortgage deal. That is a fact.

Justin: Then you would have missed out on historically low rates that are outpaced by the increase in property values. Unless it's 2008. In which case, all these everyday people were going about their lives, and the next day, they were losing their houses.

And bizarrely (or you could read it as *despicably*), the Federal Reserve took over these mortgages, which then allowed bankers like the will-he-or-won't-he jumper to buy up all these properties at a massive discount. How do we know it was at a discount? Because if money is printed just to buy the properties, there will always be more buyers than sellers. Any two-bit banker knows what happens next: property values start going up again.

Laz: As it happens, there are many who became very wealthy, and some even became billionaires on exactly this strategy.

Connie: Fake news. If wealthy capitalists hadn't moved in and bought up these houses, the recovery would have been even slower.

Justin: At the risk of cutting through this tension, I think I'll move on … Sure, that banker guy had lost his shirt on that one bad play, but in no time at all, he would be on top of the world again. Why? Because Bankism ensures that he is on the winning side of the banks. As a banker, as long as he doesn't get scapegoated as one of the guys who "ruined things," he'll be fine.

Laz: Isn't it interesting that there were a few scapegoats following this economic disaster, but almost no one went to jail?

Connie: It's not that interesting. No one broke the law.

Evan: Technically, she's right. Also, banks need to keep lending money even if it's subprime. How else are they going to keep the economy "growing"?

Laz: Strong use of air quotes there, Ev.

Evan: I use them because "growing" is definitely a relative term. We'll get into that later.

At the end of the day, what matters is that the banks run the Federal Reserve, which controls the money-printing presses, which means whenever the money runs out, they can just print more. Even an economic collapse wasn't going to change that.

And you know what? My epiphany was right. Not even an economic collapse changed that.

Yes, Lehman Brothers went the way of the dodo, along with Bear Stearns and some others. But Bankism remains alive and well thanks to quantitative easing.

In my experience, whenever someone uses the words *quantitative easing*, people start to get all tense and terse. So instead of letting the three of you get after each other, you know what might be a good idea? It might be a good idea to turn it over for a full section from one of our genuinely remarkable ideological thinkers: the love of my life, the woman with three first names, Connie Anne Kelly.

The Great Sham of Quantitative Easing

It's introductions like these that should make it clear why Justin has such a hard time finding someone to marry him.

Anyway, let's get ideological. Let's discuss the perspective on all this from the right.

If banks are indeed the source of all the world's problems, then the Great Recession is the catalyst to our story.

Once, I got a little too drunk on Wall Street, and I fell and broke my nose against the sidewalk.

Justin: It's true! I was there. The ride to the hospital was like a slasher film. I didn't even bother trying to clean and sell that car. I just wheeled it over to the scrapyard.

Connie: I was wearing these ridiculous heels at the time, and they … Anyway, that doesn't matter. Point is, if you fall and break your face, sometimes it's better to just stay down instead of getting back up and trying to keep walking.

Justin: I can vouch for this piece of wisdom too. She should not have kept trying to walk.

If Justin would stop interrupting the section I'm supposed to have all to myself, I'd say this: banks are not too big to fail. One could fail and we'd all be perfectly fine. The reason quantitative easing happened is because the banking system, which my boyfriend cleverly calls Bankism, has taken over the world and will not allow itself to fail.

Bankism is a debt-driven, loan-dependent system that often has to tell little lies just to keep itself running.

It's like that forward-thinking numbers guy from Justin's analogy in the previous chapter. Bankism is a debt-driven, loan-dependent system that often has to tell little lies just to keep itself running (and quite frankly, no one is alive today that has any experience with a world that is not debt driven). Here's the lie in this case: if we want to prevent the economy from disintegrating and the whole of the civilized world from collapsing into a Mad Max–style hellscape, then we have no other option but to bail out these massive banks.

But here's the truth: the trillions of dollars we wound up using to bail out those too-big-to-fail banks was a number designed to ensure liquidity so that banks had cash. Resulting from this flood of cash was a lowering of the value of the dollar. That's right! Following the economic collapse, money became too valuable. That's why Justin was so damn lucky to be standing on a pile of cash at the time. Banks had too little money on hand to go around, so they simply injected more of it into the system, lowering the value and replenishing their loan-giving coffers.

But the big question is, why did banks not have enough money on hand to go around? Because banks lend the same money out over and over again. No one should be surprised that an institution that engages in that kind of practice would run out of money. There used to be a thing called a "run on banks" because people used to fear that banks would run out of cash, because there was no way for the banks to pay back all the money that was held in savings.

But then in 1933, the FDIC was created, which insured accounts of Federal Reserve member banks and basically means that the Fed can print money to replace the money banks had loaned out from their customers' savings. Put another way, the Federal Reserve Act basically handed the management of the money supply over to the banks (all at the hands of the biggest banker in history, J. P. Morgan). Banks, the creators of the quagmire that is Bankism, were given the keys to bail themselves out. Pretty nice little trick, huh?

Quick recap: banks created these portfolios of junk loans called subprime mortgages. These assets wound up well underwater. So when that tanked the banking system, the Fed just invented new money out of the sky and used this new sky-money to create quantitative easing to buy back those portfolios full of junk loans. And here's the worst part—quantitative easing is a Pandora's box we'll never get shut again. People paid close attention to it in the year or two following the GR, but it has been used time and time again in the decade since—and it's been used in spades during the COVID pandemic.

However you look at it, here's the reality: politicians and financial regulators bailed out the system that created the financial crisis, mostly because it was the only thing they knew how to do. They never bothered questioning whether the banking system itself needed fixing. No one ever legitimately pushed the question, "Should we really be going back to a system that creates these kinds of problems every few years?"

And here's the funny part! Bankism also has led to a situation where politicians can now say anything they want about how to make the economy better. One can say, "Raise taxes," while the other can say, "Lower taxes," in an effort to create jobs or pay down the debt, and they can't both be right and both be wrong.

So instead of challenging the status quo, from 2007 to 2008 the Fed did nearly everything in its power to revive the lending markets, including lowering the interest rate from 5 percent to zero (literally the lowest possible rate it could give) and buying up over $300 trillion in agency debt from mortgage-backed securities that were precariously invested.

The Fed wasn't alone either. In 2009, as one of the first major acts of his presidency, Barack Obama signed a bill allocating a $787 billion stimulus package aimed at the financial markets, an act that contributed to a $1.26 trillion government debt by 2012. Ask me how I feel about that ... Okay, don't.

In any case, this debt sounds completely awful, but it pales in comparison to the pandemic response, which basically gave people more money than they earned in the jobs they'd lost, essentially allowing them to live on their couches for months, all at a staggering cost of $6 trillion.

We base all our experiments on the capacity of mankind for self-government.

—JAMES MADISON, quoted in *The Nonviolent Right to Vote Movement Almanac*

That quote from Madison has me all aflutter, so if I may go off on a brief tangent …

As the government decides whether millions of people have enough money to eat and afford a home, at what point do we realize that the government has taken sovereignty from its people? When Mitch McConnell's debating whether to vote or not to vote, yes or no, on whether people live or die from famine and homelessness, how is this not a dictatorship? The idea is supposed to be that the government is beholden to the people and it has no other source of power except the sovereign people.

For two and a half centuries, we've proven man's ability to self-govern, but today, we watch as the government is beholden to the debt collectors while the sovereignty of the people has been lost to the same banking system.

Today, we watch as the government is beholden to the debt collectors while the sovereignty of the people has been lost to the same banking system.

It's like Plutarch warned: "The real destroyer of the liberties of the people is he who spreads among them bounties, donations, and benefits." Bankism spreads these bounties, donations, and benefits, and the true freedom for Americans has been lost.

But if I can get past my feelings about the loss of our liberty, I can see that what is even worse is how the system creates a scarcity of money and therefore a scarcity of everything else. The Federal Reserve is responsible for keeping the credit markets working properly. And since the commercial banks own the Federal Reserve, it should be no surprise that they were the ones to receive the bailout.

So when it comes time to save the economy, nobody even thinks about doing something different instead of immediately scrambling to repair the old broken system. Sure, quantitative easing was a new idea, but only as a means to keep the old broken system going.

At the end of the day, the politicians, in their naivete, got their action steps from the very people who needed to be bailed out. And the only institution that could readily remedy the situation was the Federal Reserve.

The Great Recession of 2009 proved that the banking system isn't just based on credit, as J. P. Morgan famously said. Rather, money could also be had through quantitative easing, which is the purchase of debt assets like bonds and mortgages. It basically takes all the risk out of owning debt, which is great for banks, corporations, and the government, but it comes at the price of sovereignty and liberty.

Bankism robs us of sovereignty and liberty because the government claims it can simply refinance a debt it will never be able to pay back. This is only true as long as other countries are willing to supply us with the same-priced goods and services in addition to buying our debt, a.k.a. treasury bills. If their prices go up, then the bill is due, and America will have lost its ability to refinance the debt.

However, it is worse for the individual, who is forced into debt by the high cost of living. They can be placed in jail for not paying their bills, not to mention suffer homelessness, starvation, and desperation. Goodbye, liberty.

Evan Brings the Water

Okay, okay. Things are getting a little finger-pointy around here. Take a deep breath, everyone. Again, we're not out to blame the bankers or the big banks, but rather the system they operate in. Banks and bankers are just doing their jobs and trying to make money, after all.

So, hey? How about we turn it over to an apolitical actor named Evan for a bit and see if maybe cooler heads will prevail?

Evan: Hello! Evan White here again. And I'm bringing another analogy.

Imagine a pond full of water.

Justin: What else would a pond be full of? Toxic waste?

Evan: Well … sometimes, yes, a pond is full of toxic waste.

Justin: Man, you're right. (shudder)

Evan: The water in this pond represents all the money the Federal Reserve has loaned out to banks or otherwise printed for distribution.

Now, let's imagine that surrounding the pond are the banks themselves. Picture big, square-shouldered buildings with some columns out front, but otherwise they're completely uninspired architecturally. Banks are boring. But for this analogy, they're drawing water from the pond, temporarily borrowing it. These banks then loan this water to each other and to their customers, who are grateful to have some water to drink and use to water their crops.

The more the banks take out of the pond, the more water they have to put back in. Banks make money by borrowing and lending from this same pond of water over and over again. If one of these banks makes a bad loan with their water, then not only does that bank not get its payment, but the bank itself will not be able to make its payment on the water it borrowed, which means that the water starts disappearing and the pond starts drying up. In the past, there would be a panic and people would worry that the banks would run out of cash. Now, the Fed responds by creating more water and putting it into the pond. This sometimes leads to the overflowing of the pond—which, in this analogy, equates to inflation.

Like the water in a pond, there is only so much money to go around. But the banks have discovered a remarkable system for loaning out water and then recycling it so they can loan it out again—eighty times and counting!

Think about that for a second. Loaning the same dollar eighty times is like juggling eighty balls at once … and with only one hand. No wonder quantitative easing wound up looking super necessary in 2009 and is even more necessary during the COVID pandemic.

What happened during the Great Recession? The pond dried up. And how did they fix the problem? They poured four and a half times more water into the pond than existed there before. Four and a half times! How did they manage to fit this much water into that same space?

Quantitative easing. Think of QE like a giant hole in the ground at the base of the pond. It just sucks all the extra water down and away. Where does it all go? Ha! That's the funny part. All the banks, those clever, boring-looking institutions, have built reservoirs under their foundations, and it is into these reservoirs that all the QE hole water gets drained.

In the real world, the banks call these reservoirs *reserves*. Following the GR, these reserves had to grow by law. Decision-makers looked at the problems following the GR and said, "What we really need is to create a system that ensures our banks never run out of money/water again. We've got to make damn certain the banks always remain liquid, or the whole system will collapse … again."

Justin: If you're a discerning reader, which I know you are, you'll want to put a pin in this idea of bank reserves, since it's particularly useful for controlling the money supply and inflation. For now, what this says about money is interesting; these reserves are simply money for the banks to sit on so they don't run out. The only reserves they used to have came from people's savings, but now it's just money that was printed from thin air.

And let this brew in your mind until the latter pages of this book: once bankers decided to lend out money from savings over and over again, money stopped being tied to the value of gold and became something else entirely, since gold can only exist once, and definitely not eighty times. When we switched from the gold standard to this money by fiat, it was almost like you could hear the sound of a big gong echoing in the sky to signify a major dent/shift in the fabric of the universe.

Evan: Oh, a gong! Fun! In the end, it's quite simple. Prior to the GR, all the money in the world used to come from a pond full of a finite amount of water called asset-based lending. After the GR, thanks to the birth of QE, banks got to benefit from always having that reserve in their subbasement, along with their ability to sell bad debt whenever they got into trouble. Banks dried up the pond by creating junk assets based on bad loans, and the response was for the Fed to buy up those junk assets and trade them for more water to fill up the banks' reserves—except that water is real, while printing money is not; it's just a number in an account.

Justin: For all you readers who are not bankers, pay attention. What he's saying here is that the Fed bought all the bad loans—by the way, a bad loan is defined as money that is not going to be paid back. This essentially means that the Fed printed money to buy something that was utterly worthless. I bet you could make money this way too. So could I. Hell, I know of several things in my attic that could be described as priceless, if you know what I mean.

Laz: Or, hey, I was a homeless guy back in 2009. Maybe the Fed should've bought my shopping cart full of junk that I pushed around everywhere. Same thing, right?

Evan: Exactly the same thing.

Justin: What a system! It's so remarkable that I feel compelled to overexplain what's happening here.

Banks started off by simply offering a safe place to keep money. They took that money and loaned it out safely so they would get paid back. As the number of loans increased, society slowly became dependent on banks making loans. We have named this Bankism.

As time passed, the banks needed to come up with new ways to pump more money into the economy or the economy would fail to pay back the earlier loans. In this way, a debt-driven spiral of ever-greater debt was created. It has become increasingly difficult and frankly unwise to live without debt. Today, debt financing costs much less than expected asset appreciation. Therefore, not using debt is not smart.

The problem: debt has to be paid back. When banks wind up making bad loans, which is inevitable, the Federal Reserve is forced to buy these bad loans because they don't want the economy and the banking system to fail. When the Federal Reserve creates new minted money, it winds up flooding the owners of the bad debt with cash, causing assets like stocks to surge in price, just like it did during the economic collapse that followed the COVID crisis. It also replaces the money that was supposed to be earned but no longer is because the economy has failed—again. So while banks are sitting on a massive cushion of cash ensuring their sovereignty, the people of this country whom they are supposed to serve are pushed into a life of indebted servitude. As Connie said, we have therefore lost sovereignty on the national level and liberty on the individual level.

A System Based on Debt Cannot Survive

My friend, there are too many things wrong with a banking system that is supposedly independent of the government and the economy while also controlling both of those things.

As long as this debt-driven economy exists, greater and greater amounts of credit will be necessary to fuel growth. The problem with debt and credit is that they have to be paid back, which means less spending power and more work to make up the difference in the future (for everyone). Unless, of course, there's more debt. And round and round we go!

The other problem with needing more and more debt is that eventually bad loans not only start looking attractive to bankers, but they start looking essential. And because of QE, bad loans are without risk. In other words, some marginal bank somewhere is incentivized to start fudging its principles for making a good loan, because if it doesn't make the loan, then it can't pay its bills and it will go out of business. Put another way, the banks are always getting pushed toward making bad loans. Think about it: they can either fail now or fail later, so they choose to fail later by making bad loans now.

Put yet another way, it's like the whole system is designed to kill itself. And here we all stand, the rest of us, making all these sacrifices just to keep it alive.

The Great Recession's most significant revelation was this: the banking industry operates under a huge conflict of interest. Many say that the actions taken in the aftermath of the Great Recession saved the economy and returned the world to "normal." But is this a good or sustainable version of "normal"?

Commercial banks owning and operating the Federal Reserve are like private prisons owning and operating the legal system. The conflict between the business interest of banks and a moral, reasonable society are staggering. That conflict led directly to the GR. And yet we've learned in the years since—and especially during the pandemic—that the GR only scratches the surface. The banking system may very well be responsible for the imminent demise of humanity.

And so it was with that fluffy thought in mind that I stared up at that banker/jumper on the day the banking system died (temporarily). Here, this gentleman was very seriously pondering whether to make himself dead (permanently).

There's a certain energy that comes with watching a living being stand on the precipice of death. The only other time I'd experienced this sensation was during a bullfight in Seville, Spain. Barbaric as that tradition can seem to some, there is no denying the rush of adrenaline and the almost inherent thrill that comes from watching something die.

That same feeling rippled through the crowd below the jumper's building. By now, the police had arrived and had cordoned off a wide perimeter, behind which everyone was forced to stand. Of course this action was absolutely necessary so as to prevent the jumper from crashing into anyone else on the street below and ending more than one life in the process; it also struck me as an odd sort of action, in that it must have looked to the banker/jumper as if the police had just cleared him a nice landing pad to splatter into.

So there I was, a newly minted billionaire surrounded by energized and terrified and overwhelmingly curious onlookers—and there we all were, surrounded by a new reality that promised a nearly decade-long recession and a brand-new form and use of money from the banking system—and there stood the jumper, tears flowing down his cheeks, his lips moving desperately as he shouted into the sky, a banker too high above the ground for any of us to hear.

Here was a man who needed saving. He represented a banking system that absolutely did not need saving. In the end, that tragic day took the life of the former and not the latter. I will spare you the gruesome details, but I just have to say that witnessing a man jumping to his death is in no way something I would recommend. The sight still haunts me every time I think about it.

But the sight also instilled in me a new perspective about the world in which we live. Any system that could create this level of sheer desperation could not possibly be a healthy, functioning system. Bankism would pull the rug out from under the fortunes of many people, cause billions more to suffer deeply through the Great Recession, and even cause some to take their own lives.

It was then that I realized the problem: a debt-driven world is fundamentally flawed. How fundamentally flawed? I'm glad you asked …

CHAPTER FOUR

THE TRICKLE-AROUND MOUNTAIN

We don't really purchase what others produce with "money," but with what we produce.

—NARAYANA KOCHERLAKOTA, former chairman of the Minneapolis Federal Reserve

Time to get serious. Time for the big analogy! Evan, where you at?

Evan: Picture a massive mountain.

Justin: There he is.

Evan: This mountain is so tall and so large that it houses the entire American economy. At the top of the mountain, there is a spring. Just like a spring in the real world, this spring is almost like magic because it's as if the water appears out of nowhere. The difference is that on our mountain, the water that emerges from this spring is in fact all the money put into circulation by the Federal Reserve.

Now, just like with any spring at the top of a mountain, this water has to go somewhere. The Fed directs it to two places: commercial banks and the federal government in the form of debt. As this money is directed to those two places, we hear the sound of it roaring over the mountain. The more this money flows, the louder the roar.

The commercial banks take their water and loan it out, which only creates more noise. The government uses its water on all the agencies it funds, creating more noise. The corporations and business owners and consumers who receive loans spend it on work to be done, which creates more noise. Employees receiving income from their employers spend it on housing, cars, food, their families, entertainment, and so on. The more they spend, the noisier the mountain gets.

Connie: Aha!

Justin: Are you having an epiphany to go along with this interjection, my dearest?

Connie: Something like that. What's happening is, I've caught you jokers in an unoriginal idea.

Evan: Unoriginal?

Connie: This mountain is one of those deals where we put rich people on top and poor people on the bottom, and then all the money has to trickle down via loans and spending, right? Because there's a word for that already. It's *Reaganomics*.

Justin: Did you seriously just cross yourself in reverence?

Connie: Reaganomics is sacred to me. You know this.

Justin: I do, but—

Evan: It's a good point, Connie, but it's not precisely on target. Yes, there is a kind of trickle-down happening on this mountain, but we're not talking about Reaganomics. Why? Because the American economy doesn't work that way. The idea that tax cuts lead to a clean flow of money from the upper class, through the middle class, and down to the lower class is a pipe dream.

Connie: (grumbling about the words *pipe dream*)

Evan: No grumbling necessary. Because the left has it wrong too. They think taxing the rich will lead to a clean flow of money from government tax revenues into welfare coffers and into the hands of the homeless. That doesn't work either.

And the reason that both the right and the left can be wrong is simple: you're all picturing the mountain incorrectly. You're assuming that the water on this mountain follows the pull of gravity, like actual real-life water. But economics is not a gravity-based system. It's an ecosystem. The water on this mountain doesn't really trickle down. It trickles around.

Economics is not a gravity-based system. It's an ecosystem. The water on this mountain doesn't really trickle down. It trickles around.

Justin: Explain.

Evan: The movement of the water on this mountain is not about gravity. It's about the roar of the water. Yes, when it emerges from the spring, the water trickles to very specific places—commercial banks and the federal government—but once it gets into the hands of corporations, businesses, and people—once it starts getting spent—it trickles in a much more random fashion.

Justin: Help us visualize.

Evan: Will do. But that'll require an analogy on top of an analogy.

Justin: Kind of like an analogy pile.

Evan: I guess so.

Justin: Pile away.

The Hot Dog Stand

Evan: Imagine that somewhere on the side of our mountain is a hot dog stand.

Laz: Mmmm.

Justin: You've got Laz salivating.

Laz: What can I say? I'm a celebrated lover of hot dogs.

Evan: So the vendor of this hot dog stand thinks that he'll draw more business if he makes his stand more eye catching. He decides to have it painted. Problem is, business hasn't been booming lately, so he's going to need to borrow some money to pay for the upgrade. He goes to the bank, who loans him $100. The hot dog vendor uses this hundred to pay a professional painter, who does a fantastic job. The stand looks great.

Now the painter has this original $100. And his problem is that he works so hard that he never has time to clean his house. So he decides to use that $100 to pay to have his house cleaned. The professional housecleaner he hires does an excellent job, and now the painter has a clean house and the housecleaner has that $100 in her pocket.

The housecleaner decides that she would be more efficient in her job if she had a better vacuum cleaner, so she uses the hundred to buy one from the local mom-and-pop vacuum cleaner store.

Connie: They still have those?

Evan: Probably there aren't many left. But I'm trying to keep the analogy simple by not involving Amazon or Walmart just yet. In another chapter, we'll talk about how all these complicated supply chains make things even more fun. For now, though, it's all person to person in our analogy.

Anyway, now mom and pop have the $100. They're going to use it on their first romantic date in weeks. They go to a restaurant and spend it on a couple nice plates of pasta and a bottle of wine. Now the restaurant owner has the $100, and she decides to …

Well, you get the idea. That $100 isn't trickling down in this scenario; it's trickling around.

Connie: Okay, fine. You've illustrated the situation. Trickle down, trickle around. You're still just talking semantics.

Evan: Then you haven't yet spotted the real problem with this mountain that is the American economy. So let's add one more analogy to the pile.

The Unending Circle

Evan: Let's go back to that original $100. Now, imagine ten people standing in a circle. One of the people in the circle receives a $100 bill from the Federal Reserve's spring by way of a commercial bank loan. He passes that $100 to his right in exchange for goods or services. The second person passes the $100 to her right in exchange for different goods or services. This same $100 changes hands again and again, until it has completed a full rotation through ten people and returned to the original loan recipient.

In our hot dog–stand analogy, eventually that original $100 gets back to the hot dog vendor, who uses it to pay back his loan. The bank then loans that money back out, and another random trickle-around circle begins. In the real world, where money doesn't change hands as directly and freely, that $100 actually spends a little time in a bank before passing from one goods/service provider to another. And while it sits there, it can be loaned out again and again. It's baffling.

But you see the trick here? In our circle of ten people, that $100 loan leads to $1,000 in spending. By flowing a mere $100 into the mountain's economy, the Federal Reserve has increased the GDP by

$1,000. It sounds so miraculous! Especially when you consider that the banks can keep loaning that hundred again and again. If they do this ten more times, the GDP grows by $10,000, and it's all still just $100 changing hands!

Connie: I'm having a hard time seeing what's so wrong with this unending-circle situation. In fact, it sounds kind of great.

Laz: I have to agree with Connie here. Also, the hot dog–based system is fine by me.

Evan: It's water based, but if you want to get hung up on the hot dogs, that's fine. You're both wrong, though. The system is not in any way great or fine. It's just really good at looking and sounding great or fine. All that beautiful water flowing from the top, that spectacular roar of the water changing hands and trickling around the mountain, lends the impression that there is lots and lots of money in circulation.

But there isn't.

Laz: So what?

Evan: I'll tell you what: this artificial impression of abundance leaves all the power with the single entity controlling the spring at the top of the mountain.

If the Fed decides that what this economy needs is for it to stop loaning out so much money, it can tell the banks and the government that the flow is going to have to slow down a bit. This in turn compels the banks to say to that hot dog vendor, "No, you can't have a $100 loan. But you can have a $90 loan."

Now the painter is going to have to settle for painting the stand for $90 instead of $100. The housecleaner is going to have to accept that same reduction in pay for her services. Mom and pop will have to lower their expectations slightly for date night. Round and round the $90 goes until it gets back to the hot dog vendor, having changed hands ten times.

Here we see how the Fed's decision changed what would have been $1,000 in spending to a mere $900 in spending. All of that economic activity—all of that considerable deflation of the value of work—all of those people having to settle for less work, which means they make less money for their goods and services—it all traces back to a seemingly arbitrary decision by the Fed.

That's the big illusion on this mountain: the notion that the entity controlling everything is just making small adjustments to help keep the whole system healthy. But those small adjustments lead to massive changes in the roar and the flow of money.

The other big illusion is that no matter what, there's all this spending going on and all this economic activity, but it's all happening based on the smaller amount of money supply being fed from the spring by, well, the Fed. The single entity at the top makes these seemingly small changes—all of them designed to keep banks from running into any serious economic trouble, by the way—and these small changes have a gigantic impact on the people who live on the mountain.

> **The single entity at the top makes these seemingly small changes—all of them designed to keep banks from running into any serious economic trouble, by the way—and these small changes have a gigantic impact on the people who live on the mountain.**

Let's Name This Mountain

Connie: Isn't this a bit of an oversimplification?

Justin: Help us to know where your head is, Con.

Connie: Not everyone's getting a $100 loan. The hot dog vendor, sure. But what about the massive corporations near the top of the mountain?

Evan: Sure, they're not getting $100 loans. They're getting multimillion dollar loans. But the way it travels is essentially the same. Some of it gets spent on goods and services that help the corporation do what it does. Some goes out by way of income to employees. Yes, job creation. And all this money changes hands, moving around and sometimes down the mountain. But no matter how that money gets broken up, it's all still part of that original multimillion-dollar loan, and it all eventually makes its way back to the commercial banks to get loaned out again in a new form. It all still contributes to the singular roaring sound of money changing hands on this mountain.

In this way, if you want to get slightly more complicated, we shouldn't be visualizing clean circles of people passing money around the mountain. We should imagine a patchwork of random pockets of businesses and people passing money around in all directions.

And if we can borrow anything from Reaganomics, Connie, it's this: at the bottom of the mountain, there is little to no spending happening—the people down here, for any number of reasons that are usually beyond their control, have no means to contribute to the flow of water. They have no spending power. These people survive almost exclusively on aid from the government.

In this way, a huge amount of the water the government receives from the Fed's spring winds up getting carted down the mountain to help these people near the bottom survive. The rest of the mountain ignores them, as they don't have any spending power.

Connie: I have some thoughts on that.

Laz: Same.

Justin: I'm sure you do. But let's allow Evan to finish before we start the debate, okay? Evan, let's wrap this analogy up with a clever name.

Evan: I'm glad you suggested this, because I actually have a name for it already. Spent all night trying to come up with it.

At first, I thought it should probably be called the Trickle-Down Mountain, because it references how water flows, it offers a subtle dig on an outdated understanding of the American economy, and it just sounds catchy. But the water on this mountain doesn't exactly trickle down, does it? Once it starts getting spent, it trickles randomly from business to business and person to person.

This mountain creates the illusion of there being lots and lots of money that has nothing to do with the Fed and commercial banks. People just don't realize that it's all the same relatively small amount of money being allowed to flow out from the spring at the top. This economy isn't about gravity pulling water down the mountain; it's about the roar of water moving around.

Justin: Well, don't leave us in suspense, man.

Evan: I decided that it should be called the Trickle-Around Mountain.

Justin: I think you missed a point, buddy. The water coming out of the spring at the top of the mountain is magical because it comes from nowhere, and yet somehow it becomes the equivalent of the work people and businesses do for each other.

Connie: Wait. How does it become the equivalent of work?

Justin: Once the banks have loaned out the water/money, it becomes something important—when just seconds earlier, that water/money was nothing at all.

As the people exchange the money from one product/service to another, they were actually exchanging what they produced for what other people produced. In essence, they weren't exchanging money, but rather their work products.

This means that it is the banking system that allows people to work for each other, and it is the banking system that determines how many jobs and how much work is to be done. Put simply, it is the banking system that determines the value of work.

Cue that gong sound again, Evan. Because the universe has just taken a new dent.

Evan: Cueing the gong …

Justin: All joking aside, and let's just put this in bold font, **ask yourself why banks are needed to determine how much work we can do for each other.**

The answer, if there is any relevant rationale, is that work translates into wages, and controlling wages—the dollars per hour for work—is a very effective way of controlling inflation and deflation.

Which brings us to another important thesis to this book: because of the nature of the Trickle-Around Mountain, wages are no longer an effective means of improving the standard of living. In fact, looking at wages is counterproductive. Why?

Just Ask Bernie...

Today, in America, we are the wealthiest nation in the history of the world, but few Americans know that because so much of the new income and wealth goes to the people on top … Today, in America, millions of our people are working two or three jobs just to survive. In fact, Americans work longer hours than do the people of any industrialized country. Despite the incredibly hard work and long hours of the American middle class, 58 percent of all new income generated today is going to the top one percent …

Today, in America, nearly 47 million Americans are living in poverty and over 20 percent of our children, including 36 percent of African American children, are living in poverty—the highest rate of childhood poverty of nearly any major country on Earth ...

Today, in America, youth unemployment and underemployment is over 35 percent. Meanwhile, we have more people in jail than any other country and countless lives are being destroyed as we spend $80 billion a year locking up fellow Americans.

—SENATOR BERNIE SANDERS, speech delivered at Georgetown University, November 19, 2015

It's All About That GDP

Connie: I'm going to ignore how Laz is now salivating again, this time over a Bernie Sanders quote, and just say that, Evan, I love this analogy.

Evan: Aw.

Justin: Evan's blushing, you guys.

Connie: The reason I love this analogy is that it proves everything I've been saying for years. The American economy is a beautiful system. It's a meritocracy. You can receive money, make money, and spend money. And you become a part of this grand ecosystem on the mountain. If you do well, you move up the mountain. If you don't, you remain at the bottom. The system works!

Evan: Well, sure, as long as you assume that life and the economy is always fair. Think about it; you can only contribute to the mountain's economy if your skills are considered useful. If your skills are outdated or otherwise considered not useful, then you can't contribute. And you wind up trapped at the bottom with no way to climb.

Laz: This is exactly why it's so important that the government does what it does. And it's why the government is such a beautiful system, to borrow your phrase, Connie. It's using something like 75 percent of the resources it borrows from the Fed (which is converted to treasury bonds) and/or receives in taxes from the public to take care of these people who are trapped.

When the meritocracy leaves people out, there are shelters and food kitchens, welfare and food stamps. Disability. People can get by even if their skills aren't considered useful and they can't get a job. The safety net takes care of them, and they can still contribute to the mountain.

Evan: You went off the rails on that last piece. People relying on the safety net can't contribute to the mountain. They receive only what they need to survive. They don't contribute to the roar of spending in any meaningful way.

What contributes to the roar of the mountain is the inefficiency of the government at work. Let's put it this way: every homeless person in San Francisco costs the city $25,000. There is no reason for a reasonable government to continue allowing homelessness to happen if we're spending $25,000 on each homeless person. Yet, the government is so inefficient that here we are with record homelessness across the country.

Regardless, people without money do not contribute to growing the GDP.

Laz: You say that like growing the GDP is the only point of the Trickle-Around Mountain.

Evan: It is the only point. What other point is there?

Connie: Oof.

Evan: It's true! Sure, we have all this money changing hands. Some people are getting rich and others are getting left out. The banks are loaning the same money out over and over again. But if you step back and look at the mountain as a whole, what is the point? The only point is to grow the GDP. As long as it's growing, we have the illusion that the system is working. How could it not be when the GDP is growing so reliably?

But what is GDP exactly? It's supposedly a measure of how the economy is doing. But since the economy is based exclusively on this trickle-around flow of water, and since that flow all comes from the Fed and the big banks lending out money, the GDP is actually a measure of how banks are doing.

If the sole goal of all economic policy in the United States is to ensure that the GDP keeps growing, that's another way of saying that the sole goal of all economic policy in the United States is to ensure that the banking system keeps growing.

If GDP is the only measure of our economic health, then it's also proof that the only point of our entire economy is to benefit the banks that run it. There is literally no other point to our economic system.

Oh, and by the way, that means that the sum total of everything we do, all our work, adds up to propping up the banking system. This is really a lot worse than it sounds because the entirety of people's existence for the last hundred years has NOT been to make their lives better or even to Make America Great; it has been to make the banking system great.

Personally, this is not what I want written on my tombstone.

Laz: Yowzer.

Evan: Meanwhile, there are plenty of negative side effects—some of which we're just going to have to save for another discussion.

For now, though, remember that growing the GDP is the only point of this economy. And keeping GDP growing requires all this repetitive lending. All this debt spending. All this government contributing such a huge percentage of resources just to help people at the bottom of the mountain survive. Something like 12 percent of the American economy is government spending on the poor. Isn't that a massive waste of resources and work, just having to help people survive? Does that sound like an efficient system?

Laz: Boss, I'm not following here. How is helping people a waste of resources? We are human because we empathize. Robert Reich, in *To Serve Society*, says it so well: "Most human beings want to be part of something larger than themselves. They crave moral purpose and social solidarity. If we overlook this, we fail to understand the means and meaning of social progress."[2]

Evan: It's a point well taken, Laz. I, too, want to be the benevolent helper. I really do. But the problem with government is its inefficiency.

In 2016, it would have taken only $171 billion to move all Americans out of poverty status (otherwise known as the poverty gap), and yet we spent $364 billion on the thirteen safety net programs.[3]

The stories and facts about government inefficiency are endless. It has always been that way and always will. Just look at where the government initiates its activities, in the embattled haze of politics, in the form of massive bills thousands of pages long that are impossible to understand. We need a whole judicial system in place to make sure it's executed correctly and to the letter of the law.

This is why any goodwill from the government is ultimately counterproductive.

Laz: That's a hard pill to swallow!

Justin: This is where we have to go back to a simpler time. Back to the Founding Fathers, who saw the world before the banks took over. They knew that the government had to serve the people in the

---

2 Robert Reich, "To Serve Society," https://robertreich.org/post/54441489916.

3 "Ideas for Cost Savings," http://federalsafetynet.com/cost-savings.html.

most limited—and yes, small—way possible. Because what they saw, time and time again, was that government is either incompetent or malevolent in the use of brutal force.

The smaller the government, the better.

Connie: Now you're speaking my language.

Justin: Then may I quote Ronald Reagan?

Connie: Oh, God, yes.

It's time we asked ourselves if we still know the freedoms intended for us by the Founding Fathers. James Madison said, "We base all our experiments on the capacity of mankind for self-government." This idea that government was beholden to the people, that it had no other source of power except the sovereign people, is still the newest, most unique idea in all the long history of man's relation to man. For almost two centuries, we have proved man's capacity for self-government, but today, we are told we must choose between a left and right or, as others suggest, a third alternative, a kind of safe middle ground. I suggest to you there is no left or right, only an up or down. Up to the maximum of individual freedom consistent with law and order, or down to the ant heap of totalitarianism; and regardless of their humanitarian purpose, those who would sacrifice freedom for security have, whether they know it or not, chosen this downward path. Plutarch warned, "The real destroyer of the liberties of the people is he who spreads among them bounties, donations, and benefits."

—RONALD REAGAN, Rendezvous with Destiny speech, October 27, 1964

Connie: (blushing and batting her eyes) Maybe I do love you, Justin.

Laz: But, boss, we can't just ignore the needy.

Justin: This isn't the end of the book.

The Conservative and the Progressive Argue about the Government

Connie: Can we talk about the government for a minute?

Justin: By all means.

Connie: Because I feel like they throw another monkey wrench into your analogy.

Laz: You think the government throws a monkey wrench into everything.

Connie: Guilty as charged. But this time, I'm right. All those people at the bottom receiving handouts in the form of welfare and food stamps? They don't just die out. Okay, fine, the banking system makes it difficult for enough water to flow down to them naturally. But in response, we're just trucking or hobbling all this bottled water down the Trickle-Around Mountain (maybe we should call it the Hand-Me-Down Mountain) from the government tier to the low-spending tier.

So the fix should be obvious: if we restructure the economy so we can stop feeding those lazy folks at the bottom, the government will need less money/water at the top, which frees up more money/water to trickle around to the people doing actual job creation and actual work.

Laz: Whoa, whoa, whoa. As a former representative of a class you just called "lazy folks," I feel like I need to chime in here. Entitlement programs aren't handouts. They're patches to fix the major problems Bankism creates. The way they flow the water/money down the mountain leaves less work for people who may not have gotten lucky enough to land a job.

Plus, I would be remiss if I didn't mention automation. People keep losing jobs to technology. That's a fact, and it isn't going to go away.

So why should anyone suffer from the consequences of a man made system? Nature provides to animals that do not work, so why should a man made system be harsher to people than nature is to animals?

Connie: Nature isn't harsh? Ever hear of a drought, a hurricane, or an earthquake? Nature is quite brutal.

Laz: Yes, but what happens once the natural disaster is over? Nature provides again. Animals find their way. Ecosystems replenish themselves.

But what happens after a man made disaster like an economic depression? The banks get bailed out and people are left fending for themselves.

Connie: You can't lend money to people who can't pay it back. It's that simple.

Laz: This is true, but it's pointless to lend money to people who already have money while most of society remains in duress.

Connie: Why is it pointless? People and businesses wouldn't borrow the money if they weren't going to use it. And when they use it, what will they use it for? They'll hire people and make fewer lazy people.

Laz: There you go with "lazy" again.

Connie: I'm sorry to be harsh. But you get the point. Once someone has a job, then they are no longer lazy because they are working.

Laz: My eyes just rolled a full revolution. You're trying to justify eliminating all safety nets because people are lazy and there would be a job for them if they weren't lazy.

Connie: I don't think I need to justify rewards going to the hustlers of society.

Laz: So everyone receiving government aid is lazy or a hustler? What about seniors and social security? Medicaid and Medicare? Or what about the people who received enhanced unemployment benefits or Paycheck Protection loans during the COVID crisis? Are all these recipients lazy hustlers?

Connie: No, they just contribute to a large voting bloc. So there's nothing you can do about it. We're a democracy, after all.

Laz: But the safety net is primarily made up of these three agencies. What's the point of pinching a few pennies and punishing the rest?

Connie: Pennies? Those are taxpayer dollars.

Laz: It would literally cost less to just have health insurance for everyone.

Connie: But people need to have a reason to work. Health insurance is a good reason.

Laz: Why do you have such a big interest in everyone working? You barely work yourself. I mean, what the hell is a political advisor anyway?

Connie: I have money. I don't need to work. And when I do work, it's for my rich friends who pay very well.

Laz: I get it. You've never had to sweat your entire life to put food on the table, and your hands are like satin.

Connie: Why, Laz, aren't you the charmer?

Laz: I wasn't trying to be charming. The problem isn't with desire or even ability. The problem is that everything on this Trickle-Around Mountain is controlled by the Federal Reserve, which controls the water by lowering or raising interest rates in the hope of creating more or fewer jobs.

If I can share a quick story here, let me tell you about how I became homeless in the first place. I was living in Seattle. Had a great job, but I was in debt up to my eyeballs. I won't tell you who my employer was, but let's just say you've heard of them.

Anyway, when the Fed lowered interest rates, my employer could suddenly afford to buy all these robots that made my job obsolete. The loan was just so cheap that the brass figured, why not invest in our future and make our labor costs that much cheaper?

So they did. I lost my job to a robot. And then I lost my house and everything else I owned when my skills proved unnecessary and I couldn't land a new job in time to stave off all my creditors. I'd call it a sob story if I was alone. But I'm not. So, so many people have lost their jobs to robots. Many don't wind up on the streets like me—they aren't so unlucky—but some do. And it's all because of some seemingly minor numbers adjustment at the top.

No one at the Fed ever considers how raising interest rates means millions of people get kicked to the street. They don't think about how their small number of adjustments leads to kids missing meals and going on these so-called handout programs like free lunch at school.

Evan's analogy is great because it shows how the Trickle-Around Mountain provides enough separation between the big bankers and their decisions that cause the people at the bottom of the mountain to suffer. And because both lowering interest rates and raising interest rates hurts jobs from either job cuts or automation, the working class never gets a raise—at least not in the last fifty years.

Connie: You're describing unemployment as if it doesn't have any benefits to society.

Laz: How could unemployment possibly have benefits to society?

Connie: It stabilizes the cost of labor.

Laz: You mean it drives down the cost of labor.

Connie: Tomato, tomahto, potato, potahto. Corporations need cheap labor if they're going to get anything done. How else would they make a profit? And when they profit, their stock price goes up, which means they can borrow more money from the banks and create more jobs.

Laz: But those corporations will only take that loan if the Fed lowers interest rates, and the whole vicious cycle begins again.

Connie: What other choice is there?

Justin: Exactly! What choice does the Trickle-Around Mountain leave us? Let's put down the boxing gloves, you two. You're both right. There's just another way of looking at it.

Laz: Enlighten us.

Justin: First, a quick question: what would fix this Trickle-Around Mountain most efficiently, taxing the rich or cutting taxes?

Laz: Taxing the rich.

Connie: Cutting taxes.

Evan: Predictable answers.

Justin: And you're both wrong. The answer is that neither is efficient because both strategies just feed back into the same trickle-around system, where all the money flows around the mountain exactly the same as before. The winners and losers of the system change slightly, but overall, we're still talking about a system that benefits the banks first, second, and third.

Connie: So the system is broken.

Evan: That's the thing. The system isn't broken. It does exactly what it's supposed to do: it benefits banks in good times and in bad. It's just that this goal is completely ridiculous.

The system isn't broken. It does exactly what it's supposed to do: it benefits banks in good times and in bad.

If all we're trying to do is keep the banking system healthy, then it doesn't matter which side of the traditional left-wing/right-wing argument you come down on. Either way, the Trickle-Around Mountain needs poor people at the bottom and banks and producers at the top. Taxes, unemployment, and welfare are all necessary evils in this society. They're all unavoidable side effects of keeping the water flowing through the Fed and the big banks.

Meanwhile, these supposedly lazy or untalented people at the bottom of the mountain are actually just trapped. Most of them are the poorest people in society, people who aren't receiving any water directly from the source. They receive it all in the form of charity or government programs. In this way, they have nothing to earn or spend. Without anything to earn or spend, they have no hope of climbing the mountain. They remain idle, receiving just enough from the government or charity to prevent complete social collapse.

But Connie Doesn't Feel Trapped

Connie: You used the word *trapped*, and I have to take issue with that. This is a free country, after all. I'm never really trapped in one place on the mountain. I live in New York, but if I wanted, I could move to Miami.

Evan: But both New York and Miami are a part of the mountain. Where you fit on the part of the mountain that is Miami will look pretty similar to your position in New York. It'll be the same job and same spending capacity, just in a different location. What you call freedom to move to Miami is really just a matter of changing scenery. You're still in the same spot on the Trickle-Around Mountain.

Connie: Fine. I'll switch careers when I move to Miami.

Justin: Could you please switch careers *and* we'll move to Miami?

Connie: You're being flip. But no, really. It's possible in this country for someone to move to a new location and get a bigger and better job. It happens all the time.

Evan: But even if you do that, you've really only just moved slightly on the Trickle-Around Mountain. You're still a cog in the same machine. And before you say it, yes, it is possible to go from poor to rich in this country.

Justin: I was born into the lower middle class. And now I own a helicopter. I can take off from the roof of my luxury high-rise and land on my yacht. It's awesome.

Evan: Granted. It *is* awesome. But it's also extremely rare. Your story is celebrated for a reason: it almost never happens.

Connie: You know, I'm wondering why it's such a bad thing to not have a choice about having to work and support the mountain. I mean, I'm as freedom loving as the next red-blooded talking head, but there comes a point where you just have to say, "That's life."

Evan: The problem is that the mountain is causing a host of doomsday scenarios to play out.

Connie: Oh, c'mon. Are you talking about global warming?

Evan: Among other things.

Connie: That's all just left-wing conspiracy propagated by the Chinese and the solar and wind industries. Tree huggers be damned.

Evan: Fine, but there are too many catastrophes playing out on this planet, like the Sixth Great Extinction, and sooner or later this train is going to go full steam right into the living hell of one of them.

Connie: Don't even get me started. You're beginning to sound like Laz.

Evan: You want to keep it on economics? Then how about these massive recessions that crush productivity? How about the massive government, corporate, and personal debt that this country is slowly being drowned in?

Which leads us to the second counterpoint, which is that the climb is all kind of pointless.

No matter where you reside on the mountain, you're still just contributing to the mountain and the dominance of the banking system. Whatever you do for a living, however much or little money you make, and no matter where on the mountain you decide to live and work, you're still just contributing to the pointlessness of the whole.

Our only purpose, no matter who we are, is to help grow the

GDP and sustain the banking system. How uninspiring is that? Would life not be better if we knew we were all working together toward a better future?

Connie: So we're all working our entire lives just so the banking system can exist and thrive?

Evan: Everything we do, every advancement we make, is really just so the banking system can persist and grow. That's our sole purpose as people living on and contributing to this mountain.

Connie: That's completely insane.

Laz: If I can chime in here, I think we need to broaden our scope a bit. No offense, Connie, but just because you don't feel trapped on the mountain doesn't mean people aren't trapped. You're missing the point.

The years I spent being homeless is the real trap. When you don't have money, you have no options. You beg and grovel, you lie and cheat, borrow or steal. When you need to eat, you bend the rules. Laws become obstacles to survival.

As bad as it was for me, I saw far worse. Exploitation is everywhere in the homeless community. What women and children agree to when they need money is appalling.

Let's face it—the main driver of exploitation is fundamentally economics. At some point, your life isn't worth more than the next meal, because you will die without that meal. People without money have few options. This is what drives the sex trade, child labor, labor camps, sweatshops, cults, religious fundamentalism, fanaticism, abortion, and every instance where people are manipulated, abused, and taken advantage of.

Let me quote someone with some legitimacy:

Poverty kills far more people than all the wars in history, more people than all the suicides in history. Not only does structural violence (defined as an institution that harms people by preventing them from meeting their basic needs) kill more people than all the behavioral violence put together, structural violence is also the main cause of behavioral violence.[4]

—DR. JAMES GILLIGAN, HARVARD MEDICAL SCHOOL,
author of *Violence: Our Deadly Epidemic and Its Causes*

Laz Considers Moving to the Woods

Laz: This is not the first time I have considered moving to the woods and becoming one of Evan's woodsmen. The woods seem like a quaint place when you're homeless.

Evan: They're not my woodsmen. And anyway, not even that allows you to escape from the Trickle-Around Mountain …

Laz: You mean I can't even be a woodsman anymore?

Evan: There's no option to remove yourself from the mountain, because the mountain is all-encompassing. There are no services you could possibly need that you can receive without paying for them. You could live in the woods, sure, but you would be totally cut off. Even if you found a way to live off the land to where you only needed money to pay off the land, pay your taxes, or pay for the occasional medical assistance, you would still need to get money somehow. And the only way to get it is to plug in to the economy.

Either that, or you just have a stockpile of it you can live off indefinitely. But even then, you still have to spend some of that

---

4   J. Gilligan, *Violence: Our Deadly Epidemic and Its Causes*, G. P. Putnam, New York, NY, 1996.

money—whether on land or internet access or healthcare. And even if you're a woodsman supposedly living off the grid, when you spend money, you're helping to perpetuate the banking system.

It's just like the point Connie raised earlier. Even if you're financially free to move from place to place, you're still stuck on the mountain because the mountain is the only place you can spend the money. You can't take your money to the woods or to some fantasy island somewhere because it doesn't spend there. In even the most extreme self-reliance scenarios, you're still living on the Trickle-Around Mountain.

You're also trapped by greed.

Laz: Explain.

Evan: Decisions on the Trickle-Around Mountain are made by banks, and their only purpose is self-perpetuation and self-enrichment. We're all just fighting for the trickle of water that banks provide. When your life depends on the trickle, your central purpose becomes about money. Greed is a natural function of money being all there is. Money is everything you need to survive, and so greed and indifference of the poor follows.

As much as we would like to believe in the freedom of a naturalist's life, there is no realistic alternative to living on the mountain and succumbing to this needy and greedy system. Where the woodsman took care of his neighbor because it made sense, that was more like trading favors. Today, there is no account for favors; there is only money. And people without money can't return the favor, so everyone loses their sympathy, and instead a loathing of the poor festers.

In this and many other ways, we've all kind of lost our freedom because we're all dependent on or otherwise contribute to the banking system.

This causes problems society-wide because that dependence reduces the ability to make genuine differences in this world. You want to reduce the carbon footprint? Good luck, because none of the higher-ups on the Trickle-Around Mountain are willing to pay for that. And even if they were willing, they wouldn't be able, because you can't compete for a place on the Trickle-Around Mountain while also tackling big problems like climate change. You want to eradicate poverty? That's a nonstarter, because poverty is a huge part of what makes the mountain function.

So many people in this world want to do good things and advance society, but they can't because we're all so dependent on the trickle of money from the banks.

Laz: So I guess I have to keep going in to work, then.

Connie: I feel like I need to stand up for the banking system. I mean, we would all be woodspeople if it weren't for the banks. And I for one like getting my nails done while I'm at the spa.

Justin: Yeah, I like that too. Nothing better.

Connie: The truth is that the banking system puts people to work, it drives efficiency, and it makes these awesome lifestyles like Justin's and mine possible.

Evan: There are definitely benefits to the banking system, and we never said it was all bad, nor are we suggesting abolishing it. We are simply saying that it can't be the sole purpose for our existence, because our ability to exist is being jeopardized by this banking system.

If a few small tweaks to the system can create massive change, massive benefits, and still allow you to get your nails done at the spa, all while making humanity sustainable, would you be game?

Connie: Doesn't sound like I have anything to lose and I have everything to gain.

Evan: Exactly. But I do have to push back on your sentiment about banks creating efficiency. The truth is, when you don't know where you're going because your only purpose is to grow the GDP, you basically wind up chasing your own tail.

I'll expand on this more later. For now, if we don't do anything, you'll lose everything. And until we change our way of thinking, we all have to keep working on this mountain. We're all trapped. Completely, totally trapped.

Connie: Actually, this is a common talking point for my party. People have to pull their own weight. You can't have half the population sitting around, because that means the other half of the country has to work twice as hard. The mountain, as you describe it, makes me see that very few Americans are actually pulling the country forward. The country is being pulled forward by the cheap labor of other countries.

Evan: Now you're getting it, Connie. The quality of the work on the mountain matters. GDP is pointless if you're chasing your own tail. But it gets worse ...

On That Uplifting Note ...

Now that Evan has all of us sufficiently bummed, it's my job to point to the silver lining in all this.

This is fixable! But there are BIG obstacles to overcome. And sometimes even I get overwhelmed.

We just need to rethink our understanding of what money is supposed to be. It isn't just about creating work and making a living. You can work anywhere on this mountain. The problem is that the whole mountain is limited because it's all there is. You can't take the money you make and move off the mountain to go live on an island or something, because the money is useless there. You have no choice but to live and work on this mountain.

We thought we were free, but we're not. We're forced to live on this mountain. The work we do, we don't have any choice. We're just living for this GDP growth, just living to benefit the banks, and for no real purpose that impacts our own personal daily lives or the future lives of our children. We're stuck.

This is the Orwellian truth—after all, what is the difference between somebody telling you what to do and not having a choice in what you can do? Our Orwellian system limits what trickles around and how it trickles around. It lashes us to this need to create jobs that will keep all those millions of people working and consuming at least comfortable enough to continue taking on debt and paying it back. And if you're near the bottom, the government provides you just enough to survive and not ponder open rebellion.

I know we've been at this a long time at this point, but let me just overexplain this again.

Left-leaning people are right to think we need to help those who struggle in this Trickle-Around Mountain Bankism world. The problem is that first, the government is terrible at doing anything. Second, the reason there are so many people struggling isn't because they are unfortunate or untalented; it's because Bankism forces poverty, misfortune, and for a certain percentage of people to be essentially useless. This in turn forces the government's hand to create safety nets and welfare programs, which ultimately lead to massive debt and the loss of sovereignty.

On the other side of the coin, right-leaning people think that wealthy people, a.k.a. job creators, will provide opportunities even though history has shown that the opposite is true. Wealthy producers cut wages and lay off their employees for even small profits. The profit incentive has no scruples; just look at the history of slavery, which was driven by profits and banks. Nevertheless, to them, Ayn Rand's selfishness principle and defense of the producers seems like the right answer. They never address stagnating wages and a shrinking middle class or poverty and the real reason big government's safety nets are needed.

The debt-driven economy breaks the government, as it has to respond to the shortfalls of Bankism by borrowing money, because even the highest tax rates can't flip the bill of all the people left out. This government debt actually means that the people owe more taxes than they have paid, and the only way to pay those taxes is by earning and working for it. This is the definition of indentured servitude.

There is more—debt is not something that people are built to take on. We are not genetically built to be burdened by debt. Is it possible that the psychological burden of debt is driving obesity and chronic illness in America?

Finally, to sum it all up, it is important to visualize the Trickle-Around Mountain as just that: a single mountain. Because then you can see that there is no purpose to the mountain. The only measure we have, and the only measure we use, is GDP. The total cumulative work done is for the purpose of propping up some banking metric. This is the enlightening part of the exercise: besides a few personal goals that we may or may not meet in our lives, all those years spent on getting educated and working are for the sole purpose of keeping the banking system going.

It is fair to conclude that the biggest failure of intelligence in human history is happening right now. The greatest minds and the leaders of the world fail to see how the American banking system has turned the work of humanity into nothing more than activity, as measured by GDP. They don't recognize how Bankism has made it impossible for humanity to plan its future or do much at all about the suffering of the poor all around the world.

There will be an instinct, in the minds of my discerning readers, to try to rationalize Bankism as necessary. It's that old line of thinking: "This is the way things have always been done. These are the factual realities. So what choice do we have?" In this case, it's all reinforced by the notion that this is what academia is supposed to be doing—we've invented a whole art/science around our understanding (however limited) of economics.

Well, as it turns out, economics is not a study of the banking system. And perhaps academics is part of the problem.

Everyone is beholden to the way things have always been done. We have systems set up and designed to support that one central, deeply flawed system. It seems so very difficult to change the Trickle-Around Mountain because, well, it's a friggin' mountain. They're notoriously hard to move.

So stick around for the next chapter, where we'll talk about a few more of the ills that this seemingly immovable mountain creates for our society.

CHAPTER FIVE

THE FROG AND THE WOOL

The basic tool for the manipulation of reality is the manipulation of words. If you can control the meaning of words, you can control the people who must use them.

—PHILIP K. DICK, "How to Build a Universe That Doesn't Fall Apart Two Days Later"

I'm going to step on Evan's toes here and bring the metaphor this time.

Evan: Ouch. I thought this was my thing …

Justin: Would it help if I built my metaphor around something water related, like you always seem to do?

Evan: Only slightly.

Justin: Then slightly it is!

Picture a frog in a pond. Actually, let's picture a whole slew of frogs in a pond. They're all hopping around, valiantly contributing to this complex ecosystem full of different life-forms that all rely on each other to survive and thrive.

For more years than we could possibly comprehend, these frogs have been doing just that in this very pond. There's been tens of thousands of generations of these critters here in this place. And look how cute they are! And how useful, too, since they eat flies and other bugs we don't enjoy having around while we're trying to sun ourselves pondside.

Because we have been observing them for the past few generations, we know that most of these frogs eat ten flies a day, and almost all of them reproduce successfully. They tend to birth just a mess of tadpoles, many of which avoid danger long enough to become nematodes or whatever before growing into frogs.

Evan: Actually, they grow into what are called *froglets*, which are like frogs with a long tadpole tail. A nematode is something entirely different. A nematode is sometimes called a roundworm, even though it's more like an insect than a worm. Anyway, nematodes have nothing to do with the life cycle of frogs.

Justin: Nerd.

Evan: Hey, I'm just sayin' …

Justin: But wait! Something is wrong. Suddenly, our thriving frog colony isn't thriving so well anymore. With every breeding cycle, a larger and larger percentage of their tadpoles hatch with, like, two heads or three tails or something. They're weird, is what I'm saying. Something has gone very wrong.

Now, if we're good scientists, what do we blame for this change? We know that these frogs have thrived for tens of thousands of generations. So do we blame this latest generation of frogs for their plight? Do we call them lazy or stupid and say they need to try harder to breed right?

Or do we investigate the surrounding ecosystem, discovering that recent weather patterns have eroded the land to the point where some strange pesticides from the neighboring farm have begun trickling into the pond and contaminating frog eggs?

Put another way, when something is suddenly terribly wrong with the system, do we blame the system or the living beings that the system is causing problems for?

Of course we blame the system! We find the cause of the frogs' weird breeding situation, and if we're activist enough, we take measures to fix the problem. Then, we sit back and watch the frogs thrive.

This is the way it should be, am I right? Whenever something goes wrong, you find ways to fix that wrong thing so that it won't go wrong anymore. This is the way it works for any physical science. Find problem, work toward solution, identify solution, fix problem.

Unfortunately, there's at least one science out there where this isn't in any way the case. Evan, would you be so kind as to identify the science I'm talking about here?

Economics. It's economics.

Evan: Since you stole my metaphor thunder, I would be happy to take over on the explanation. Of course you're referring to economics. I would split hairs here a bit by pointing out that economics is considered a social science and not a physical science, but still, your point is salient.

Justin: Thanks … I guess?

Evan: Whatever you call this supposed science, the way we think about economics is rather silly. It's as if the word *economics* has been defined incorrectly—and, moreover, that it was defined incorrectly on purpose.

Justin: Excellent use of *moreover*. Words like that really class up the joint. But anyway, why would it have been defined incorrectly on purpose?

Evan: To fool the workers of the world. It's just like your frog metaphor. Our definition of "economics" suggests that people are to blame for their situation; this is precisely so the banking system can't be blamed for the economy.

When the economy is in the toilet—which is to say, when conditions lead to imbalances that create shortages of money, jobs, and opportunity for lower-class people—the tendency is to blame those lower-class people:

> **Our definition of *economics* suggests that people are to blame for their situation; this is precisely so the banking system can't be blamed for the economy.**

"Why don't they just get a job?"

"Clearly, they're not working hard enough."

"The problem isn't with the system; it's with widespread laziness and the expectation of a handout."

Connie: Stop. My ears are burning.

Evan: This kind of thinking pins all the blame for economic failures on the people those failures impact most. It's all backward, like saying the frogs' ecosystem is dependent on the frogs' behavior. Okay, sure, a frog could behave in a way that damages the ecosystem. It could go on a hunger strike or something and allow the pond to be overrun by insects. It could commit suicide-by-swan and just jump into some bird's mouth.

Justin: Yeah, what does eat frogs in the wild anyway?

Evan: At the risk of being called a nerd again, it's usually birds, snakes, or lizards, but sometimes rodent-like creatures will eat them too.

Justin: Nerd.

Evan: Any way you slice it, it's preposterous to think that a frog—or even a community of frogs—could have as much impact on its ecosystem as its ecosystem could have on it. It's like looking at Justin's scenario, where the pesticides were creating the two-headed, three-tailed tadpoles and blaming the frogs instead of erosion or the farmer or the company that sold the pesticide to the farmer.

And yet that's how we view economics. We pin it with the label "social science," which is a fancy way of saying it's a psychology based on certain behaviors. Then we place the responsibility for everyone's financial situation on their individual behavior. Meanwhile, the people and entities who actually control the economy take zero responsibility for the sometimes catastrophic failures their economic policies create.

Crazier still is that the people on the bottom—the ones who are most impacted by poor economic decisions from the top—have been conditioned to accept their lot in life. The banks and the system they have created control the economic environment, which in turn dictates just about everything in life, and the people themselves shoulder the blame when something goes wrong, and their reward is the plight of their miserable lives.

But it isn't just poor people who are being blamed for their miserable lives; rich people are too. Have you heard of income distribution, redistribution, spreading the wealth? These are all concepts born out of this fake science of economics. Wealth distribution only seems reasonable because economics blames the individual and not the banking system. In simple terms, the income one person makes has nothing to do with the income someone else doesn't make. One person earned income and another person did not. The government having to play a role in taking from one person to let another person survive is not about fairness; it's about using laws (force) to make up for the dysfunctional banking system, a.k.a. the dysfunctional economy.

Laz: What about the superhigh CEO pay compared to the line workers?

Evan: It's a symptom. Asset values likes stocks are driven up by QE and low-interest loans. CEOs are compensated by the value of company stocks; line workers are not. It's that simple. It's the irrational valuation of assets that is creating these disparities, but there is so much cash and it has to go somewhere. The question that arises is, would you build a house of cards three feet high over your own hand and then place a five-pound weight on top of it all?

Laz: Ouch. That sounds like a bad idea.

Evan: People are like the frogs we've been discussing, just accepting this new pesticide in their ecosystem and allowing it to slowly kill them off. Except unlike frogs, people honestly buy the lie that they themselves are responsible for the pesticide.

Meanwhile, people have no choice but to live in this environment. You can't leave the Trickle-Around Mountain. The idea that they are responsible for the kind of life they lead is ridiculous, because they can only really have a life on the mountain.

But the blame goes wide too. People are blamed for global warming, pollution, diseases, and all the evils that are produced by the economy. People are told that if they didn't drive to work, then there wouldn't be climate change. If they didn't drink out of plastic water bottles, there wouldn't be pollution.

In this way, the idea of a social science for explaining economics is brilliant: they blame everyone, so no one is responsible. The only problem is that it's not true, and eventually, like with the poisoned frogs, this line of thinking is going to kill us all.

The Wool They Pull over Our Eyes

Here's another of my famous epiphanies: if you think you are responsible for how much money you make and how much you pay for what you need in life, then you are empowering the banking system to control you.

This is why calling economics a "science" is such a kick in the teeth. It's not a science by any stretch of the imagination. When you have all the world's top minds in a particular "science" going on TV and essentially saying they have no idea how the economy will react to a certain economic decision or prevailing sentiment, you are not talking about a science at all.

An actual science is measurable. There are inputs that lead to predictable outputs. The proper ratio of lift, drag, thrust, and weight leads to an airplane getting off the ground. A certain amount of electricity fed into this wire will bring the light bulb to light. Too little and it won't get bright enough. Too much and it just might explode. These numbers and inputs have relationships to each other, and those relationships always lead to predictable outcomes.

But with economics? In a recession, what happens when government lowers taxes or cuts food stamps? Sometimes things improve. Sometimes they don't. There's no way to predict!

What happens when a virus springs up in China and quickly becomes a pandemic? The markets tank, productivity slows, and people stop buying things. Okay, how do you get out of this cycle? You borrow a gazillion dollars. And then, when that doesn't work, you borrow a gazillion more. And this isn't done to save the poor from starvation, or to keep small businesses from going under, or to preserve jobs—ultimately, it's all designed to save the banks from annihilation.

Economics is in no way a science. This is (conveniently, as it turns out) why they call it a "social science." Adding that word *social* is supposed to allow us to blame the frogs and not the banks. Further, it's why they put the economics department in the arts building and not the sciences building. You don't get a bachelor of science degree in economics; you get a bachelor of arts.

You have to ask yourself if we consider economics an art simply because doing so works to the benefit of the rich and powerful: "We would fix the system so more people would benefit, but the system is an art. There's just no predicting what will happen if we make changes." Meanwhile, there is one incredibly predictable element to this art: the banking system must not fail, no matter what.

There is no doubt that engineers and scientists could optimize the American economy just like they optimize every other system to which they contribute. But if they did so, we'd lose all that money the banks are making by exploiting the inherent flaws in the "art."

If we get nothing else out of this book, then how about this? How about we stop calling economics a "social science"? It just makes no sense to let something be called a science and not be scientific.

Evan: I agree with this, and I studied this so-called science for eight years in college and grad school.

A Brief Conversation between Our Four Heroes

Justin: Now that I'm all revved up, let's do a little more kicking at economics, shall we?

Connie: I've never quite decided whether I love it or hate it when you get all revved up.

Justin: Hey, Evan? As our resident economist, I'm going to pose this question to you. What does every economist ever point to as the clearest indicator that the economy is growing?

Evan: Gross domestic product.

Laz: Ah, the almighty GDP again.

Justin: Yes, and even if we can set aside the idea that we're all just living for the GDP for a moment, there's still some craziness to plumb here.

It starts with this idea that if the country is showing growth in its GDP, then clearly it's doing better this year than it was last year. The idea being that more activity is better than less. But how ridiculous is this measure? Currently, the healthcare system provides the majority of growth in the American GDP. So in other words, the more sick people we have, the more growth we see in the GDP.

Meanwhile, these same economists who point to the reliable GDP just shrug their shoulders about the complexities of the economic cycle. Recession, recovery, expansion, peak, recession, recovery, and so on. How stupid is this? We're adhering to a system that guarantees we'll be running in circles forever. Any fool knows that running in circles is a waste of time and energy.

Connie: Most people think that GDP growth means more jobs and more productivity.

Justin: But that's exactly it! The banks have pulled the wool over everyone's eyes, if I may reference the title of this section of the book. The only thing GDP growth means is that the banks are remaining profitable, or at least meeting their objectives. This is because GDP growth directly correlates to more successful loans being made (because if the loans were not made, the GDP would plummet). It's insanity!

But even our understanding of this overly simplistic measure is flawed. This is hugely by design. Big banks, in their efforts to obfuscate the situation, create all kinds of think tanks and donate to both political parties in an effort to propagandize this false notion that life is always getting better on the Trickle-Around Mountain. Hundreds of millions of people worldwide live on less than a dollar a day. Millions perish from poverty every year. And yet we're led to believe that we're seeing all this progress thanks to the existing system. After all, look at GDP growth! It's so reliably positive, year in and year out!

And it gets crazier! Most economists can't even agree on what constitutes good GDP growth, and even fewer can agree on the strategies we should follow to get to good GDP growth. They all have their own theories. None of them know what's up or down in the economy at any given time. I mean, how could they? All of them have been trained to blame the frogs for the economy. So they just kind of guess.

We're all supposed to accept this? Even though there is nothing else in the universe that behaves this way?

Laz: So what's the answer, boss? How do we pull the wool back?

Justin: It starts by embracing, as a society, that we are not working toward anything meaningful. We're simply working toward sustaining the banking system. That is our purpose.

We pull the wool back by realizing that a growing GDP doesn't mean that We the People are actually doing better. A growing GDP simply means a growing banking system.

Wherein an Ultraliberal Makes a Plea to the Government to Look Beyond GDP

Laz: I can't seem to stop thinking about the Trickle-Around Mountain. So thanks for all the sleepless nights, Evan.

I'm picturing all those poor people at the bottom of the mountain. Maybe it's because I used to be one. I don't know. But what I do know is that I keep getting hung up on this notion that the government spends supposedly the majority of its income and debt on covering the welfare state. And okay, yeah, social security, Medicare, Medicaid, unemployment, and so on do make up somewhere between 60 and 80 percent of the budget.

Connie: Good gravy!

Laz: And whenever we think about these numbers, we also tend to overlook the money spent by state and local governments to set up their own programs. The cost to society of taking care of homeless people, the unemployed, the elderly, and the sick is admittedly massive.

What did you say it was in San Francisco, Justin?

Justin: It's $25,000 per person.

Laz: Given those numbers, even I, an avowed liberal, can recognize that the government as it is currently constructed is basically designed for the purpose of taking care of people who can't find a contributory place on the Trickle-Around Mountain.

Connie: You mean they're too lazy to find a contributory place on the Trickle-Around Mountain.

Laz: Here's the thing, Righty. You and I have always seen eye to eye about this concept. Where we differ is that one of us believes these programs are necessary while the other calls the frogs lazy.

Connie: Willing to call a spade a spade …

Laz: And the need for this care from the government keeps growing. Even so, every year we're told the GDP is growing and so this clearly means that the economy is healthy. But what the hell kind of healthy system keeps churning out more and more poor and unproductive people every year?

The problem is the Trickle-Around Mountain. It doesn't care about people at the bottom, what they need, and how they can help. The Trickle-Around Mountain makes top-down decisions, which means no consideration for the bottom. So when companies cut jobs, it's because cutting jobs keeps the water from trickling out of their coffers. And that leaves the government as the only way to get money down to the people who got screwed by some executive decision.

And speaking of top-down decision-making, a not-so-funny example of the top-down decision-making hierarchy of the TAM (Trickle-Around Mountain) is that the people doing all the work get paid the least. The person who is in position to get the money from the bank gets to choose how that money is spent. First, he is going to pay himself handsomely, and that's why CEOs make so much more than their employees.

Second, because the banking system creates plenty of unemployed, he gets to pick talented people who have no choice but to make just a small fraction of the value they are contributing.

So, the next time you pass a construction site, you can be sure that the guy holding the clipboard is making ten times more than the guy doing all the hard work.

GDP is a terrible, terrible measure of economic health. It is a crutch that everyone at the top, the government included, uses to prop up this broken system and keep it running well past its expiration date.

Justin: Your mixed metaphor game is on point, Laz. Maybe we'll put your name on the cover too.

Laz: Really?

Justin: No.

Wherein an Ultraconservative Shocks the World and Blames the Government

Connie: Since we're trying to be inclusive with this book, I'm going to ignore the obvious sarcasm in the title of this section.

Justin: That would be for the best, yes.

Connie: Let's talk about another problem with economics: too many people conflate it with the government itself—as if the government runs the economy. But the truth is that these two entities are like oil and water. Any time the government steps in to fix the economy, everything goes sideways.

This is probably because the government's response to anything—whether it's a Democrat or a Republican in the White House—is to throw money at it. Think about the War on Drugs. A massively expensive boondoggle that has produced basically nothing.

Laz: Hey, look! Another thing we agree on!

Connie: Yep. Let's pause to sing "Kumbaya."

Laz: Really?

Connie: No.

It's time to wake up, people. The relationship between government action and economic outcomes is inverse. Politicians aren't crafting sound economic strategy; they're simply throwing darts at a wall and then rearranging them to match their political motivations. It's economic policy by sound bite.

While I'll defend until they day I die the notion that tax cuts for the wealthy creates jobs for the working man, increases tax revenues, and even reduces deficits, even I have to admit that it only works if politicians do what they're supposed to do—and lately, it doesn't look like many of them are hugely incentivized to do what they're supposed to do.

As long as economics remains a supposedly unpredictable art form, politicians can pass legislation that directly hurts their constituents. Because after all, they can always shrug their shoulders and blame the unpredictable economy. Plus, they can hide behind the big words, strange ratios, and impossible-to-understand concepts that economists have created to explain the economy. The harder it is for the average person to understand why the latest turn in the economic cycle is happening, the less responsibility a politician has to take for the consequences of their policy actions.

This leads to an odd sort of sameness between politicians from both sides of the aisle. Bernie Sanders can stand up and sound vastly different from Donald Trump, but because none of them are trying to actually change the banking system, and because they are all reaffirming the TAM, they're basically all the same. Centrists, in all their rationality and compromise, actually think they can get the mountain to function properly through compromise, which is hopeless.

So this lack of responsibility or lack of feedback to politicians and their parties means that they no longer are trying to do what is right for their constituents. Mostly, this is because they don't even know the difference. This makes politicians easily corruptible. They can do what they want, so they might as well do what their largest donors want them to do.

On the other hand, when their policies accidentally lead to positive developments in the economy, they can puff out their chests and look like geniuses. For instance, people like my boss can tout the low unemployment rate and the record stock markets as evidence of his success as an executive (and he has been a wildly successful executive—fight me).

It also further locks the TAM into a persistent fixture in human life. The TAM produces winners who pay the politicians to make them even bigger winners and, above all else, to make sure they continue being winners. Any drastic change to the system could unseat them. In essence, if you have everything you want, then why change anything?

It's a pretty remarkable con, when you think about it.

We Can Put the Science Back in Economics

After all that bickering, you might be thinking that I'm a proponent of the idea that economics can never be a science. Quite the contrary.

There's plenty of scientific opportunity here. We just need to reimagine the way we think about money so it behaves in a more natural way that can be scientifically measured.

The first step is to not look at human behavior as the main input into what makes the economy the economy. We need to be able to examine and control other inputs like the water with pesticides from the neighboring farm. In our frog pond, once we have determined that pesticides are creating two-headed tadpoles and threatening that whole ecosystem, we can then take measures to correct the problem. Maybe we approach the farmer and insist that he use a different pesticide. Maybe we restructure his irrigation system so he's not feeding chemicals into the water. Maybe we selectively breed the frogs that still manage to thrive in this newly polluted ecosystem.

Point is, the economy can indeed be scientific, as long as we ignore human behavior. It can be understood and viewed as predictable, just like the frog pond. For the frog, the input was pesticide—a poison. Same with our economy, except that the poison in our water supply is an overabundance of debt. If we can figure out a way to distribute only clean water ... to create a system that isn't driven by debt ...

As scientists, we can determine why things are going wrong and then take steps to fix them. Meanwhile, economists can't do this. They may think they have ways of determining why an economy is going wrong, but really, it's just guesswork. And they have no idea how to fix things. The price the human race pays for this inability is massive. Millions of people die every year for no reason. The mismanagement and misdirected resources of the human economy lead directly to suffering and loss of life.

Why are we still doing this? Why do we continue to stand behind a system that is supposedly random, when the real problem is that we have wool pulled over our eyes and haven't realized that the purpose of our entire existence is to grow the GDP and benefit the banking system?

If we thought the most important thing for the frogs was to keep the water level rising every year, then sure, we could measure our success in the level of water. But it would do nothing to stop the pesticides or the three-headed frogs the system kept producing.

Similarly, increasing GDP does nothing to stop poverty and suffering. The unpredictability of the economy is simply caused by the inputs that are used and the outputs that are measured, all of which are tailored to the growth and health of the banking system.

But it doesn't have to be this way!

In the end, the economy becomes a science when the desired outcome is not a measure of the health of the banking system (a.k.a. GDP) but instead is a measure of desirable human outcomes like cost of living, average income, and a sustainability index.

If we offer a lower interest rate, people will be more compelled to take out a loan.

If we print or recirculate more money, demand will rise and it will increase inflation (unless there is competitive pressure preventing price increases).

These things are true and predictable. All of them bridge the political-ideological divide. The only problem is the social scientists at the top of the mountain telling us how unpredictable all of these things are. But the reason these things are unpredictable (and also unstable, unfair, inefficient, unsustainable, and downright stupid) is that the economy is almost entirely based on keeping the banking system healthy and growing.

Saying this in reverse, if we wanted the economy to be stable, fair, efficient, sustainable, and smart … well, then, the bankers would be out of a job—at least in the Federal Reserve, because that was the responsibility they were given in the Federal Reserve Act of 1913. More on this subject later.

For now ... what if we flipped the script? What if we created an economy that served the people instead of just perpetuating the banking system? What if we created an economy that had more than one input? What if we could put together a predictable, reliable, ultimately scientific system that virtually guaranteed the end of recessions, greater predictability of investing (which means, believe it or not, that planning for retirement becomes easily achievable!), and a constant, sustainable existence?

What if we could make this supposedly uncontrollable and unpredictable system controllable and predictable?

CHAPTER SIX

OH GOD, WHAT'S THE POINT?

*Once you arrive at the end of the world, it
hardly matters which route you took.*

—ISAAC MARION, *Warm Bodies*

Connie: Evan, why isn't a young man like you busy adding a woman to your life?

Evan: Connie, you were there. I know it's been a few years, but I watched that lunatic, Dylan Elan Powers, shoot Nora (reference to Book 2 of The Wolfe Trilogy). I watched him break into Valence's theater and just start shooting. I will never forget his name. I loved Nora, and having her die in my arms after that bastard shot her is something I will never get over.

Justin: I'm thinking this is a Blanton's conversation.

Laz: Hey, if you're buying.

Connie: Where did that highball come from so suddenly, Laz? Do you carry it around in your pocket?

Laz: You don't carry glassware in your pocket?

Justin: Will you two just let him speak? Just drink this and shut up.

Evan: Keep them coming, okay?

Justin: Of course.

Evan: (drinks) God, that's good. Every time I start to wonder why I still stick around under your employ ...

Justin: You're thinking of leaving? What? No! Connie, why did you have to ...

Evan: I'm kidding, Justin. Just trying to lighten the mood before I have to talk about holding my girlfriend while she died.

Connie: What makes these young men just go crazy anyway? Why do they want to ruin other people's lives?

Justin: C'mon. You know that already. They have nothing left to live for, so they go out with a flurry of bullets.

Evan: You're right. And it's making me think that maybe we should be drinking cheap stuff, given the circumstances.

Justin: Right back with some Wild Turkey.

Evan: The world seems to be producing an ever-larger number of young men without a future.

Connie: So you're saying it's not the guns?

Evan: No, I'm saying that when that young man shot the love of my life, I became like him—hopeless. I mean, truthfully, my lack of a love life isn't about mourning Nora. In the years since, it seems like it's even harder to succeed and even more things can go wrong. Just look at this pandemic.

And before you jump me, I should say that the presidency has nothing to do with it. There's just so much wrong with the world, and every year, it gets worse. It's absolutely true that no matter what our political affiliations or social backgrounds are, we're all just helpless in doing anything about it. I mean, what the hell's the point?

Connie: Of dating?

Evan: No, I'm not talking about having some fun. I'm talking about a serious relationship, family.

Laz: Well, there's sex. That's kind of nice.

Evan: Ha! True. But that can be had without a committed relationship. Pre-COVID anyway.

Connie: Oh! Do tell!

Justin: Please don't. How's the Wild Turkey?

Evan: Exactly what I needed. And anyway, sex aside, I guess the point of dating is starting a family, and that just doesn't seem like something worth doing anymore. It's difficult to be thirtyish and trying to have a relationship while outwardly not wanting the responsibility of a family.

Connie: So you have enough on your plate just taking care of yourself?

Evan: It's more than that. It's all the other societal problems. The American Dream seems lost. The environment is deteriorating rapidly. How do I know my kids wouldn't wind up living in poverty—or, worse, I wind up causing my whole family to live in poverty? Plus, everyone's so tuned in to separate media bubbles, how is change even possible? I'm not just worried about money here. I'm worried about a total societal collapse.

Laz: Well, then. On that happy note …

Connie: Yeah, do we have a fun analogy for this chapter or something? Maybe another one with water? Like a Jacuzzi or something?

Justin: No, I think we'd better let the man talk this out.

Evan: Think I'd better take a full section, then.

Justin: Then take one.

Evan: Booze first.

Justin: I always did appreciate what a pro you were when it came to whiskey drinking.

Evan: Should I slow down?

Justin: You kidding? Laz, Connie, keep up.

As He Pounds Wild Turkey, Evan Takes a Full Section on How Depressing It Is to Be a Young American

I keep coming back to this idea that they drill into your head anytime you study generational change. It's a popular concept, this idea of perpetual progress. Yes, there are ups and downs, but you can always count on the general trend to be upward. The stock market is as reliable as the sun rising in the east and setting in the west. That thing has always climbed. So has GDP, in good times and bad. And that can't be disputed. What's the other piece of wisdom? Every generation is supposed to have it better than the last.

> **For the last few decades, everything has gotten harder for the average person.**

That part can be disputed. For the last few decades, everything has gotten harder for the average person. Year after year. Many observers are suggesting that my generation, millennials, will be the first one where that other piece of wisdom isn't true.

Just on its own, this is enough for me to bug out on. But I'm also a trained economist—for whatever that's worth—so I believe in trends. If life isn't better for me than it was for my parents, then what are the odds it'll be better for my children? If we all keep serving as pawns on the Trickle-Around Mountain, I'd say the odds aren't great.

Think about the major life events that I've endured and that my kids would one day endure as well. I owe more than $100,000 just to my grad school and another $50,000 to my undergrad. There's a chance I'll never pay that off. What caused the system that made me feel so compelled to do something that financially ruinous? The TAM.

Most people who suffer through this level of debt—and that's most people, by the way, whether it's student loans, mortgages, credit card debt, and so on—feel lashed to their jobs. Stuck on the mountain. Nowhere to turn and no way to improve their lives. The way things are, there's no reason to believe that this situation will be any better for my would-be kids.

The dark truth here is that living in America today does not provide the ingredients for life. There are too many forces working against the very purpose of life.

Every decision in life has become remarkably difficult. And why? The dark truth here is that living in America today does not provide the ingredients for life. There are too many forces working against the very purpose of life.

Life is supposed to be about perpetuating life, about sustaining a family, about pursuing happiness. But is any of that actually possible right now, at least if you're not in the top echelon? Are any of us even able to pursue our dreams in this system with any chance of their becoming a reality? This is why I'm not alone in this thinking. Nobody wants to have kids or raise a family or even get and stay married. What's the point?

Yeah, Let's Talk about That

Justin: Shall I pour another, then, Bukowski?

Evan: (holds out glass)

Justin: You've just about got me ready to walk off a bridge. So how about we discuss the differences between your generation and the generations before yours? Maybe if we get to the heart of that, we can start to see some hope for your future as a father, if not just as a ladies' man.

Evan: I guess.

Justin: What are some of the differences?

Evan: It's all about work. Back in the '50s, which I would argue is the last time the American economy was truly functional, people would go to work at jobs with reasonable pay. They would have enough money to bring home to their families with some left over to save for a brighter future.

Some of these families could even afford to get by with only a single parent going to work. The other managed the home and raised the children.

Justin: Can you even imagine?

Evan: Right? I mean, ignore the overworked, hypermasculine breadwinner and sheltered housewife trope and just try to imagine a scenario where only one of the two people in a couple—whether that one person is a man or a woman—needs to collect a regular paycheck in order for the family to survive and thrive.

Justin: It's. Completely. Insane.

Laz: Here's an interesting aside to that thought: can you pinpoint the exact moment in history when both parents suddenly had to work in order to make ends meet? Or can you identify the exact cause?

Justin: Well, I guess at some point in history, we thought of the age of eighteen as the time when a child became a grown-up no longer in need of parental support. But that isn't true anymore. Today, more than half the people between the ages of eighteen and twenty-nine live with their parents. When did that change? When did a high school degree become not enough for a decent job? I mean, the richest man in history, Cornelius Vanderbilt, only had three years of formal education. When did that cease being enough?

In today's world, tens of millions of people need multiple jobs just to pay for rent, food, the car, and raising real live children. Hell, sometimes you feel like you need to drive for Uber just so you can afford the lattes you need to stay awake for your night job.

Laz: I met so many people during my homeless-guy days who struggled with this same thing. People don't think about this, but you wouldn't believe how many bachelor's degrees, master's degrees, and even doctorates you'll meet living in a homeless shelter. And I'm not talking about the staff. I'm talking about the residents.

Justin: We were just discussing this the other day, Laz and me. It's crazy. While I pour you another, tell them why you think it's happening.

Laz: Thanks, boss. There are a bunch of reasons. But I think the first one is like what Evan mentioned. Education has become this huge debt trap that people have to overcome. We've gotten to a point where people have to have more education and work harder for longer hours and less pay. Meanwhile, they have all this student loan debt to pay back. For many, many people, the debt picture just gets out of control.

Justin: Why is it that people need more education to get by while the education hurdle keeps getting higher and more expensive?

Evan: Student debt is actually necessary to keep the economy growing. It's just one more place Bankism has created to keep pumping in more and more debt. The education bar keeps getting higher because the Trickle-Around Mountain forces people to have to learn to adapt to it. People have to conform to the needs of the mountain. This keeps getting harder, so the bar for education keeps going up. The Trickle-Around Mountain keeps getting more advanced, not to make people's lives better, but to keep the banking system going. And the banking system needs to keep making loans that can be paid back. This means some invention or technology must be able to economically displace some old technology.

Laz: Some people say it's all about automation taking jobs, driving down wages, and making life miserable for the working class.

Connie: By "some people," Laz means "Laz."

Laz: Hey, I'm not alone here.

Justin: That problem about having to work harder for less money probably contributes too. It all leaves us with so little time to do the things we enjoy. Forget sneaking out to have a picnic or go surfing once in a while. You hardly have time to even daydream about that stuff anymore. And while you're working your fanny pack off trying to make money, you're not actually able to save any of it. Life satisfaction is at an all-time low in developed nations.

Speaking of life satisfaction, we circle back to the original question. I'm told that nothing is more satisfying than raising a family. But Evan isn't alone in his thinking. Raising a family seems to get harder and harder in developed nations. We know this because average family size keeps shrinking in those places.

Evan: In Japan, the situation is so bad that they have actually calculated the date when the world's last Japanese person will be born.

Justin: Can we just take a second to honor Japanese culture?

Connie: Ugh. Here we go with this again.

Justin: Yeah, here we go. Japanese people are smart, hardworking, perfectionist … and their sushi—am I right? Yum!

So what the hell is going on in Japan? Suicide by overwork-

OH GOD, WHAT'S THE POINT?

ing. They call it *karoshi*. Is this what's in store for America's indebted future? What is it about massive debt that tears society apart? Why does national and total debt make life so hard? These are supposed to be just numbers in the sky, totally meaningless.

Well, no, obviously they aren't meaningless. Debt on this level is as deadly as the coronavirus. You can't see it, smell it, or know where it is, but the effects of big debt are suffocating.

Connie: You're really proud of this analogy.

Evan: And he should be. It's good. You know what else is good? Wild Turkey.

Justin: There we go. Another?

Evan: Yes, but I'm done talking. You keep talking. Analogize, man.

Justin: What's your boss call the coronavirus, Con?

Connie: The Wu Flu?

Justin: No, the other one.

Connie: The China Virus?

Justin: No, the less racist one.

Connie: God, I don't know anymore. The invisible enemy?

Justin: That's the one! Debt is like an invisible enemy. Like a silent killer. The larger the total debt, the more work has to be done to pay back the debt. And because debt has contracts of obligation attached to it, the work *must* be done.

So, if I owe a lifetime's worth of debt, and I have to work sixteen hours a day to pay it off … well, then it isn't suicide by work; it's death by indentured servitude. It's more like the Japanese have to work so hard to pay off their debts that it's killing them.

In that kind of environment, Evan isn't alone. Nobody is going to raise children.

Let's just overexplain this, because the politicians seem to be playing games with debt like it's just a number. And don't get me started with the gang of economists theorizing about Modern Monetary Theory (MMT). But debt has to be paid back in the form of work, so even if interest rates are low or it's perpetually refinanced, the debt obligation is there. It turns up in the form of increased cost of living, which is another way of saying you have to work longer and harder just to live.

Then there are those who argue that as long as the debt is in dollars, Americans will not have a problem because debt can be devalued through inflation. This is also complete nonsense. This is another way of saying the value of the dollar will become worthless. This would mean a complete collapse of America as an economic superpower, which would perhaps be the only thing worse than having every citizen enslaved to work their whole lives because of debt obligations.

Laz: Aha! We need more people doing more work to deal with our mounting debt. Immigrants are needed to do that. The US population would be shrinking without immigrants—and especially poor immigrants who are having all the babies.

Connie: I haven't had nearly enough whiskey to debate you on immigration.

Justin: Then let's just duck that debate and have this one: why are poorer people having more babies?

Laz: Because if you live a really, really impoverished lifestyle, then your access to proper nutrition, potable drinking water, and decent healthcare is so slim that your children die at a rate far higher. Meanwhile, because you live in such poor conditions, you need more children to help pitch in with the labor so your family will survive. Also, it's in many ways the only retirement plan available to you. Without living children to take care of you after you pass the age when you can reasonably work, you're pretty well screwed. All of this means having more children as a means of survival and as an insurance policy against when some of them pass away.

Evan: God, that's so depressing. So we are stopping immigrants who actually have big families from coming into the country because we don't have enough work for them. Yet the citizens of this country are having to work so hard just to get by. This doesn't seem to make sense. We need more people working to pay off all that debt.

Justin: Does this sound like a country with a plan? Does it sound like the human race is destined for peace on Earth? I know I'm not supposed to rant, and I know these concepts aren't super uplifting, but let's just blame it on the booze.

Think about this: suicides and overdoses are at their highest rates in history. Every year brings more mass shootings than the last. And terrorism and gun violence aren't going anywhere anytime soon.

Connie: Speaking of light and fluffy subjects, is democracy dying?

Justin: Yeah, I hope not. I still believe in the good old USA and its unparalleled ability to face down adversity and turn it into something shiny and amazing.

Connie: That is heartening, yeah. It started when we punted some tea into Boston Harbor. And we've been doing similar stuff for the two hundred and 250ish years hence.

Laz: But we're fumbling it across the board, if I can stay with Connie's football analogy. The states are fumbling it fifty out of fifty. And it's completely irrelevant who's running the government or how many outreach programs they pay for and why. Republican/Democrat, red/blue, right/left—none of it seems to matter in the face of the modern world's problems. Whatever your background or part of the country, you're still more than capable of fumbling.

Connie: And no matter who's in power, total debt keeps rising.

Evan: So does personal debt.

Laz: Ugh, don't remind me about personal debt. I've been avoiding my credit card statement for months.

Justin: I think credit card companies frown on that, bud.

Laz: Then how about some more whiskey?

Justin: Sure. While you pour, let's acknowledge that the local, state, and federal governments are fumbling it. And it isn't because of social media or traditional media or political gridlock. These are all symptoms—not causes—of all our problems that need a Big Solution. There has to be a different way of thinking—sincere, out-of-the-box thinking—that can reveal a bigger and better solution.

> There has to be a different way of thinking—sincere, out-of-the-box thinking—that can reveal a bigger and better solution.

I mean, we could sit here all night listing problems.

Evan: The quality of education is on the decline in the US while education costs are increasing rapidly.

Justin: Oh, you took that literally. Aren't we all depressed enough as it is?

Connie: Maybe if we make a drinking game out of it.

Laz: Now you're talking.

Justin: Hold on, Evan's had, like, six already, and I'm not sure he can—

Evan: Every time someone lists a problem, we take a shot. Justin, you pour.

Justin: But we—

Connie: Healthcare is a disaster. Costs are going up while more people are getting sick from chronic diseases like cancer, diabetes, obesity, and name-your-favorite-ailment-of-modern-life issue.

Evan: Drink!

Connie: Go on, Justy. Pour.

Justin: We don't get all four of us in a room that often anymore. I was kind of hoping we could, you know, at least pretend to work on the book. Instead of just thinking about all this depressing stuff?

Evan: You know what I'm not thinking about right now while we play this game, Justin? Nora.

Connie: Pour.

Justin: Done.

Laz: War rages in every corner of the globe.

Evan: Drink!

Connie: (singing) "War! Hoo! Good God, y'all. What is it good for?"

Laz: (more like yelling) "Absolutely nothin'."

Connie: You have such a lovely singing voice.

Evan: Drink!

Connie: But no one listed a, you know, sad thing.

Evan: Drink!

Justin: You heard the man.

Laz: The US has withdrawn from the Paris Climate Accord.

Evan: Drink!

Connie: Oh, boo-hoo. I'm not drinking to that one. We need the jobs. The Paris Climate Accord is a jobs killer.

Justin: You should drink to that one, though. We're talking about the future here. We're standing on the sidelines doing very little to combat global warming, resource depletion, the melting of the Antarctic ice shelf, ocean acidification, and massive plastic pollution. That's just a few of the effects the human race is having on nature. And even if the US did everything it could, it still wouldn't be hardly enough to fix these problems.

Evan: Drink!

Connie: He was still kind of talking about the same problem, but okay.

Justin: All this economic and environmental upheaval leads to more people displaced from their home countries, which creates more refugees and immigrants. And a lot of developing countries are so poor that their populations are exploding, which can only mean mass migration and more refugees in the future.

Evan: Drink!

Laz: Gotta tell you, Ev, I don't think I can keep up with you. Not as young as I used to be.

Justin: None of us are.

Connie: Speak for yourself.

Justin: I'm done. Evan, you done?

Connie: He passed out.

Justin: Well, that was fun. We all got good and drunk as we sorted out how future generations will be inheriting a world that is economically and environmentally screwed.

Who feels better now? No one? Cool.

Then let's plan to have some fun tomorrow morning, shall we? Let's play a different game. Let's look at how ridiculous our world has become as a result of Bankism.

CHAPTER SEVEN

BANKISM SUCKS

*It isn't acceptable to pursue emission reduction policies
that add substantially to the cost of living, destroy
jobs, reduce incomes, and impede growth.*

**—ANGUS TAYLOR, energy minister of Australia, even
as his country suffered through four of the largest forest
fires in the history of the world simultaneously**

Since we're all properly hungover and depressed about our prospects in life, let's have some fun with this chapter. Here, let's do our level best to imagine how Bankism controls the United States and how it keeps us trapped on the Trickle-Around Mountain.

The key thing to remember as the four contributors to this book get back to arguing with each other is that some of this is going to sound like a pipe dream, but really, it is in no way a pipe dream. Part of the trick of Bankism is that it looks extremely complicated. That is by design. If it looks extremely complicated—and if we can be led to believe that economics is such a vast and unpredictable so-called science that there is simply no way to accurately foresee how the business cycle will turn—then it prevents people from asking too many questions about who the system is supposed to benefit and who it hurts.

The true value of Evan's Trickle-Around Mountain analogy is that it helps simplify that complicated system by allowing us to better visualize it. If I can mix metaphors and move away from the mountain for a moment, most people (even high-level economists) see the economy as trees, where they really need to be looking at the whole forest. Now that we can see the forest—or the mountain, as it were—it becomes easier to spot the many problems and dysfunctions it creates for our society.

So, with this chapter, we're going to examine exactly who the TAM benefits and hurts, and we're also going to imagine how a society that functions on something other than the TAM would benefit everyone. And I mean that. Everyone. Poor people. Rich people. Republicans. Democrats. Conservatives. Progressives. Neighborhoods. Towns. Cities. States. Every race, ethnicity, religion, and social class of people. Literally everyone.

Just in case you've put the book down for a while, how about a quick recap of what Bankism does to all these people?

It pretends to control only matters related to money, but on a societal level, it in fact completely controls the country, and on an individual level, it completely controls what we can do in our lives.

It has created an economy where inequality is a permanent feature.

For it to function properly, we must have wealthy people and poor people. Rich people borrow money and poor people work to earn the borrowed money. That's the only way the system can function. So the saying that a rising tide lifts all boats doesn't actually make sense, since in the cases where the tide goes too high, the Fed will just pull the plug and plummet the boats back down.

The illusion of an unstable and unpredictable economy is essential for the system to hold up—otherwise, how could we possibly explain scenarios where millions of workers get laid off and the response is to make it easier for rich people to borrow money? What if workers realized that money was created by just signing a document and that they in turn did all the work for that money? They couldn't even say no, because after all, they have to eat. It's completely unfair. The working class never stops to question why they are doing all the heavy lifting while the bankers and elites sip piña coladas in the tropics. But then again, even the elites are stuck on the mountain without options.

All of this false complexity props up the notion that all money must flow through banks because no one but banks could possibly know or understand how to track something as mysterious as money. This is by design, because, oh boy, do they make a ton of money by being the only ones able to track it. As a tech billionaire, I can tell you that my laptop could track

All of this false complexity props up the notion that all money must flow through banks because no one but banks could possibly know or understand how to track something as mysterious as money.

every dollar and every currency for the whole world. Computers are that powerful now. So for the bankers to retain control and remain super profitable, the obfuscation of the social science of economics must be maintained.

Banks making loans is what controls the economy, and when they stop making loans, then jobs decrease, money quits circulating, and the economy gets reduced to nothing. When they make too many loans, we experience inflation and price increases. So yeah, sure, there is some functionality to what they're doing, but it's not rocket science.

Given the above list, this is quite clear: without banks controlling the flow of money, we would have a much more stable economy, one without recessions, one without panic-driven boom and bust cycles. We would have the ability to enjoy long-term, sustained economic activity without the business cycle. Just as importantly, we all, no matter what our backgrounds or current financial situations are, would benefit—financially, professionally, and socially—from a life outside the TAM.

So with all that in mind, let's open up the floor to our panel, and they can all just shout out the topics they would like to discuss as they relate to a country without Bankism.

And Now, a Volley of Impassioned Shouting

Connie: Well, I guess we should get the big one out of the way. In this imaginary scenario where we can suddenly just get rid of banks altogether, what does that do to politics?

Laz: Please say it will make Republicans honest for a change.

Connie: Watch it.

Justin: Yeah, we're not here to point fingers. There's plenty of dishonesty going around on both sides of the aisle. The question is why? And also, given how unstable this country has gotten during the COVID crisis and the racial inequality protests happening in almost every city, I'm just as interested in the question of how we've managed to get so divided in this country. Why is there so much finger-pointing? Could banks have anything to do with that?

Evan: I suppose the rapid succession of questions means you're teeing it up for me to answer …

Justin: And Evan chimes in. I tell you what, buddy. I wasn't sure if you'd actually get out of bed today. That was a hell of a night you had.

Evan: It's been a struggle, yes. And if you could just talk a little softer please, that would be …

Justin: Yeah, okay. And maybe Laz could go make you a Bloody Mary or something.

Evan: …

Justin: Evan's gagging, you guys. Let's avoid the hangover jokes.

Evan: Appreciated. So my answer, then.

Justin: Please.

Evan: Thing about politics and politicians is this … Bankism is a neat trick because it manages to control everything about our society while also letting other, more public-facing people take the blame when things go wrong. As ugly as politics have gotten in recent years, you kind of can't blame politicians for all the finger-pointing:

"It's the Republicans' fault!"

"No, it's the Democrats' fault!"

The truth is, it's no one's fault. We can argue the semantics or the high-level details all we want, but in reality, politicians have just gotten a raw deal.

Justin: Even in the middle of a hangover, you've somehow managed to make both Connie and Laz go from red faced to hesitantly nodding in just one stretch. Maybe you can explain what you mean here …

Evan: Yeah, okay. The Trickle-Around Mountain is constructed in such a way that it looks like politicians are in charge of the economy. People vote based on how well the president is doing with the economy, but that's kind of sad and hilarious at the same time because the president has absolutely nothing to do with the economy and how it performs in any four-year period.

As we've seen, it's the Fed that controls the economy. It is the one entity that can expand or contract the roar of the water flowing down from the peak of the mountain. And even it has very few controls—either raise or lower the interest rate. So the economy on the TAM is this roaring, raging thing that is, for the most part, beyond anyone's control.

Whenever things get really crazy, politicians can push for (or against) quantitative easing or COVID relief packages to help bail out a broken system that has overleveraged itself again, but apart from that, politicians are taking all the blame for losing a game even though they spend the whole thing standing on the sidelines.

Laz: But politicians almost never do anything substantive. They just argue.

Evan: Exactly. When their success is measured by job creation and control over a system they have no control over, what other choice do they have? Name a big idea that our government should be pursuing. Go on. Name any idea.

Justin: Reducing or eliminating plastic packaging.

Evan: Yeah, if we reduced or eliminated plastic packaging, that would be objectively good for the oceans. Wouldn't it be nice if we could do that in a way that didn't cost companies money and jobs, so that both progressives and conservatives could have something to be happy about?

Connie: You should get hammered more often. There's a charming sort of wryness to you when you're booze-sick.

Evan: I'll consider it. Anyway, of course we can't pursue outlawing plastic. Why? Because outlawing plastic would raise the cost to produce many if not most products. Those higher costs cause prices to go up, which angers the consumer while also reducing sales. Higher cost plus fewer sales means less profitability. Less profitability means a need to cut costs, which most employers do by laying people off.

So, if you change policy on plastic, you directly raise prices on goods and eliminate jobs, both of which are losing propositions for both parties and in any constituency. A politician gets reelected by making his or her constituents feel as if their life has improved or at least that the status quo has been maintained. Big ideas that would benefit humanity as a whole but lead to job loss and an increased cost of living? Those ideas die before they even start.

Connie: Now you're going to say something about the military industrial complex.

Justin: And why not go there?

Connie: Because it'll get Laz and his kind all worked up.

Justin: Why shouldn't it get him worked up? It should get all of us worked up. Yes, the jobs in the military industry are great, and it's a huge contributor to GDP, but at what cost? All these wars and deaths and bloodshed? That shouldn't appeal to any politician.

Evan: That's exactly the problem. Continuing in wars and conflicts for the sake of keeping the machine turning is not something anyone should want to do. But again, even though the way toward positive change is obvious—even though Republicans and Democrats alike have campaigned in recent years on stopping these endless wars and reducing the sense that America has become the world's police— politicians are handcuffed by their lack of options. Every state in the union has significant interest in the military industry. Millions of jobs are dependent on defense spending by the government. When orders for guns and bombs dry up, people lose their jobs.

Connie: You're conflating the issue. Are you honestly saying we should lower the defense budget? Do you want to leave America vulnerable to its enemies?

Justin: With all respect, Con, this is one point of slight hypocrisy from your party. Before you eviscerate me, it's the same hypocrisy on Laz's side, just from a different perspective. But humor me for a moment. Why is it that Republicans are all about reining in spending for everything but defense?

Connie: To keep America safe. To put America first.

Justin: And to Make America Great Again, Again?

Connie: Hey, you said it.

Justin: Frame it however you like, but it's all about jobs. We're spending many multiples of what we should be spending on defense, not because we're putting America first, but because we're putting jobs first. We're throwing all this money at an industry that doesn't need so damn much of it, all because we want to keep people employed. Think about it. What's better, spending on welfare or spending on defense? At least the spending on defense actually gives a return on investment, jobs, and a stronger military.

Connie: I'm still failing to see the problem here. Keeping people employed is what everyone wants.

Justin: But in this case, it comes at the expense of human life. Soldiers die because of these investments. Our new and old enemies die too.

Laz: It also contributes to the endless war syndrome. I mean, if more bloodshed means more jobs, then that makes it all the easier to justify jumping into new wars or skirmishes with other countries because it only enhances profits and creates new jobs.

Connie: Starting to get a little nauseated by the hippie nature of this conversation.

Evan: Okay, then let's remove the politics from the matter and just look at economics. The TAM causes jobs to be elusive. Having or creating jobs is seen as this prized achievement. But there's the sleight of hand at work. Bankism prizes jobs because more jobs equals more potential people to make loans to. But when that happens, it leads to inflation, which the Fed corrects by changing interest rates, which then forces companies to downsize to remain profitable. Jobs are lost.

No matter how you look at it, governments are not responsible for jobs. Politicians are not responsible for jobs. Bankism is responsible for jobs. And because everything is designed to benefit banks, jobs ebb and flow no matter what we do, what policies we try to change, or which wars we enter or exit.

Laz, Connie, this is another one of those scenarios where you're both right and you're both wrong. Everyone can agree that a world with less plastic and less bloodshed would be a better place. The problem is there's nothing we can do about it as long as Bankism keeps running the show.

Justin: That's so depressing.

Evan: Yes.

Connie: So you're saying that all the world's problems—or at least all the ones we deal with here in the US— can be blamed on this need to borrow ever larger sums of money, which in turn creates work.

Evan: In some ways, yes. The trickle-down effect on the TAM, however randomly it operates, is primarily driven by work. But here's the thing: remember how that $100 the bank loans into the economy is passed around and around, looking like it's more money changing hands than really is? And remember the part about how it all winds up back in the hands of the bank, who then reuses it by loaning it out again?

Yeah, this is your earned money they're reusing or printing from scratch. And the effect of this is that the money you earned isn't actually accumulating; it's reused. So instead of having work be worth more because there is too much work or having money be worth more so that wealth accumulates through savings, the system is designed to maximize loans, which benefits the banks but not the worker and his savings account. The amount of money in circulation is limited so banks can increase the amount of loans they can make.

Meanwhile, the bank also benefits from every dollar you actually manage to put into a savings account by loaning that out too. Everyone has always been told about how important it is to have savings, but savings accounts are basically "rent out your money" accounts. So you earn this money from work, you put that money into savings, and the bank uses that money to make itself more profitable, which in turn reduces the value of the money you put into the savings account, which by extension reduces the value of wages, which is the work you contribute to the economy.

You see the trick here, or am I too foggy headed to explain this properly? Your own money undervalues your own work! So if you're not getting high interest in that savings account, then it really isn't worthwhile to keep your money in the bank. But there is no choice, because they can just print more money to replace the money under your mattress.

Justin: I haven't seen high interest rates since the '80s.

Evan: Correct. You are not getting high interest. But anyway, since you're not getting that high interest, it's actually more sensible not to keep your money in a savings account. If you do this, the bank just uses your own money against you. And that's why stocks and assets are so overvalued.

Laz: What does it look like in a non-TAM world?

Justin: There are so many personal savings benefits from abandoning Bankism. For one, planning for retirement becomes more straightforward and not based on luck, because if banks aren't reusing your hard-earned money, then your money and your work are more valuable because you can get a higher interest rate. More on this later.

Evan: And remember our depressing conversation about how people who get married suddenly find themselves competing against other married couples to buy a house and a car, and to send their kids to private school? Even groceries, clothing, and other essential items are more expensive than they need to be because of the artificial competition Bankism creates. The TAM drives up cost of living and drives up asset values, which is the only way to accumulate wealth on the TAM, unless you're some supertalent like an NBA player. But then, talent is also a form of asset.

Connie: Jeff Bezos would like a word. Accumulating wealth on the TAM is very much possible.

Evan: Ah, but there's another neat trick happening there.

Justin: Look at this guy coming out of his hangover already.

Connie: It's nice to be young …

Evan: Yeah, yeah. Anyway, Bankism forces wealth to be created from assets. The only way to become wealthy on the TAM is by owning and compiling assets that the bank sees as valuable. Jeff Bezos isn't the richest man on Earth because he gets a big salary; he is the richest man on Earth because he owns Amazon shares and assets.

Compare this to the richest person in history (before the onset of full-blown Bankism): Cornelius Vanderbilt. Here's a man who did not become the richest person in history by building assets. He amassed his vast wealth by selling tickets to his trains and ferries in what amounted to a remarkably limited business model. His company constructed and operated a few transit lines between New England

and New York and another out to Chicago. They also had ferries between Staten Island and Manhattan and Hoboken and Manhattan. I'm simplifying, of course. There were other moneymakers, but unlike Amazon, they were all extremely profitable. This is how Vanderbilt became much richer even than Jeff Bezos—all because he could earn a significant profit on every ticket. Of course, it helped that back then, before modern Bankism, his money was tied to gold, and he also possessed actual, physical gold that he could put in his own safe.

Just look at all the work Amazon does for pennies. Vanderbilt made dollars on every ticket sale; Bezos lost money for years on every delivery, and even now, it's fractions of a penny, of which Jeff sees very little.

Connie: You're saying all this as if guys like Bezos don't have any spending power. Which is ridiculous.

Justin: True. Dude can spend. But that's one of the more bizarre effects of the TAM. There is this need for the wealthy to spend, because that's what creates jobs and circulates money. All of that looks acceptable because it contributes to GDP growth, which is the only actual measure of economic health. But when you look at it from a resource perspective, it's outrageous that only a few people hold all these assets and wealth. These people are then strongly encouraged with tax breaks to waste massive amounts of resources to help the economy.

Laz: Can I ask a question? Why are there homeless people right now?

Justin: Because abject poverty is an essential part of Bankism. The system doesn't work without a large pool of people looking for work. Before Bankism took over the world, everyone had the opportunity to

Before Bankism took over the world, everyone had the opportunity to make a living anywhere, at any time, by using their skills and resources to sustain their own life.

make a living anywhere, at any time, by using their skills and resources to sustain their own life. Without Bankism, the economy is not debt-driven. Instead, inflation is controlled by the amount of currency in circulation and not the labor markets. This means that mass layoffs don't happen because some bank made a bad loan. It means tuition would still be cheap because there were no loans to pump up the price. It means housing would cost less because there would be no low-interest mortgages to pump up the price. It means the cost of living would be so low that homelessness would be much easier to address.

Laz: Do you mean anyone could afford a decent life anywhere?

Justin: Yes, in a TAM-less world, we could have entire towns in the middle of nowhere that were self-sustaining and independent of the greater economy.

Laz: This all assumes things like systemic racism disappear along with the mountain. I'm having a hard time swallowing that idea.

Evan: Yes, Bankism actually creates the kinds of inequalities that lead to systemic racism. Think about it: trickle-around does not mean trickle-around to everyone. It's trickle around from one type of person to other people of similar ilk. Money and wealth rarely change hands between demographic spheres. So there is an inherent prejudice in the trickle-around effect.

What this means is that whole neighbourhoods are either moving up or moving down, all based on where the money is trickling. If a neighborhood is no longer favorable, then bankers will reduce the amount of the mortgage a house can get. If an important company moves to another location, then the trickle-around is reduced and the neighborhood goes bust.

Instead of broad, consistent improvements in the standard of living, you have isolated pockets of wealth created by heavy trickle-around, and it's all built mostly around assets and other financial products.

Connie: Gentrification beautifies cities and increases the value of property. Period.

Evan: But gentrification is just another symptom of the TAM. When it happens, rent goes up for the poor as rich people move into a neighborhood, causing poor people to have to move. Poor people never have the credit to buy and take advantage of the increasing asset prices. This leads to more inequality and also to the rise in cost of living across the board. This forces some people into poverty because they can't afford the rent.

Justin: Which in turn contributes to many of the problems that perpetuate systemic racism.

Evan: Exactly. For example, because Bankism causes inflation in cost of living, forcing more and more people into poverty, more and more people wind up turning to crime as a means to survive. If a person has no other options to climb the mountain, it is only a matter of time before they start breaking the law.

Crime is a great example of the effect of being stuck on this mountain. Crime is driven either by poverty or a lack of opportunity. Either you're in a situation where you literally need to steal to eat, or you just can't get out of your current economic position because the job and education opportunities are not available or affordable for you.

The stuck-ness of our situations is what creates people like drug dealers. They just want to move up in the world and see this as their only opportunity. In response, governments wind up having to employ more and more police, which of course doesn't solve the underlying problem. Without addressing that underlying problem, we'll always have crime, and we'll always have a need for more and more police. The larger a police force gets, the more we accentuate that "us versus them" mentality upon which racism is based.

From a politician's perspective, it's better to increase the budget for police than to increase the budget for welfare since the taxpayers who pay for it get something tangible out of increased funding for the police. Plus, it creates jobs. But with facial recognition, mass incarceration, and the militarization of the police, we wake up to the nightmare of a police state that is trained to use lethal force first.

Connie: And this is how we wind up with race riots in the middle of my employer's roaring economy.

Justin: Roaring? It was in the toilet by the time the BLM movement began.

Connie: Only because of COVID!

Evan: And also literally everything else I've been ignoring this hangover to talk about.

Laz: Can we talk more about the inequality the system creates? Because it's not just racism. There are massive inequalities in standard of living too.

Connie: For instance?

Laz: For instance, Justin, what'd you have for lunch today?

Justin: Why does that matter?

Connie: He had salmon risotto.

Laz: Fancy. Healthy. All organic?

Justin: Of course.

Laz: Want to know what I had?

Justin: I'm not sure I do …

Laz: Big Mac and large fries. But I went with a Diet Coke, so I'm staying healthy, you know?

Connie: You can take your tongue out of your cheek now.

Evan: God, I could go for some fries right now.

Justin: It is one of the tried-and-truest cures for your present condition.

Laz: Anyway, you can see where I'm going here. I'm not poor by any stretch of the imagination, but I have a certain budget that keeps me eating shitty food. Meanwhile, Justin's eating salmon risotto.

Connie: I'm not a billionaire, and I eat something similar most days.

Laz: You're upper middle class. Of course you shop at Whole Foods. The point I'm making is that there shouldn't be such a huge difference between the cost of healthy food and food that's terrible for you. Why is that the case, Evan?

Evan: Why is fast food unhealthy?

Laz: Sure. Let's start there.

Evan: Because in a country where everything is driven by profits, the only incentive a company like McDonald's has is to make their food "super delicious" but just edible enough that they don't get sued. For distributors of produce and for supermarkets, the incentive is to create, buy, and sell foods that have been inundated with preservatives, so they last longer and don't have to be thrown out in such massive quantities. Meanwhile, pesticides make crop yields higher for the farmer, who makes more money. And all of this at the cost of your health.

So all at once, the TAM is ensuring that the majority of people struggle to make ends meet. Meanwhile, it incentivizes companies who cater to these people to create profitable food. Health is a minor concern. Profitability is what drives the decisions.

Rich people can choose organic, but people struggling to make ends meet can't, so they take the cheaper, less healthy option—the affordable, high-volume, mass-produced option.

Justin: So the system is indirectly lowering the quality of food, which makes more people sick.

Evan: Absolutely. Because the true drivers of the TAM remain behind the scenes, the profits made by the food industry on low-cost food is lost to the healthcare burden put on society. It's that whole blaming-the-frog-for-its-own-environment thing again. The TAM creates a food supply system where the average person can only afford to eat food that is bad for them. This strains the healthcare system. And the reaction is to tell people they're fat, eat too much, and should start eating less, but healthy food that they can't afford. How exactly are they supposed to do that?

Connie: So it's like society is just chasing its own tail, going in circles.

Evan: Yes, like I said earlier. All so the banking system can maintain its control over the economy.

Justin: You're not going to like this, Laz, but if we're going to look at the entire Trickle-Around Mountain and society chasing its own tail, then we have to come to the conclusion that the government—specifically big, socialized government—is a big part of the problem, along with all the other problems caused by the banking system.

This is the way I see it: the cost of living is tied to the efficiency and the effectiveness of the work that people do in society. The more inefficient and ineffective work the government does, the more expensive the cost of living is going to be. Why? The system is forcing the government to spend more on police, welfare, and safety nets because Bankism creates poverty.

The cost of living is tied to the efficiency and the effectiveness of the work that people do in society.

And it's not just government that's inefficient. Every industry is driven toward counterproductive pursuits like moving work and factories to other countries, unionized workers, and unaccounted-for costs such as pollution. Let's face it—despite many threats to our very existence, politicians are choosing jobs now over a sustainable future. It doesn't get any less efficient than that. There's an even bigger inefficiency caused by TAM because the goal is GDP growth. Only the number of transactions matter, which means that there is no purpose, and without purpose, you can't improve.

The point is that life would be so much better if we all worked productively toward a better, more sustainable future. Bankism compounds this problem by turning healthcare into sick care and creating this behemoth of inefficiency that is the modern healthcare system. There is simply no way that more sick people growing the GDP is not also going to raise the cost of living.

Connie: Don't you think you're kind of oversimplifying the healthcare situation? I mean, it's not all about quality of food. It seems to me that if Bankism is to blame for everything on this mountain, we wouldn't have the healthcare system we have. To me, that's still a broken system we can blame on the government.

Justin: Whatever happened to your boss's healthcare plan, by the way?

Connie: (grumble)

Justin: This is the true power of the mountain that we've only just scratched the surface of. The system is so obfuscated by academia and politics that it actually extends to all the knowledge we think we have about society. Whatever you think you know about healthcare, you know it because it's exactly what you need to think in order for the system to continue surviving.

Connie: For example?

Justin: For example, ask any doctor, and they will tell you that preventative care is twice as effective at staving off disease and costs hundreds of times less to implement. Why is it, then, that there are almost no systems in place to support and fund preventative care?

Laz: Here's where Connie blames the government again.

Connie: Actually I was going to blame big business.

Justin: Give us all a moment to pick our jaws up off the floor. But yes, you're right—in a sense. The reason the US is structured so completely toward reactive instead of preventative care is that there's just so much more money to be made in trying to heal the sick rather than keeping people healthy. Call it that old cynical line about how there's no real incentive to cure cancer by preventing it because there's too much money in managing the disease.

Evan: We're all knocking into those trees you mentioned at the outset, too, Justin. Big money in reactive care is a tree. Single-payer versus private insurance is another pair of trees. The government's role in this whole mess is a tree.

Justin: Show us the forest, brother.

Evan: The forest is that Bankism limits profit-making to where money is trickling around from bank loans. Companies have to be as profitable as possible so they can pay back their loans and reward their investors. They need to be able to pay back their loans so they can take out more loans so they can grow. The cycle continues.

In other words, we don't have to focus on preventative care in this country because there is no money there to pay for it. Banks can't loan a gazillion dollars to a company that has a method of keeping people healthy and cancer-free. They can only do that for companies that can charge $1,000 for a one-gram pill that staves off existing cancer for a little while. This is how pharmaceutical start-ups become billion-dollar stocks with no profits to show for it while gyms and health food stores need to panhandle for start-up money from friends and family.

For every company that contributes to healthcare—pharmaceutical companies, hospitals, medical device suppliers, research companies, and even the government—it makes so much more sense from a business (profit) perspective to let people get sick and then make a hundred times more money treating the sickness.

Yes, that cynical line of Justin's is true. But it's what makes it true that is interesting to me. Bankism makes large profits only possible in a limited number of markets. So companies are always going to chase the highest profits, no matter what they do to earn them. Bankism doesn't allow for businesses to focus on profits that serve the common good because there is little to no profit in doing it.

Put another way, Bankism ties the hands of society from taking care of itself. This goes back to the earlier analogy of being stuck on the Trickle-Around Mountain. We are all stuck, including businesses, unable to change the way we do things or what we do because of these rules that govern Bankism and the TAM.

Justin: What's really crazy is that the situation causes all these strange bedfellows to emerge. The medical education system in this country works hand in glove with the healthcare industry. Pharmaceutical companies, in search of their ever-soaring profits, partner with colleges and universities, but not out of some kind of noble effort to marry research with education. They do it because it allows them to tell the universities what to teach.

When med students graduate and begin working as doctors, they do so armed with the toolbox their education delivered them. That toolbox is filled with drugs, medical devices, and profitable solutions that were pushed on their schools by big medical companies. Those same companies influence the decisions at the hospitals and clinics employing these doctors as well. Those hospitals and clinics, needing to be profitable themselves, are similarly incentivized to favor treatments that make the most money.

Evan: Everyone who contributes to the picture is in it for the same thing. They all want and need to profit. As a result, you have a stagnant system locked in place. The Trickle-Around Mountain makes it impossible to improve healthcare or focus on preventative medicine. It's all just so dependent on people getting sick and having no choice but to pay exorbitantly to get well.

Laz: You're saying all this like it's Bankism that's causing people to be on drugs.

Evan: In more ways than one, that's exactly what I'm saying.

Laz: But there are good sides to this system. My doctor has me on statins, and I'm feeling better than I have in years. He says they're totally safe too. Says they should put them in hamburger meat as preventative care. Lower people's cholesterol even as they're eating something that would otherwise raise it.

Evan: We really shouldn't have to tell you that this is a case in point, Laz. This notion of putting the most profitable drug in history into meat as a preventative measure? Why not just educate people on healthy diets? Outcomes and quality of life will never improve in this country as long as we continue to educate for sickness. And we're going to continue educating for sickness as long as there's more profit in sickness. Once again, Bankism forces healthcare to be sick care, as there is just relatively little money in keeping people healthy.

Justin: Healthcare isn't the only industry influencing schools either. It's to the point where the purpose of higher education is no longer about truth or advancing society. It's all about learning how to fit in to the mountain. We might debate what's wrong with the economy or healthcare, but schools don't teach what might be a better solution. Instead, they teach whatever lessons will be needed to get a job on the mountain, which correlates with where the profits are.

We've already talked about pharmaceuticals and medical devices, but do you think it's an accident that Google gives schools free laptops and Apple hands out all those free iPads? They want kids learning to use their products. Getting them while they're young makes them loyal for the rest of their lives, and so they buy your product or service, and when they do this, their profits rise for a generation.

Laz: Speaking of companies being incentivized to profit, can we finally get to my piece of this?

Connie: Here he goes with the robot uprising.

Laz: It's a serious concern.

Justin: Just stay out of the sci-fi weeds, buddy, and we can talk automation, sure.

Laz: Can we agree that this isn't just a crackpot thing? Whether you agree with me that AI is a terrifying problem or not, many people see the problem with automation. They see all the people being displaced by robots and technology.

Ever since Henry Ford created the production line, work has been dismantled into simpler tasks. Eventually, those tasks become so easy that a machine can do them. Modern technology just takes the assembly line a step further by replacing jobs that require basic thinking.

Connie: So what? The people who lose their jobs should just try something new. Go back to school. Open a business. I mean, look at you, Laz. You did it.

Laz: I had a little help from your billionaire boyfriend—help that most people don't get.

Evan: Anyway, that's beside the point. You're both still arguing from a political perspective. The cost of ever-expanding technology isn't jobs. Technology itself doesn't create or destroy jobs—only the Federal Reserve does that. It's just that they're in a particularly job-destroying period at the moment because the persistently low interest rates they've been putting out means several key things.

First, there's the most sinister part of it. Low interest rates lower the cost of technology. How? Low rates mean cheaper loans to big businesses. From the businesses' perspective, cheaper loans mean that investing in technology is less expensive. Expanding into new technology allows them to cut costs and improve profits—every company's goal.

So we wind up in a spiral where technology is replacing so many jobs that the average person now has to compete against that technology. If they earn too much money, they are replaced. This leads to high unemployment, which drives down the average worker's ability to demand a decent wage. They have to accept lower pay just to compete with automation and the fact that there is more unemployment.

Meanwhile, those same lower interest rates make it more difficult for the average person to earn anything on their savings. This leaves them strapped for cash at all times, which only furthers their desire and willingness to accept lower-paying jobs.

Justin: And on top of this, the higher the unemployment rate and the more low-paying jobs there are, the fewer people there are for banks to loan money to.

Evan: You hit the nail on the head there. So then the government and the Fed swoop in with quantitative easing, which not only bails out companies, but also supplies them with cheap loans that drive down the cost of technology further. More job loss follows, and the cycle continues. We wind up in this race toward a dystopian future of great inequality and massive wealth gaps.

But the craziest part of this is that automation makes it less expensive to produce goods. This should mean that goods are less expensive. In a system that wasn't designed to benefit banks, automation would be a good thing. It would lower cost of living across the board. But instead, automation replaces jobs, which forces the Fed to lower interest rates, which has caused wages to stagnate for a generation now. And that means less money for the average person for the things they need.

Connie: Maybe we just need one of those big ideas to break us from the cycle. Think of all the new industries created by computers, the internet, and, hell, the iPhone.

Evan: There is a tendency in this country to always believe that progress will save us. Maybe the iPhone 15 will save the world. Yes, all the technologies you mentioned have changed day-to-day life for most people in this country, but have they led to a better lifestyle for anyone? I mean, objectively speaking, is the average person better off today with a computer, high-speed internet, and a phone that contains the sum of all human knowledge?

Laz: I know a lot of people who would say that no, they are not better off.

Connie: Admittedly, so do I.

Evan: This is because technological progress of this kind doesn't actually benefit the individual—at least not on a lifestyle and economic level. It changes the amount of information that the average person can access. And it in some ways opens up the potential for innovative thinking from a grassroots level. But ultimately, none of that matters because every innovation still serves the banking system. Any technological advancement just feeds the machine whose only measure of success is GDP growth.

This is why the only progress possible is the profitable kind, which is limited to wherever money is trickling around on the mountain. Resolving global warming, feeding the poor, eliminating poverty— there are plenty of technologies and technology-driven strategies that could do all of these things. But doing so is not profitable, so the banking system makes it impossible on a grand scale. Instead, banks float loans for the iPhone 15, a wildly profitable product.

Connie: So you're vilifying Apple now? Is Steve Jobs now a public enemy?

Justin: Or am I, for that matter?

Evan: Not at all. Don't get me wrong. I'm not saying these companies were wrong to chase profits. That's what companies are supposed to do. Steve Jobs, Justin, any tech billionaire—they all did what any brilliant leader would do.

Connie: The jury is still out on whether the word *brilliant* applies to Justin.

Justin: Hey!

Evan: The problem is that all money flows from the Fed, and the Fed's only real concern is keeping banks profitable. It's not big business or their leaders who are to blame; it's the banking system. Businesses need profitable sales to exist, and as long as Bankism determines where those sales can come from, we'll be stuck in this same self-destructive system.

Connie: I'm having a hard time swallowing this premise because there are so many outliers.

Justin: Such as?

Connie: Well, charities, for one thing. They're not profit driven.

Evan: Charity is an excellent example of the kind of dysfunction we've been talking about. Here we have companies pinching pennies to create the most efficient supply chains possible. Inefficient companies are put out of business if they do not lower their cost. Where competition is the friend of the consumer, charity is none of that.

Charity tries to supply poor people with essentials with donations from wealthy people. To do this, the charity has to set up its own supply chain, management team, and work force. Charities are, by nature, inefficient. All you have to do to see how inefficient they are is to look at how poorly they deliver anything compared to for-profit companies.

Connie: Okay, fine. How about schools?

Laz: If you think schools aren't all following this same need to be profitable, you're not paying attention. I mean, do you know what tuition costs at most private universities? I do. I looked into it after I lost my job to a robot and started "trying something new." Turned out I couldn't afford it.

Evan: We can't blame universities for this, though, either. It's not like they're paying their professors NBA salaries. It's not like their cost of doing business is going up. More and more students are applying to these schools, so they increase their prices. Why are more students applying despite the increases? Because banks are giving out loans so that more kids can pay more and still apply. And the system, being that it's controlled by banks, completely loves having millions and millions of young people who need to take out loans for higher and higher school costs because that keeps pumping money into the economy.

So, what happens with all this money being pumped into higher education? Students go from being students to being guests. The cafeteria turns into a food court with Starbucks and gourmet eating options. The campus starts to sprawl as more and more land is purchased and buildings go up. Give a nonprofit a lot of money to spend, and they will.

On the other hand, if they don't make these luxurious upgrades, they will fall off the whatever list of most desirable places to go to school.

Again, businesses are not to blame. They're just doing what the system allows. It's banks. The system is designed, start to finish, to benefit banks. If we want a better country free of all these problems, then the answer is changing the system so banks aren't running it.

Connie: If we're done blaming banks for literally all of this country's ills, then I have one more objection.

Justin: You always have one more objection.

Laz: I'm going out to grab lunch. Anyone want anything?

Evan: Fries! My God, please, fries. And one of those breakfast biscuits with bacon and egg.

Laz: Not sure they serve those simultaneously, but I'll try.

Evan: I love you, Laz.

Laz: Aw. I'm touched.

Justin: Yes, we all love Laz. I'll have one of those Diet Cokes you were on about earlier. But before you go … Con, what's your objection?

Connie: The United States is only one country. There's a whole big world out there, full of its own problems. In fact, many—if not most—places are worse. Are banks to blame for that too?

Justin: What a perfectly timed question! Let's discuss it in the next chapter. And you know what? Let's do it with another analogy. Everyone, quick—change into your bathing suits.

Laz: McDonald's in the pool. I had a feeling this was gonna be a great day.

CHAPTER EIGHT

THE JACUZZI PYRAMID

The root problem with conventional currency is all the trust that's required to make it work. The central bank must be trusted not to debase the currency, but the history of fiat currencies is full of breaches of that trust.

—SATOSHI NAKAMOTO, Bitcoin.org

Justin: See? I told you it would be nice to get out here.

Connie: I have to say that this doesn't seem super professional.

Laz: Ah, lighten up.

Evan: I agree with Connie. Even though I understand why you brought us all here, it is kind of challenging to think and talk about high-level economics while sitting in a hot tub with three coworkers and a pile of fast food.

Justin: It's got to be doing wonders for your hangover, though.

Evan: Admitted.

Justin: You're all too uptight. It's just that things got a little tense in that last chapter, so I figured it would be a good idea for all of us to meet up in a place we could relax.

Connie: So you thought that sharing a tub of bacteria-riddled water with three coworkers while all of us are half naked would make us all relax?

Justin: If you guys would give me, like, half a minute to explain myself …

Anyway, by now, I've heard from all of you independently and behind the scenes that you think we've been focusing too intently on the US economy. Connie's point at the end of the last chapter about how the Fed doesn't control all of the whole world's economies was an interesting one. Her other main point has been that there's a pretty simple solution to getting off the Trickle-Around Mountain: just move to another country.

Ah, but that's the next big trick of Bankism, my love. The notion that there are all these different, competing economies running on different, competing political systems like capitalism, communism, socialism, extremism, and on and on—all of that is a fiction. Why? As explained earlier, all countries control their currency through central banks just like the Federal Reserve. But for the rest of the world, the situation is worse because the entire world, every last country in it, has to contend with the dominance of the American dollar.

It's kind of like they're all controlled by their own versions of the Fed, which are in turn controlled by our version of the Fed.

Connie: So what does this have to do with the four of us uncomfortably sharing a hot tub?

Justin: We'll get to that in a bit. But first, you know what would really liven this situation up?

Connie: Maybe you could turn on the jets.

Justin: In due time. First, I'm thinking a nice history lesson will get this party going …

A World at War

Hello, folks. Laz Hammond here. Former homeless guy. Current hot tub–bound history buff.

Travel back with me to 1944.

We're at the peak of fighting during World War II, so Europe is essentially in ruin. The tide was beginning to turn in favor of the Allies, so now the conversation on our side turned to money. How could the countries contributing to the fight against the Axis powers exchange money fairly—not just during the war, but after it was won, and all that critical reconstruction could begin in earnest?

World wars tend to decimate international economic systems, so here the chief players in the conflict saw the need to discuss how they might rebuild that international economic system.

This, of course, was all a very reasonable idea. As an aside, isn't it fun how all the best horror stories begin with the hero's very reasonable idea?

Given that the US wasn't suffering through any actual fighting on its own shores, delegates from the forty-four Allied nations agreed to hold their gathering in Bretton Woods, New Hampshire, at the very fine (read "palatial") Mount Washington Hotel.

I'll spare you the deep history lesson and gory details. What matters most is that, over the course of three weeks in July 1944, delegates from the member nations established the institutions and rules that would govern the international monetary system for decades to come. In fact—and this is maybe an unintended consequence …

maybe—most of the way we think about money today is the result of this agreement.

The agreement itself might technically be over, but the dominance of the American dollar it created very much lives on. In short, it created a global system that has always had a life of its own, mostly because the people and economists of the world have always believed that this is the best way to run a global economy.

Thanks to Bretton Woods, we now have the International Monetary Fund, a bank that would become the World Bank Group, and a monetary system that kept monetary exchange rates within 1 percent of each other from nation to nation by tying every nation's individual currencies to the value of gold. This would force countries to cooperate financially while also preventing competitive devaluation of currencies.

For all you wonks out there—and I'm looking at you, Connie—I should clarify that the Chinese devalue their money by making massive loans to small municipalities that use these loans to build infrastructure, like cities big enough for millions of people—and in a few cases, these cities wind up not housing anywhere near millions of people. This particular brand of competitive devaluation of currency is kind of China's jam these days.

Back to Bretton Woods. A few important things to note here. First, at the time of the agreement, there was another power who just so happened to be housing treasures from all over the world in a palace called Buckingham, so guess who benefited most from this agreement?

Second, it was determined that all those countries who didn't have enough gold to play this game would instead use the US dollar (behold, Connie! The real trick that Made America Great!). Third, the Soviet Union, who'd sent their fair share of delegates to the conference, wanted no part of this arrangement, because they saw clearly how much this program would benefit the US (and Wall Street specifically). No matter, though, because enough other countries had no trouble signing on the dotted line to ratify the agreement.

Flash forward to 1971, when the US said, "You know what? We're done tying the value of the dollar to gold." This violated the Bretton Woods Agreement, so all those policies officially came to an end.

But here's a fun twist! They really didn't come to an end. The world kept following essentially the same system—and it still follows it today. The only difference was that now most of the world's currency wasn't valued against gold but rather the US dollar. Guess who benefited most from this arrangement?

Yes, it's true that the US found itself standing alone as the world's most dominant economic power in part because of Bretton Woods, but what's truer is that US banks were the entities that benefited most. Because all currencies now worked as a function of other currencies, this allowed the big currencies like the US dollar to dominate small currencies. The agreement essentially stacked the deck in the favor of US banks.

Why does Bretton Woods make the banks responsible for all the inequities? Because most central banks and commercial banks around the world hold the US dollar as a reserve currency and use the dollar as a means to trade with other nations. This is why America can export paper dollars all over the world, and it's also why Zimbabwe cannot.

Connie: Hold on there, Laz. I'm going to take over for a minute, because I think there's another piece of war history that plays every bit as great a role in this whole thing. And it smelled a little socialist to me.

I'm talking, of course, about the Marshall Plan, a program designed to help Western Europe recover from the devastation of World War II.

In 1948, the plan started distributing $15 billion to the reconstruction effort. That $15 billion sounds like a hilariously small amount of money these days, especially to reconstruct an entire continent. For perspective, that's just a little north of my boyfriend's net worth. At least that'll be his net worth if he decides to vote for my boss in 2020. How's that roaring stock market treating you, sugarplum?

Anyway, over the next four years, that money went to rebuilding the cities and infrastructure necessary for Western Europe to reindustrialize and reopen trade between friendly nations. Once again, because the US was fronting most of the money, they got to reap most of the benefits. Laz doesn't seem to think that was such a great thing. On this matter, among many others, Laz and I do not see eye to eye.

That's not the most important imbalance the Marshall Plan ushered in either. More important was that it placed certain countries at the head of the pack economically. Great Britain and West Germany suddenly found themselves in the driver's seat of the European economic picture. Meanwhile, all the nations that had either fought with (looking at you, Italy) or been occupied by Nazi Germany found themselves under the thumb of the currencies of other bigger, more powerful nations.

As just one example, Denmark was forced to tie its currency to the West German deutschmark. This effectively left this otherwise sovereign country without a central bank of its own. And that system remained in place even after the EU was formed. Denmark, whose currency was based entirely on the deutschmark, now saw itself dragged by Germany into the era of the euro. These days, Denmark basically doesn't have the ability to make monetary policy, as they aren't in control of their own central bank—and this despite the fact that the people of Denmark voted to not use the euro as their currency. Let this be yet another lesson in the horrors of not allowing countries, states, or people the freedom to make their own destiny.

Justin: Okay, I've heard that tone. Before we get too deep into one of your famous libertarian rants here, Con, can I just point one thing out? Isn't Denmark supposedly one of the happiest places on Earth?

Connie: Sure, but its economy is incredibly strained. People can't borrow money on the same level they do in Germany or the US because their currency is directly tied to the euro, which is tied to the US dollar, which thanks to the US's decision to quit tying its value to gold, means that the dollar itself is the euro's reserve currency. It's great for America, but it's kind of unfair overall.

Justin: I'm so glad you went here, because as you know, Denmark is a particular fascination of mine. What fascinates me most is that, despite seventy-five years passing by, the people of Denmark do not protest their loss of sovereignty or even the indignity of having to do more with less. They just seem able to do that—do more with less—and be completely happy about it. If I'm being totally honest, I'm jealous of that quality.

Laz: I'm happy to help you with that, boss. You could give me some of your money, and then you'd be free to try doing more with less.

Justin: I had a retort for this, but first we have to wait for Connie to quit laughing.

Connie: Sorry. I'm honestly not sure I've ever laughed so hard at anything in my life. Thank you for that, Laz. Give you some of his money? Ha ha!

Justin: Anyway, while we're thinking about Denmark, let's consider the poor developing nations, because they make Denmark look like a huge winner in this hierarchical economic game. Developing nations were invited to join the fun by taking on big US dollar loans (loans that they are still paying off today). Poorer countries, meanwhile, were invited to join the modern world, but they had to play by the rules, too, and to their detriment.

Thank you, Laz and Connie, for that fascinating history lesson.

In the end, the main lesson is that the world's leaders set out to create very reasonable solutions to some very serious global problems.

But there's an issue with global systems: they create global problems even as they're solving other global problems.

To do this, they created global systems. But there's an issue with global systems: they create global problems even as they're solving other global problems. It's all baked right into the pie too—if everyone's money is tied to everyone else's, then one country's economic problems can have a direct and sometimes catastrophic impact on other countries. See the Great Recession, where an economic collapse in tiny, economically upside-down Greece helped wreck the whole planet's economy. Of course, this was an unintended consequence of two very reasonable ideas in Bretton Woods and the Marshall Plan.

But really, the biggest unintended consequence is that these systems essentially took all the power away from people and governments and placed it in the hands of a very different new entity: an integrated global banking system.

Okay, Connie. Time for the moment you've been waiting for. Time for me to help Evan illustrate his new analogy. Time for me to turn on the jets ...

Evan Makes a Mountain into a Hot Tub

What does dollar dominance mean? What does reserve currency mean? Why are any of these concepts so important?

If you return to picturing our Trickle-Around Mountain, you're aware that this is just the economy of the United States. But here's the thing: all economies are connected these days. Think of dollar dominance and reserve currency as other countries' dependence on the dollar. American-driven Bankism has made other countries need dollars that trickle from the American Trickle-Around Mountain.

Since it's challenging to picture water trickling off one mountain and onto another, let's bring a new analogy, shall we?

Justin: I'm so excited about this analogy.

Evan: I'm starting to regret it, since it's clearly the reason we're all sitting uncomfortably in a hot tub.

Laz: By my count, only half of us are uncomfortable.

Connie: (groan)

Evan: Think about this Jacuzzi we're sitting in as the American economy. All the water in this tub is the money that exists in that economy. The jets pumping in water are the banks making loans. The sound of the bubbles and the roar of the water? That's people using money for goods and services.

But since this Jacuzzi is the American economy, something weird is happening. Water keeps spilling over the edge and dripping out of the tub. Where is the water going? It's going to Europe for German-made cars. It's going to Japan for electronics and China for a host of consumer goods. Each one of these countries has its own Jacuzzi to catch all this water spilling down from the US. The more they catch, the more their jets pump in loans, and the more their water spills over the sides of their Jacuzzis.

So now the water flows down to the next tier, to a dozen or so Jacuzzis like England, Brazil, India, Australia, and so on. They catch these dollars, which allows them to make more loans until they start overflowing their Jacuzzis.

Below that tier are all the small poor economies around the world. The problem for these jacuzzis is that the second tier catches most of the dollars and much less trickles down to the third tier but, because they're at the very bottom of the pyramid, they don't have anywhere for their own currency to trickle down to. So it just starts accumulating and losing value. The important thing to notice is that the dollars tends to trickle around and, once again, it is not a gravity-based system. The jacuzzi pyramid winds up being just like the Trickle-Around Mountain, with rich countries up top and poor countries at the bottom. The rich countries get to exploit the poor countries for resources just like rich people get to exploit poor people for labor. Bankism truly runs the world.

Poor developing countries wind up with their jacuzzi water flooding if they make too many loans, which means trade becomes impossible because it costs too much. These developing nations are desperate for trade because they do not have the infrastructure to be self sufficient. And since banks can't make enough loans to create work the people sit idle without jobs. Too many loans made in their own currency and, bam, flooding, leading to people not being able to make ends meet and the whole economy suffering. In essence, bankism forces these poor developing countries to not be able to function and their only hope is that they have some natural resource that they can trade for dollars.

This is how the banking system can be global while every country's economic system can look different. It's all based on a global banking system, and no matter how you build your Jacuzzi, it's still designed to work the same way. The basic job of every central bank is to control the amount of water in the Jacuzzi, or the money supply, as economists named it.

Each country has its own Jacuzzi, banks pumping in money and banks taking out money and trying to balance things out. While America sits on top, they can just basically buy from wherever they want and do whatever they want with their money because the rest of the world uses the US dollar. And so they never have the problem to the degree that the third world countries have.

Dollars also get recycled from the American government borrowing money. Other countries buy this debt in the form of treasury bills because America is considered a stable country that can pay the debt back. So any dollars floating around in other countries get sucked up by the American government spending more than it collects in taxes. This makes everything seem great now, but America owes money to other countries, which they are working hard for. They will want to be repaid with something of equal value. A debt only delays the work required to make the repayment.

Meanwhile, the rest of the world needs US dollars in order to balance their trade surpluses or their trade deficits, essentially buying back their own currency to prevent it from being devalued in inter-national trade. Put another way, the rest of the world has to manage their Jacuzzi water. The United States does not. And so that makes America the leader of the world because it can loan out more money than any other country without causing inflation.

Okay, then, let's look at the Jacuzzis at the bottom of the pyramid. Their first problem is that they have dollar-based debt courtesy of the IMF; their second problem is that their currency is considered unstable, so if they import anything, they get instant inflation. This means they are basically isolated from the rest of the world and stuck not benefiting from the advancements of other countries.

Since they don't get these advancements, their only hope is to export their natural resources in exchange for dollars to either pay back their debt or stabilize their currency.

This is part of why your boss's campaign slogan was so confusing to me, Connie. America first? America has always been first. We've been at the top of the pyramid since the end of World War II. So if we actively seek ways to withdraw from our position in the world, then we fail to lead the world, which is a huge problem, because our money basically controls the world.

Justin Towels Off

I don't know about the rest of you, but I'm getting a little warm. Time for me to towel off.

While we're doing that, let's consider a new mantra:

US dollar dominance on the global stage means that every other economy in the world is a function of the US dollar being exported for goods. Other countries need the dollar to pay off debts, trade with other countries, and control the value of their own currency, and therefore they need the dollar to print and lend out their own currency.

This means the global economy is limited by the US economy, specifically US asset prices like the stock markets and real estate, which are leveraged for loans and printing money. But once again, the economies of other countries are explained by social science, not basic math, so the US doesn't get the blame. Countries are described as basket cases, corrupt, and financially unsound. They are asked to use austerity and cut spending so they can prevent inflation and prop up their currency.

Globalization has been defined as international business. In reality, globalization is the effect of a global banking system driven through dollar dominance. This causes people to blame international businesses for moving their workforce elsewhere when in fact the banking system gave them little choice.

America isn't first because of political policy. It's not because we have a powerful military, or because we have always been some kind of shining beacon on the hill. America is first because of the dollar and its position at the top of the Jacuzzi pyramid of global trade.

Connie: I can see why it's hard to believe a currency can make a country a superpower. In the past, currencies have ruined empires. Just look at Rome and its currency, the denarius. Or what about all those countries with hyperinflation like Zimbabwe, Venezuela, and Argentina?

Evan: This is true. Currencies are fickle, but when the whole world treats the dollar like it's gold, then it isn't fickle anymore. This is why the Bretton Woods Agreement was ingenious from the perspective of American bankers and the efforts to win World War II.

Connie: The American dollar is gold? I thought it was just a piece of paper.

Evan: It's not even a piece of paper, but I'll explain that later. What's important is that the world treats the dollar like it's gold even though it's not. Originally, each piece of paper, each dollar, was backed by gold, but Nixon ran out of gold in 1971 and refused to sell any more. This was several decades after the Bretton Woods Agreement, and by this point, the dollar had been used in place of gold for so long that there was essentially no substitute.

In other words, Nixon's refusal to sell the gold in Fort Knox did not change the fact that the dollar was used as the currency of international trade and a reserve currency regardless of the value of gold.

Connie: That actually sounds really shrewd and amazingly brilliant. No wonder America is number one—and still great, if you catch my drift.

Evan: There's more to the story than America becoming the world's superpower. Without gold limiting the amount of money banks could loan out (because Nixon's fiat money basically ended fractional gold reserves as a standard), all this new money created inflation. The dollar was being debased by the banks lending out too much money.

Connie: Kind of like how debasing the denarius destroyed the Roman Empire.

Evan: Correct! And thanks to this debasing, America went through a long period of stagflation with both Carter and Reagan as president. But Paul Volcker (the Fed chairman at the time) fixed this by increasing the interest rates on loans, which basically shut down all borrowing. This came at a price that the workers of America are still paying for today.

Since gold no longer constrained borrowing, interest rates were the only tool the Fed could use to tame inflation. This meant people were out of work and not making money. The ability to ask for a raise was squashed by high interest rates. Many people blame stagflation of the late '70s on the price of oil, but let's face it—the price of oil went up because the dollar was flooding the world.

Connie: But this sounds like a good thing. The Roman Empire fell because they made too many denarii. The US controlled the amount of dollars being created for loans by raising interest rates, and this saved the country from going the way of Rome and the dinosaur.

Evan: True, but it was a deal with the devil. Let's look at the Jacuzzi again. When Volcker raised the interest rates sky high, it basically turned off the Jacuzzi pumps, but in a weird way. The pumps didn't pump water in, but all the outstanding loans kept sucking dollars out.

Countries all over the world who had borrowed money in dollars from the IMF and the World Bank were ruined. They had no way of paying off their dollar debts, and all the dollars that were flooding the markets quickly dried up. Basically, the economies of the entire world slowed just so America's dollar could sit on top of the world's Jacuzzi pyramid.

Connie: Again, this sounds pretty good for America.

Evan: But look at the water in the Jacuzzi! The water stopped roaring, jobs dried up, wages started falling. Once the dollar had the upper hand, the interest rates were slowly lowered, but only in small enough increments to ensure that wages didn't go up. And here we are thirty-five years later with wages having remained stagnant the whole time and a massive governmental safety net to help all those people who were squeezed out of a job.

Connie: This doesn't explain why the cost of living has gone up.

Evan: In order to get the economy working again, the banks had to loan money back into the economy. Those loans had to be backed by assets. This means loans went to wealthy people. Wealthy people bought and sold all the nicer assets, making them go up in value. Low wages allowed for wealthy people's companies to make more profits; the strong dollar allowed imports to enter the market at great discounts, which helped the poor working class get by; and this eventually led to assets like stocks and real estate going up while inflation was tamed.

Justin: I know exactly what you're gonna say, Con.

Connie: That this also sounds good for America?

Justin: We know each other so well.

Connie: U-S-A! U-S-A!

Justin: Hold the phone, though, Connie. Remember how the Trickle-Around Mountain highlighted the importance of the effectiveness of the work taking place, and how GDP doesn't matter if you're chasing your own tail? Well, the events of the '70s and '80s basically set up America to be delusional about its greatness. Companies worth billions without showing any profits. Housing values going up no matter what. Record stock markets in the worst economy in history. Does any of this sound familiar?

The vast majority of jobs—78 percent—are service jobs. Think about what that means. It means we're not producing much for other countries who we owe more and more money to every year. Almost half the country doesn't work. A rapidly growing portion of more than 40 percent of Americans has a chronic illness. America is not self-sufficient. It needs other countries in order to function. It needs low-cost products from other countries like China. It needs countries like China and Saudi Arabia to buy its debt. And when all this is added up, it means America has lost its sovereignty.

Connie: I knew it! Those commies are subverting our freedoms. And that's why we have to fix the trade policies with China.

Evan: Or we can change the game—turn trade wars into mutually beneficial trade.

But let me sum this up. The majority of Americans' earnings have been stagnant, and their cost of living has gone up. People are having a harder and harder time making ends meet. And because of the Jacuzzi pyramid situation, this is playing out in other countries as well. People all over the world are seeing stagnant wages and increased costs of living—or much, much worse.

The profound reality is that America in this scenario is the default leader and dictator of what happens to the world's economy. So, despite America's reputation as benevolent and charitable, millions of people die from poverty-related death around the world, which unfortunately is indirectly caused by the dominance of the American dollar.

> **Despite America's reputation as benevolent and charitable, millions of people die from poverty-related death around the world, which unfortunately is indirectly caused by the dominance of the American dollar.**

When we talk about America first, Connie, it's either stating a fact or incredibly ignorant because the American banking system and its dollar are first, just as designed at Bretton Woods. The effect isn't all roses for America. There is plenty of poverty, and most people struggle while wealthy people think they live in the greatest country on Earth despite the fact that China is solidly in control of its future while America is not. The question is, what do we have to change in order to put people first—all people, not just the banking system and their wealthy American customers?

Justin: Good question, Evan. It's the perfect pivot to our next chapter. It's almost like we planned it!

CHAPTER NINE

THE THREE-HEADED MONSTER

Know your enemy, know his sword.

—MIYAMOTO MUSASHI, legendary Japanese Kensei

A s we debate all these realities about the world, something has become increasingly obvious to me. Yes, the status quo that emerged following World War II was remarkably clever in its subtlety, but it seems to me that it takes a whole lot more for the entire human population for multiple generations to not realize its impact.

I've never been one for conspiracy theories. So before I dive into my thoughts here, I need to point out that I'm not suggesting a grand conspiracy in any way.

Is it possible that the banking system established dominance intentionally?

There is no doubt that J. P. Morgan took the reins of the printing presses and created the Federal Reserve with the clear intent of monopolizing the printing of money for the purpose of banks and the banking system. This increased their profits while providing a service. By declaring that "money is gold and everything else is credit," J. P. Morgan not only took control of the origin of money, but he set the stage for controlling the mind of mankind for generations.

But a conspiracy theory requires malicious intent with a heaping side of shadowy organizations running things behind the scenes. Did J. P. Morgan have malicious intentions? It isn't likely, in fact. Considering that he had personally bailed out the federal government, it's likely he was feeling quite benevolent.

In the end, it really doesn't matter because (a) the new world order that cemented our modern understanding of banking and money happened two decades later in the aftermath of World War II, and (b) no matter what the intent, the outcome is a series of global disasters hitting on every possible front while human suffering persists without an end in sight.

The results are monstrous, and yet it's like we don't even see the monster.

What matters more than any of this is that we got to where we are because of the global banking system constructed during and after the war, and everyone has been following these very public rules ever since. The results are monstrous, and yet it's like we don't even see the monster.

And incidentally, this monster has three heads.

Head #1: the commonly held belief that these institutions are not things we can change. They have existed for generations, and they are therefore written in stone, immutable, unmovable, and unchangeable. The Federal Reserve Act of 1913 is over a hundred years old. It's the only thing we know. The monetary policy of the Federal Reserve is accepted without question.

So the first head is the historical institutions and the authority we believe they must have. It is considered unchangeable and unchallengeable. We must all bow down to this very specific, long-held control of money for the purpose of allowing banks to maximize the lending of money and to have some pretense for the control of the money supply.

Head #2: the social science of economics as a means to explain our reality.

The study of economics is extraordinarily complex and esoteric, to the degree that even the world's leading experts admit there's no predicting exactly what the economy will do.

Economics becomes a monster when it makes our problems, our common enemy, invisible. It makes the creation of money, the banking system, and monetary policy seem mysterious and unknowable. Economics allows the banking system to not just control people but to control the entire world.

Imagine thousands upon thousands of young minds educated to believe the lie that people are responsible for the economy rather than the banking system. Go to an economics class and watch as students raise their hands to object as their instincts tell them one thing but their professor says another. And so the professors of tomorrow are the indoctrinated students of today, and the cycle continues.

Out of these thousands, there will always rise respected experts. Those experts will take powerful roles with banks, in the federal government, in the media, with states and municipalities, and all of them will be preaching from the same bible that their understanding of economics is (a) the only way, (b) unpredictable, and (c) all the fault of consumers and their behavior.

In all ways, this army of experts trained on the same doctrines helps spread the lie that the banking system is not responsible for the condition of the economy, the country, and the planet.

Head #3: the belief that GDP is a measure of progress.

Despite its obvious futility, this third head of the monster truly makes us blind. Yet it only has power because of the other two heads. If it were not for the institutionalized power of the banking system and the indoctrinated legions of economists, this head would be laughed into the history books.

However, since economics can't explain our reality, and the only thing the banks can control is the money in circulation, the only progress that can be measured is GDP—even if GDP or the activity it measures is leading to the destruction of humanity.

When viewed in this way, it's clear that we're dealing with an incredibly formidable, pretty damn scary monster. It's probably unbeatable, right? Let's ask the gang, shall we?

How to Defeat a Three-Headed Monster

Justin: Okay, guys, we've got this. Everyone knows that the way to beat a three-headed monster is to cut off one head at a time.

Connie: This whole thing is getting a little too Dungeons and Dragons for me already.

Evan: You never played D&D as a kid?

Laz: Ev, if you're trying to get all of us to quit calling you a nerd all the time, you've got to stop saying stuff like that.

Evan: Fair enough.

Justin: Is there a better analogy you would prefer, love of my life?

Connie: By this point, we're already thoroughly invested in the monster thing. So let's start cutting off heads.

Justin: That's the spirit. How do we do that?

Evan: Seems to me that we already know what the problem is. Yes, my educational background isn't helping anyone. And I see what you did there earlier by throwing my whole set of degrees and advanced degrees under the bus.

Justin: No one's saying you wasted your time in school, by the way. Your perspective is invaluable.

Evan: Thanks, I guess. But yeah, I suppose you're right about that. It's tough to see the problems with a system if you don't first study the hell out of that system.

Justin: So since most of our readers don't have time to study the hell out of that system, how about you break down the main problems for us?

Evan: Mostly it boils down to the way we're all taught to understand money. To cut off the first head of the monster, we have to get rid of this belief that money is just credit. We've got to get rid of Bankism. To cut off the second head, we need to stop the education system from teaching economics as a social science—in other words, we need to quit blaming citizens or the people themselves for the average economic situation, which means people have some control, but banks have a lot more.

Incidentally, if we can return to my Jacuzzi pyramid analogy for a second, it's not just people who get the blame here. Modern economics teaches third world countries that it's their fault their economies aren't doing well, when in fact the global banking system prevents developing countries from making progress. It's been eighty years. How long does a country really need to develop if it wasn't systematically deprived of resources?

We have this situation where both macroeconomics and microeconomics are teaching us the wrong thing. On a macro level, it's the idea that whole governments, systems, and countries are just plain doing it wrong, and that's why their economies are in the toilet. On the micro level, it's the average individual's fault that their household economics are upside down, that they're struggling financially, or that—

Laz: Or that they've been forced into homelessness.

Evan: Exactly! Imagine a system where the message is that if you can't make ends meet, it's all your fault. We live in a world of tremendous abundance of resources, and yet all these people and countries are living in duress, suffering from these shortages that result not from actual shortages, but from shortages manufactured by an imperfect and imbalanced banking system.

Justin: I appreciate you jumping in whole-assed on the economics bashing, Evan.

Evan: What else could I possibly do here? The evidence is plain as day.

Justin: Unfortunately, there are more contributors to the problem than just economic teachings. It permeates every discipline and every way of thought. It's what some people call normalcy bias—that notion that there is a reason for everything, a plan, and that even if things look bad right now, it's all going to be okay. During the Great Recession, it was like, "Well, that sucks. But the people in charge are taking care of things. I might not totally agree with their actions, but these kinds of things happen every couple of generations and we always pull our way out of it. Everything's going to be fine."

Even during the COVID crisis, which makes the GR look like a walk in the park, there's still that allure of normalcy bias. Hundreds of millions of people shuttered at home with not even a semblance of certainty about when the crisis would end, and there's still that natural human tendency to at least hope that there are adults in charge, and everything will be fine.

Obviously, this was a particular (and in many ways unique) period of unrest not just in the US but all over the world; still, the "fixes" that dominated the conversation had everything to do with measures that would prop up the banking system and help struggling people just get by. Passing multitrillion-dollar stimulus packages designed to put Band-Aids over massive, gaping wounds that the COVID crisis exposed was completely wrongheaded. But it comes from that same place. We all accept that this is the best we can do, so we do the same things to fix the broken system again and again.

> **Passing multitrillion-dollar stimulus packages designed to put Band-Aids over massive, gaping wounds that the COVID crisis exposed was completely wrongheaded.**

Of course, the problem is that we're not looking to make genuine change to the reality the banking system has created.

Laz: Speaking of which, coinciding with the COVID crisis was the Black Lives Matter movement. Yes, that emerged as a response to systemic racism in police departments, but it raised the national conversation about systemic racism in all American institutions.

Connie: Here we go again, blaming all our problems on the silent majority.

Justin: There's genuine truth to the blame, though, Con. Whether you believe in systemic racism or not is irrelevant. The imbalances exist. They are, as Evan put it, plain as day. We can't continue blaming people—particularly people of certain skin colors—for their own economic conditions. And we can't keep blaming impoverished countries for failing to provide for their people in what amounts to a totally rigged game.

ING

Connie: Okay, sit down, you three. I need a minute here. You're all pointing too many fingers. Talking about the need to see reality for what it truly is and make genuine change. But have any of you stopped to think about why things are the way they are? Yes, the acts passed after World War II set up the US as the world leader in all things money related. It set us on top of Evan's Jacuzzi pyramid.

But let me ask you this: if we can put your liberal agendas aside for a minute, what exactly is so wrong with this? What's wrong with wanting to put America first? Isn't it in our best interest—at least the four of us and our three hundred million fellow Americans—if the US continues to lead and dominate the globe? I mean, doesn't a successful system need someone to lead?

Laz: Who decided who gets to lead?

Connie: History.

Justin: Can you elaborate?

Connie: We had this pair of world wars and a cold war immediately after. Perhaps you've heard of them. The West conquered the world. Plain and simple. After conquering the world, its leaders established the rules by which the world should work. These rules have worked for all these generations by keeping America as the most powerful country in the world.

Rip on the economic conditions that result from Bankism all you want, but Western philosophy has more than a few benefits, not just in the US, not just in the West, but everywhere.

Justin: No one's denying that Western thought drives the world, Connie. The problem is that it reinforces the notion that there is no other way. No one is even looking for answers to our problems from these eighty-year-old agreements.

Laz: And the crazy and really damaging part is that it permeates the way even non-Western countries think. Even in some African countries, a good percentage of people have this notion—whether consciously or unconsciously—that they need the West, or even just white people, in order to succeed as a country. It has become a pervasive influence that drives whole cultures. It teaches them that the West isn't just powerful, but that it is the source of all logic, all systems, and everything about the way the world works.

Connie: Without even realizing it, you guys are making my point for me.

Justin: Which is?

Connie: I'm not arguing with you about whether racism exists or whether there's a cultural imbalance in the world. I'm arguing with you about what change would mean. You want to try to change Western hegemony? Fine. But if you do that, everything will fall apart. It's not just that we've spent generations setting up and supporting systems that put the West and its banks in charge; it's that too many people all over the world have bought into this power structure. They see it as reality. As normalcy, like Justin said.

People resist change to the structures they know and trust not because they think racism or inequity is somehow right. Racism and inequity are absolutely wrong, just so you guys don't think I'm some kind of bigot. People resist change to the structures they know and trust because they believe that this kind of change would lead to chaos. For most people, it's too much of a leap to accept disruptive change to the way the world works. For most people, it's an A or B scenario: either we accept the system we have (and hope it repairs itself after these many varied crises) or we accept anarchy.

Justin: But what if we presented the people with a genuinely beautiful idea—a Big Solution—one that fixes everything without forcing anyone into big, scary cultural changes? What if we could provide a solution that eliminates the inequities created by Bankism and our false understanding of money? What if that solution could fix all these poorly functioning systems from the ground up rather than the top down?

Evan Poops on the Parade

Evan: I'm sorry to kick you in the gut, Justin, but there's probably never been a worse time to get the masses to believe in big new ideas.

Justin: Now even you are going to get cynical on me?

Evan: The writing's on the wall, I'm afraid. Blame it on the internet. Blame it on a slow cultural shift toward following the talking points of talking heads on TV. Blame it on Connie or, better yet, Connie's boss.

Connie: Watch it.

Evan: I'm not blaming it on your boss. I'm apolitical, remember? I'm just saying … some people do blame it on your boss.

Connie: Tell me about it.

Evan: No matter who or what you blame, the point is the same: people just don't know who or what to believe anymore. There's this pervasive sense that science and the experts have misled society too many times.

Justin, you started this chapter with the idea that economics is a bad science.

Justin: To be fair, I suggested that it's more art than science.

Evan: Fair enough, but the reality is that economics isn't the only science with a history of flip-flopping and often getting it wrong. A huge part of why people these days don't fully believe in science and the experts is that we're presented with evidence of science getting it wrong almost every day. Remember when bread was healthy and fat wasn't? Now fat is healthy and bread is not.

Connie: God, I miss pasta.

Evan: Well, just wait around a while, then, because if history is any guide, then it'll be healthy again eventually. I mean, first eggs were considered very healthy. Then they caused heart attacks. And now they don't have anything to do with heart health anymore and are actually pretty good for you again. Coffee is good for you. Wait, no, it causes cancer. Wait, no, it actually helps lower your risk of cancer, but only if you drink it black.

Now, I'm not saying for a second that this means science is bad. There's a system that every good scientist must follow. You simply go where the evidence leads you. Sometimes that evidence seems conclusive. Other times, new evidence emerges that suggests you were totally wrong. That's the entire basis of the scientific method. The unfortunate side effect is that this lack of genuine, lasting certainty contributes to public distrust.

Laz: So the problem isn't with science itself. The problem is that we all want to adhere to common belief systems. We want to think that there are absolute rights and absolute wrongs, and science doesn't allow for that. It's why we've all aligned so rigidly into our political camps where talking points and beliefs are handed out to serve the party.

Any talking point coming from MSNBC or Fox News, or from left-wing or right-wing leadership, is repeated almost verbatim by the people who identify with those groups. It has nothing to do with science or truth. It's all about a common point of view. And a weird side effect of the need to accept a talking point is to believe—vehemently, angrily, and sometimes violently—that the other side is evil and wrong.

Connie: Are you trying to apologize to me, Laz?

Laz: Hell no. You're evil and wrong.

Evan: The media isn't helping, particularly with opinion-driven entertainment news. It's not just that people have a hard time respecting institutions that sometimes change their minds; it's that facts are now muddled because media tends to not report on scientific studies but rather the interpretations of those studies. Science is undisputable, but it is well open to interpretation. This leads media to position information in a way that allows audiences to ignore facts, truth, and principles completely. But it's not just the media's fault, either; people want to hear what they believe. They want to be reinforced and told they are right. So if they want to keep their audience and ratings, the media doesn't have much choice.

I hate to say it, Justin—especially since you're paying me to help you deliver this Big Solution—but just showing people a different way of looking at things doesn't mean they will believe in it. We could make the case in the most logical way imaginable. It could all seem completely irrefutable. But there's still enough distrust in truth that the people won't believe it unless they receive approval from the leadership of their tribes.

The Connies of the world won't accept this idea unless it starts getting traction on Fox News or with the RNC. The Lazes of the world will need the NYT and the DNC to give the thumbs-up first. Truth is now based on talking points, and everyone gets their talking points from up top.

Laz: Maybe you should run for president, Justin.

Justin: I would, but like you're saying, I don't speak from the top. I don't provide the talking points.

Evan: I think we have to accept that your book isn't going to be accepted, even though you're doing all this straightforward explaining. You're just not the right source of the talking points for the vast majority of people. We're talking about people who don't even fully believe in science. Or even math! And nobody understands economics. So how exactly are you going to get people to accept what you're writing about when they have never even considered the framing of their existence?

Justin: Excuse me while I find a fire to burn these notes I've been taking.

Et Tu, Laz?

Laz: Personally I think we're putting too much stock in the tribal nature of modern culture.

Mostly I think it's all about apathy. We're all so beaten down by the constant arguments, polarization, and difficulty in making ends meet. It's only natural to just check out—to accept that the people in charge are going to squabble and that things might sometimes seem like they're terrible and unfixable, but ultimately, it all works out.

Honestly, I fall into this trap sometimes too. I fell hard about a year into my homelessness. At that point, I was so messed up I could hardly even bother to wake up every morning. But then I started leaning into this sense that as long as I accepted that I didn't have control over what was happening in my life, I would find peace. And I did find a sense of peace in that. It's so much more comfortable to turn the responsibility for your future over to fate or to God. It's easier to have faith than to engage.

Justin: So the kind of change I'm asking for is in God's hands?

Laz: For some people, yeah. But there's also the flip side of that. Other people believe that events in this world are preordained. Things will take care of themselves. Just have faith. I mean, look at me. A few years ago, I was homeless. Then I put my future in the hands of a higher power. And now look at me. See? It all worked out.

That's a huge part of what you're going to have to overcome—and frankly, I don't think it can be overcome—this idea that someone else is taking care of us, everything's going to be okay, so why worry about what's happening right now? Why even try to make change when there's someone else making the necessary changes for us?

Justin: So when I opened this chapter, I suggested that the only thing standing in our way was a three-headed monster related to institutional acceptance. And what you three are telling me is that I also have to go up against history, Western hegemony, the public's general distrust of science and math, modern tribalism and cultural conflict, and now also apathy and personal faith. Does that about sum it up?

Connie: Sounds right.

Laz: Yep.

Evan: I do feel like you're forgetting one or two others, but sure.

Justin: Then what exactly have we been arguing around in circles about? I mean, why have we put all this time and energy into identifying the ills of Bankism and examining the problems of the world? What was this all about?

All: (crickets)

Justin: This was just some kind of academic exercise? An attempt to sell some books?

All: (crickets)

Justin: You mean to tell me that this isn't just about slaying a three-headed monster? That there is no convincing the world that the Big Solution has merit because everyone is already too entrenched in their beliefs? You mean to tell me that we're all just shouting at the wind?

All: (crickets)

Justin: Excuse me, then, while I go curl up in a ball and cry.

CHAPTER TEN

ALL IS LOST

Bond: Do you expect me to talk?
Goldfinger: No, Mr. Bond. I expect you to die!

—from the film *Goldfinger*

t turns out that my version of curling up in a ball and crying feels a little more like that iconic moment from that iconic Bond film. Imagine your hero, bound and gagged, staring up into the darkness, where only the glint of a laser beam can be seen. It moves slowly but in a direction bearing down on his crotch, and he's straddled akimbo on a table with his legs and hands strapped to the sides. Eventually it dawns on him that—wait—this is a laser, and its business is very clearly two halves of his whole.

You know that "all is lost" feeling. Between the COVID crisis and the utter collapse of the economy, we've all had more than our fair share of it over the past few years. Well, I'm feeling it now, as it relates to this book. All the time and effort we've put in, all the arguments we've had and resolved, all the great ideas bouncing around our four contributing brains—and in the end, the bad guys are just too powerful. Established institutions, subtle economic policy, blind acceptance of the status quo, that "this is the way it's always been, and changing it now would destroy everything" mentality. There's nothing we can do to fight Goldfinger. We're done. Might as well lie back and accept this encroaching bisection.

Inch by inch. It sizzles and burns. It'll get to me eventually.

Man, waiting for death is boring, especially when it's all in your head, but I feel like I'm in a deadly trap. It just seems like there is just no way to overcome it all.

While we wait, might as well think about how we got here. Might as well ponder how humanity finds itself in this situation.

Maybe humanity is just destined to fail. Hell, maybe intelligent life itself is destined to fail. That would certainly be one way to explain why we've never been contacted by superadvanced aliens. We've never had our Independence Day standoff because every species that reaches a certain point of advancement in its civilization just winds up falling apart. All those years from my childhood, we worried and assumed that the bomb would be the end of us. Then, later, we assumed it would be international terrorism. Later still, it was a financial collapse, then COVID-19 or rioting in the streets. Turns out, it's just economic policy. Turns out, misguided policy is more than enough to subvert an entire planet's varied and interconnected societies.

We all came out of some primordial soup, followed some stupid chain of events to our current evolutionary moment, and now we're just teetering on the brink of the death of civilization. And our reward for getting this far is that human activity has reshaped the earth to such a degree it's causing the Sixth Great Extinction.

How could we possibly survive? Why would we even want to?

The smell of plastic from the laser burns the cushion. C'mon, I'm ready to get split in half.

There's too much to fight against. Too many obstacles to overcome. Too many established beliefs. Even if we manage to convince a few readers that the Big Solution has merit, and that simply changing the way we think about money will lead to stable and sustainable economic growth without having to change anything else, there are just too many deeply held core beliefs that will prevent us from swaying the establishment.

We all came out of some primordial soup, followed some stupid chain of events to our current evolutionary moment, and now we're just teetering on the brink of the death of civilization.

Connie to the Rescue

Okay, hold on. I'm getting a little sick of this pity party. Pouting after our last conversation is one thing, but you've been at this for a good twenty-four hours. Time to buck up, buttercup. This is a little too sissy, even for you. I mean, fine, you can go up in smoke, but c'mon, man, you're fighting for all of humanity.

Justin: You always did give the best pep talks.

Connie: I'm serious. This is sad. You're spending all this valuable page space in your book on feeling sorry for yourself. You've got a great idea, but the establishment is going to make it challenging for that idea to take hold. Welcome to the real world.

Justin: I'm serious too. Were you a cheerleader in high school? Because you're an extremely gifted spirit lifter.

Connie: I mean, how you thought you would be able to make

genuine change with a book in the first place is beyond me. I mean, really. Even before the pandemic, people were always too afraid of change, too entrenched in their established beliefs about how the world is supposed to work. And, Justin, you're expecting people to change in the middle of all this uncertainty?

Justin: Call me a starry-eyed dreamer, but I guess I thought maybe all this upheaval would make people more willing to change.

Connie: You're a starry-eyed dreamer.

Justin: That's very helpful, thanks.

Connie: People only change if societal conditions or natural disasters make them change.

Justin: Why aren't global warming, a pandemic, and economic collapse enough?

Connie: Don't bring that liberal crap.

Justin: It shouldn't be a liberal or conservative issue. It's a human issue.

Connie: Maybe, but it is a liberal issue. That's the reality we've created for ourselves. And anyway, global warming doesn't feel urgent enough for the average person to care. A pandemic? People can learn to live with it. And economic collapse? You said it yourself in the last chapter. People have been taught that it's all cyclical. Why change a whole system when it's bound to change itself soon enough?

Justin: God. Stop. You're making it worse.

Connie: It's like everything else in life. When something bad happens, people just need a minute to adapt to the new reality. It's true that 9/11 shut shit down for a while, but then we all just got used to taking our shoes off in the TSA line. And look at things now. We've all kind of accepted the reality that COVID will probably be around forever. It sucks, but you don't see the rest of us curled up in a ball, pretending like we're in some overrated Poe story.

Justin: Look, some of us are just trying to have an existential crisis here. So if you don't mind …

Connie: Fine. Keep feeling sorry for yourself. Maybe when it's all over, you'll finally start taking comfort in the idea of fighting to keep America first.

What Do You Call the Opposite of an Epiphany?

America first. I mean, the arrogance of this notion. My girlfriend doesn't even realize that this is a huge part of why I'm engaging with this freak-out in the first place.

She says change only comes—and is only temporary and minor—when disaster strikes? Okay, well, here we stand on the precipice of not just an economic collapse, but of a series of global conditions that could easily cause America to slip to the bottom of Evan's Jacuzzi pyramid.

Think about it. Are we really the lone economic superpower we were even ten years ago? An increase in global commerce and ever-increasing influence from China has to have many countries in the developed world wondering why we're still basing everything on the dollar in the first place.

What happens if, while we're all clinging to our established beliefs and ideals, the US dollar is suddenly dumped as the defining currency? What if this coronavirus continues spreading, continues upending daily life, continues sewing political divisions and eroding democracy?

Or what if the rest of the world succeeds in containing the virus and the US continues to fail at turning the tide? How could we ever expect American life to return to normal? And how could we possibly expect the world to continue holding our currency as the standard?

What value does a currency, or US treasury bonds, or American stocks have if our economy remains in decline, our future prospects look uncommonly bleak, and our whole society faces collapse?

If the US dollar continues to look like an incredibly vulnerable asset, what the hell value will it have as the global reserve currency?

Laz: I think I can answer that, boss.

Justin: How'd you get in here? Man, can't a guy have a panic attack in peace?

Laz: Connie said you were in here feeling sorry for yourself and I should check in. Anyway, it's not like you're behind a locked door or something. You're just sitting out here in your storage shed. You take comfort in all this dusty patio furniture, boss?

Justin: It's not just my shed. It's where I come to think. There's nowhere else on my property where I can be sure I'll be alone. Or at least where I thought I could be sure.

Laz: Like your own little Situation Room.

Justin: Exactly. Except I'm more in the mode of imagining this as a torture shed at the moment. I'm doing this whole Goldfinger thing.

Laz: Yeah, Connie mentioned something about that.

Justin: Glad to hear you two have gotten so buddy-buddy during my moment of considerable doubt.

Laz: Okay then, Eeyore. I'll leave you to it, but I do think I have an answer to your questions.

Justin: Fine. Take over, then. Not like I'm making myself feel any better out here anyway.

Laz: Cool. So your question is what value the dollar will have in this post-COVID, postapocalyptic version of the world you're imagining. The answer is none.

Justin: Ugh. You're all just such huge rays of sunshine.

Laz: You're one to talk, boss. When's the last time you had a shower?

Justin: Don't worry about it.

Laz: Anyway, when the world stops valuing the dollar as the reserve currency, you're right, man. There won't be any way to spin the lie that America is first. It won't be possible. The world will have replaced its reserve currency with gold or the euro or the yuan, and we'll be left as a country that used to be valued for its consumer culture but is now incapable of anything approaching that same level of consumption. We'll be a country that is no longer a great producer of anything. No manufacturing. No means to innovate or drive technological change. A population overrun by illness and decline, with 10 percent of us deathly sick and 50 percent unemployed or unable to do any actual work.

We'll go from first to last, from the top Jacuzzi to the bottom. Just like with any impoverished country in the world today, we'll find ourselves overwhelmed with the water generated by this new version of the global economy. We'll overflow, flood, face hyperinflation, and there will be no way out.

That's the darkly hilarious thing about all of Connie's and her ex-boss's America-first nonsense. Even before they took office, this country's "we lead the world" attitude was actually a vulnerability because, man, what if we're not first anymore? Do we have a contingency plan?

Justin: No.

Laz: No.

Justin: So you came in here to make me feel worse, then, too?

Laz: Not at all. You're not really listening to me, boss. You're just moping through it all.

Justin: What am I missing, then?

Laz: You're missing that your Big Solution is different from any of that crap Connie was talking about. Sure, people resist change. And sure, there are a whole lot of deeply entrenched systems preventing this message from really sinking in. But you've got a really big ally on your side.

Justin: Which is?

Laz: The change that the COVID crisis and this economic collapse will show the world that even in a pandemic, the rich get richer and the poor get the bill, both in terms of risking their lives for minimum wage jobs and in layoffs. Really, it's business as usual. But even worse, it seems like every time disaster hits, inequality and the wealth gap widens.

No matter which reserve currency is dominating, and no matter which country is at the top of the pyramid, everyone will still be a slave to that pyramid, to that Trickle-Around Mountain. Like no other change before it, the change you're suggesting will open people's eyes.

Justin: I'm having a hard time believing that right now.

Laz: Well, that's your loss, man, because while you're feeling sorry for yourself, you're missing the uniqueness of this moment. If and when the whole thing collapses and gets replaced with essentially the same system, people are going to wake up to a new question: do we really want to live in a world where some other country gets to dominate us because of their strong currency?

I'm telling you, boss. People are going to want to get out of this pyramid scheme and create a global economic system where there is no dominant currency, where all countries thrive. And there isn't this trickle-down effect. COVID has been an unmitigated disaster, but it could also be the great equalizer. People are going to want a level playing field for all countries.

Justin: If you say so.

Laz: I know so, man. And you know why? Because none of this is real.

Justin: What are you talking about?

Laz: This is slightly conspiratorial. Are you okay with that?

Justin: What do I care? The book I envisioned is off the rails already.

Laz: Okay, so what if the whole "stock market" thing is orchestrated? What if the Federal Reserve is buying up all the bad debt and even ETFs so that America doesn't collapse?

This is exactly what would be happening right now if the Federal Reserve wasn't printing money and exchanging it for debt assets that are worthless because the debt payments are not being made. All those unemployment checks that the economy is burning through were paid for not by taxpayers but by other countries like China buying treasury bonds. So basically, China is paying for America's meal ticket right now.

Why would anyone want to give America a free lunch? It's because of the dollar being seen as a safe haven. But how safe is it really? Between a couple of economic collapses, serious mismanagement of a pandemic, and an increasingly shaky democracy, how much more doubt is needed before some other currency seems safer than the dollar? And when that happens …

Justin: Someone else takes over.

Laz: Exactly. Someone else just slides in at the top of the pyramid. I mean, you don't even have to buy into my conspiracy theory to see that this is a possible outcome. In fact, I'm not sure it's even a conspiracy, since it's happening in broad daylight. You can choose to believe that we got here because of ineptitude or an inability to accept even the perception of failure, but wherever it comes from, the whole thing's like a perfect nightmare playing out in reality.

Justin: All the more reason to stay in this shed, Laz. The reality you're talking about has even less hope than I thought.

Laz: You're still missing the point. Point is that this whole nightmare is driven by Bankism. The rules that keep the banks in charge are still being applied. Sure, they're printing money and buying worthless debt hand over fist like never before, but it's all so that banks can continue to keep control.

You've got to finish this book, boss, even if it feels like it won't do any good. You have a real chance of changing the course of history here.

Justin: Yeah, I'll get right on that just as soon as I finish dusting this patio furniture.

Laz: Long as you're up and moving, I feel like my work here is done.

There Is No Longer Any Work to Be Done

I wish I had half of that man's sunny disposition. That dude used to sleep in a gutter. He had nothing. A robot had taken his job, his family left him, the bank repossessed everything he'd worked a lifetime to earn (on credit, by the way), and he wound up with less than a penny to his name. I've heard stories from him that still make my skin crawl to think about. The shit he's seen, man.

Meanwhile, I've never seen a day of difficulty in my life. Sure, I grew up in a small house owned by what you might call lower-middle-class parents. We had an upstairs tenant in the joint. I used to mow lawns and deliver newspapers just so I could pay for the basketball shoes my parents couldn't afford. But I've never eaten garbage.

Laz has eaten garbage. And he comes in here with that "every-thing's gonna be okay, boss" nonsense. Tell you what—the only thing I care about right now is dusting this furniture and feeling sorry for myself. So that's exactly what I'm going to do.

"Change the course of history." Ha!

This idea wouldn't even scratch the surface of changing daily life in America, let alone the world. It helped on the farm for a while, but that was a self-contained, thoroughly data-driven environment based on absolutely perfect conditions. And still it blew up. Sure, it had some help from the outside world, but it blew up all the same.

And I mean, really. Who am I kidding? How can I expect to fix the problems of this country and the problems of, like, Japan simultaneously? Japan has hundred-year mortgages, a much larger debt than the United States, stagflation forever, a shrinking population, and professional demands that amount to essentially suicide-by-work. So the notion can't be that simple. The American government can't just spend its way into job guarantees and then think prosperity would naturally follow. It hasn't worked for the Japanese. And, hey, while we're at it, Germany tried the same thing after WWI and wound up creating Nazism.

What I want is for people to recognize that we already live in a world without scarcity, and as such, our purpose in life should be to enjoy and sustain life—to create something great, to truly have the means to pursue our own happiness. I want an optimized economy, not an economy that chases its own tail.

But how do I get there when everyone everywhere has been conditioned to think that there are only a handful of different ways to run an economy, and only one of them is acceptable to the good old US of

> **What I want is for people to recognize that we already live in a world without scarcity, and as such, our purpose in life should be to enjoy and sustain life—to create something great, to truly have the means to pursue our own happiness.**

A? How do I prove to people that they have essentially been forced to live under very specific conditions set up (through some seriously remarkable sleight of hand) by Bankism? How could I possibly get them to believe that we can actually create a system where cost of living actually goes down and wages go up? How could I convince them that there is a future that looks brighter for everyone?

Evan's Timing Is as Impeccable as Ever

Evan: Did I hear somebody call my name?

Justin: You certainly are among the whitest of white men.

Evan: In a neck-and-neck race with you.

Justin: Touché.

Evan: If you don't mind my saying, Justin, you seem to be a little at war with yourself here.

Justin: You think?

Evan: I mean, you're dusting patio furniture and talking to yourself about the racial inequality baked into the economic system.

Justin: Guilty as charged.

Evan: Laz and Connie said I should come in here and pile on, so that seems like a pretty good place to start.

Justin: I swear, there are only three people staying in my house presently, all the staff are out on holiday, and I can't get a single second alone.

Evan: That's the thing, though. If you'd just quit feeling sorry for yourself for a moment, you'd see how your Big Solution even solves the massive racial inequality problem in the American economy—and the world economy, honestly.

Justin: How in the hell would it do that?

Evan: Well, it would level the playing field, for one.

Justin: Only if the playing field actually accepted the notion that there's a way to think outside our established economic box.

Evan: Granted, but getting them to do that is just a matter of pointing out how simple and natural the fixes become if you just change that one thing.

Justin: And what is that one thing?

Evan: How we think about money.

Justin: Good luck with that.

Evan: No, seriously. It used to be that the whole system we're living in made some semblance of sense, because it was based on bartering. Goods had value. The dollar had value; it was gold. All money had value; you had to earn it. But the foundation of the bartering system ended the moment our currency was taken off the gold standard. At that precise moment, the American dollar became more than a means to exchange goods and services. It evolved into a means to consolidate whole industries; it became leverage.

Of course, that benefited certain countries over others and certain minorities of people under others. It also made the dollar a tool to extract resources from poor countries.

This doesn't just mean that consolidated industry makes it impossible for the small farmer to exist anymore or that it's next to impossible to make any real money as a small business; it means that impoverished people become useless and a burden.

Justin: How do you mean?

Evan: Everything the government does, it pays for in taxes collected or in debt. This is, in fact, the only mechanism for distributing money. So it should be no surprise that our government is beholden to the people paying the most in taxes while also being left with the responsibility of taking care of all the people made useless by progress. What kind of progress makes people useless, anyway? It's so backward.

Justin: This is supposed to make me feel better, the idea that the existing system has essentially created an oligarchy? That next generations are getting screwed on the cost of living, on education, on opportunity, and on global warming?

Evan: No. This is supposed to make you feel better: you have the answer. If you take away the dysfunctional banking system and replace it with common sense, then you might just find the formula for a better world—a much, much better world.

Justin: It's not that simple. We can't just "take away the dysfunctional banking system." It's too entrenched. People are too set in the erroneous notion that there's no other way to do things. How do you shock them out of that kind of thinking?

Evan: We follow the Trump playbook. We do it with messaging. The simpler, the better. "Putting people first and banks last" isn't just simple; it makes perfect sense.

Justin: Seems a little clunky.

Evan: So there are some rough edges to smooth out. But that's no reason to bury your head in the sand—or the patio furniture dust, as it were.

Justin: Har!

Evan: Nothing's perfect right from the start, and nothing is immediately accepted by the public. Think about the combustion engine. It started as a clunky, noisy pollution machine in Henry Ford's barn. Now it's the purring, powerful drivetrain of the vast majority of the cars on today's roads. The only difference between those two versions of the combustion engine is fuel injectors—brilliant mechanical devices that optimize how much fuel goes into the combustion chambers. If a car's engine worked like the American economy, where bankers inject money to wealthy people and corporations that spend it randomly, no one would want to drive.

Justin: The question is, how do we get anyone to care about that point?

Evan: No, the question is, when are people going to wake up and realize that the American Dream is for bankers, not homeowners or small business owners? It's the bankers that benefit from every home needing a mortgage and every industry that gets consolidated. It's the people who are misled into thinking higher housing costs make them wealthy when in fact the cost of housing will remain the same after they sell their home, which means there is no net benefit unless they downsize into a new, cheaper home. The same with consolidation. The one business left standing created dozens of heartbreaking bankruptcies, never worth more than the sum of the previous parts. But no matter who was left standing, the banks reaped rewards. It's true of anything you own. It doesn't have to be, but that's the reality we currently live in. So that's the big question, Justin: when do people start questioning the reality we've chosen to live in?

Justin: You're just digging the hole deeper, man. They answer is, if they haven't already, they're not gonna. I mean, how many unemployed do we have in this country right now?

Evan: Last I saw, it was something like 39 percent of Americans.

Justin: You want to hear the stat I read this morning? Slovakia has 93 percent of its people employed. Slovakia, Evan.

Evan: Yeah, that's ... is that correct?

Justin: What makes you think people have this grand wake-up call in them when hundreds of thousands of Americans are dying from poverty every year and most of us just say, "Well, they probably should have worked harder or had better jobs." Why must we look to the past for answers to a problem that has plagued humanity throughout all modern history? Why not question the lack of progress in the fundamentals of economics? Every aspect of society advances through science, research, and development—every aspect except for economics. Why is that?

Evan: Because—

Justin: No, no. I'm on a rant here. I'll answer that one. So … why don't people question what's going on? It's not politicians or the media;

> **Banks should not be in control of that value for their purposes. It's the people. Money and people should come first.**

it's the people making the definitions of the financial system—the bankers. It's the bankers who print money to finance the skyscrapers that everyone can point to and say, "See? Progress." But money is supposed to be the exchange of value between people. Banks should not be in control of that value for their purposes. It's the people. Money and people should come first.

The best way to print more money according to these probank policies is to increase the value of assets. The houses they are tearing down are replaced by more valuable skyscrapers. Low interest rates on loans are not meant to produce more jobs for people; they simply increase the likelihood of another skyscraper tearing down more affordable houses and further displacing the poor.

If anyone's going to wake up, then we have to call out the enemy of the people, the enemy of humanity: the banks and their privatized money system. The only reason the world is full of all these problems is that we're letting them get away with it. If science and engineering were the guiding principle behind the use of money, then the social science of economics would be history, and work would be for the purpose of advancing mankind, not a mindless banking statistic like GDP.

Evan: So it seems like you just answered your own question. How we get the people to wake up is by telling them exactly that. We just have to do it compellingly, with simple Trump-like sloganeering.

Justin: But if the banks control the monetary policy, there's no chance of that happening. Politicians treat economics like it's some holy grail, but nothing affects our lives more than the words (and they are only words!) that define monetary policy.

Evan: Okay, so America just needs to understand that without work, nothing has value. There has to be a way to show them that asset prices unsupported by actual work is a recipe for disaster. It should be an easy point to make that the only thing supporting America's astronomical asset prices is debt, and debt has to be paid back.

Further, as we stated earlier, money is an exchange of work products. Credit is an exchange of unearned money for work that has to be repaid with actual work. When you work for credit, you are in actuality creating double work. There has to be work done now and work done later to pay it back. It should be no surprise to anyone that the larger the total debt, the more work that has to be done.

If debt is used to pump up asset prices, the work was never done to support the value of the money and therefore the asset. Ultimately, the work is done by workers, not bankers. This should be the battle cry: "Stop making indentured servants out of WE THE PEOPLE who are supposed to be free."

Justin: Oh please! People are working eighty-hour weeks and barely making rent and they think Joe Biden will take their freedom. It was lost long ago. Do they realize that there are indigenous bushmen in Australia who only work twelve to eighteen hours a week to get by?

Evan: We need a slogan—

Justin: Don't say "sloganeering."

Evan: Fine. An example, then. Tell them that robots are coming for their jobs.

Justin: That slogan's already circulating. Laz is out of his mind about it. People know it already anyway. And still they do nothing.

Evan: Yeah, but most people think it's the robots themselves to blame. Or the billionaires investing in them. What most people don't understand is that it's not the robots taking their jobs; it's the banks. The cost of technology is astronomical and couldn't compete against most human labor without bank loans. You know that better than anyone.

Justin: True.

Evan: Human labor, even now, is much cheaper than technology—unless the technology can be paid for with a bank loan. The bank loan allows the technology to cost less since it can be paid for over time. This allows robots to be competitive with human labor on a per-hour basis. Technology is only waging war on the working class because banks are financing the hostile takeover of people's jobs. But this is a zero-sum game for the economy since people not working and earning less means a smaller, less productive economy. See, when a robot does work, it's not worth anything. When a person does work, it's worth money. Human work is money.

These factors also narrow the future scope of technology. Tech is only deployed when it can return the initial investment. Banks don't make technology loans for something that they can't easily see paying them back. So there will never be any technology to eliminate poverty, for example, because there's just no money in that. Same with global warming. Technology will only ever advance in a direction where it can outperform people and older tech while costing less as well. And this highlights the problem with Bankism; it doesn't solve our problems because the only thing that matters are banks.

Justin: Fine. You can maybe sway some working-class Americans that the banks are behind the robots that are taking their jobs. But you haven't even mentioned what I think to be the strongest head of the three-headed monster. How do we convince the very serious economists?

Evan: That should be easiest, because we have the raw data. Quantitative debt is exploding, assets have risen to irrational valuations, and interest rates are rock bottom or even negative.

Justin: "So what?" they'll say.

Evan: An asset class that has been driven up in valuation from years of low interest rates on loans will eventually cause a correction in the stock market that leads to another financial collapse.

Justin: We'll just throw more quantitative easing at it.

Evan: The Federal Reserve does what its owners tell it to do: save the banks. It starts buying debt assets that are underwater (which means the debt leveraged against the asset is greater than the value of the asset). And by doing this, the Federal Reserve bails out the commercial banks once again using quantitative easing. In addition, in order to pump up the value of the assets, the Federal Reserve will lower the interest rates and hope asset prices recover, since that's what America's economy is based on.

Justin: I know how quantitative easing works.

Evan: Sorry. It's just that all these measures only make the situation worse. It allows for cheap credit to pay for more automation and less work done by people. It creates that illusion of wealth you mentioned, an illusion that will persist as long as other nations support the dollar in international trade. But make no mistake—it's an illusion of value. America's wealth is no longer based on work, and we are already seeing the damaging effect this can have on our society. People are choosing not to work because they aren't receiving a relative value for their work when compared to asset prices.

Justin: So we're doomed.

Evan: Maybe. The data suggest it's possible. I mean, over the last seventy years, the global population has been exploding, right alongside global debt. Production of goods and services has grown considerably in conjunction with this, but the growth rate is heading south. Global economic growth is projected to be negative by 2060. How can the population and debt be growing so fast while the growth rate is slowing? Simple: it's taking less and less work to produce goods and services. The real economy is based on work done, not asset prices.

Justin: Weren't you supposed to be coming in here to cheer me up?

Evan: I did get a little into the weeds there, yeah. Sorry about that. Point is that none of this has to be complicated. It's all about convincing people that the banks are behind all the world's ills and that we can fix those ills by changing how we think about money.

Justin: If only convincing economists were that easy. I mean, we're not even in the wonks club, and I've heard nothing that will convince economists—especially the serious ones.

Evan: Maybe it can be easy. It's all about pointing out how the field of economics was started after the Federal Reserve was created and after the Bretton Woods Agreement. In other words, it's like the banks took over the economy and then academics created this social science to explain economics while banks were in charge of the money.

In other words, they have been taught that banks are immutable, unchangeable, and a fact of life. Is it too much to ask them to question the reverence of the banking system? Until they are willing to consider all the pain that the banking system is creating, the world is in for more pain.

Justin: Then, my friend, I fear the world is in for more pain.

Evan: So you're just giving up?

Justin: Don't look at me like I just kicked your dog. Evan, seriously, man. We started out all starry eyed, but let's not forget what triggered this whole idea in the first place. We tried an experiment on a farm, and the whole thing fell apart.

Evan: I remember, but—

Justin: Your girlfriend died.

Evan: Why would you go there? You absolutely do not have to remind me of that.

Justin: Because you're standing there telling me that this whole thing is about word choice. We didn't just tell the world this system works when we built that farm. We showed them. And in response, they destroyed it.

Evan: People are always going to fear and lash out against what they don't understand. And by "they," I mean that creep Elliot Larson.

Justin: Which is exactly why I'm giving up. What you just described is a key cog in human nature. Humanity just does not have the ability to survive.

Evan: Then how do we share the Big Solution with the world? How do we convince people that their past belief systems aren't correct? Hell, how do we even finish this book?

Justin: You're still not seeing it.

Evan: Help me see it.

Justin: Evan, we don't.

CHAPTER ELEVEN

DARK NIGHT OF THE SOUL

Labor was the first price, the original purchase–money for all things. It was not by gold or by silver, but by labor that all wealth of the world was originally purchased.

–ADAM SMITH, *The Wealth of Nations*

I remember this hike being quite a bit more direct when Ron led it. Ron's my groundskeeper, so I guess it shouldn't be surprising to me that he knows this land better than I do. It is his job, after all, to know and care for every inch of this property, and this is, after all, only my second hike through this particular quadrant.

"Why not just take one of the trails you know, Justin?" you might be wondering. Because I'm tired of all the trails I know. They're so predictable, so trodden, so very much like the American discourse on the economy.

Plus, with the way my three houseguests have been turning up in every place I try to steal a minute alone, they surely would've caught up or crossed paths with me on the more predictable trails somehow. So I went rogue. Told no one I planned to take a hike, changed into some shorts I'm starting to regret, laced up my Chucks, and then took that hike straight down the western path, the one so overgrown this time of year that there's almost no chance I don't go home with a poison ivy rash on my bare legs and/or some ticks in places no one wants ticks.

But rashes and ticks are worth it tonight, dammit. I spent two years planning this book, then another year writing and rewriting the concepts, and then another year letting my houseguests step all over it as contributors, and for what? I painted myself right into a corner, identified a problem so complex and so likely to be overwhelmed by public resistance that I've lost all faith in my ability to pull it off. So maybe a little discomfort is exactly what I deserve.

What I probably don't deserve is to be utterly, terribly lost, which is exactly how I would describe myself at the moment. I've been following this admittedly narrow and overgrown path in a single direction for an hour now, so I don't know how it's possible that I've definitely passed this outcropping of rock before. But there it is, the one that looks like Barbara Streisand's nose. I've passed this already. So I'm officially wandering in circles. It's approaching sundown—whole point of this journey was to watch the sunset from a scenic overlook Ron showed me on that other hike we took out this way—and I'm officially wandering in circles.

When am I not wandering in circles lately? When are any of us not wandering in circles? All this strife and suffering in recent years, and we all just keep spinning the hamster wheel, keep trying desperately to do what we've always done and believe what we've always believed.

Here we have a supposedly intelligent species willing to look at the extreme poverty, homelessness, and millions of working poor and think, "Well, tough luck." In the richest nation on Earth, most people are able to accept that poverty is just an unfortunate reality of American life, or that the people living this way just didn't take the right path, or they need to work harder, or maybe it's just that advancements in technology and culture have left them behind. No one stands up and blames the system—at least beyond blaming politicians, usually in a wildly partisan manner, or blaming billionaires for somehow hoarding all the money, as if even the richest among us aren't also doing all of this on debt. No one pauses to reflect on the true causes of this suffering.

Few people will look at the clearly systemic problems in this country, like the shoddy education system, the bloated and imbalanced healthcare industry, the military industrial complex running wars all over the planet, or the political gridlock supposedly preventing any real change. Sure, they talk about these things, but all they do is point fingers. There are policies that could fix these things, they say, if only the other political party would see reason. But none of this has anything to do with politics. These imbalances and this mismanagement all derive from the way we think about money and from who controls that money.

But none of this has anything to do with politics. These imbalances and this mismanagement all derive from the way we think about money and from who controls that money.

So we're all willing to go to work at jobs where we're undercompensated and overworked. Hell, we're even willing to do that on top of homeschooling our kids in the middle of an unchecked pandemic. And while we're doing this, too few of us are wondering why the cost of living seems to keep rising; why every year, it seems harder to make ends meet than the last; why our personal debts continue to grow even though we're trying hard to keep up; why there's absolutely no way we're going to have enough money saved to retire on when the time comes (and that we're in no way alone on that front); and why the world keeps getting worse and worse even though we're all aware of the problems but have no solutions to solve them.

I definitely haven't seen this grove of pine trees before. This is new. Good. I'll keep moving this way, then.

Everything's so dry out here tonight. Been a while since it rained. God, here I am, wandering alone and lost through overgrown for-estland in southern California in September. Just have to hope no one threw a gender-reveal party today, I guess. Burning alive while wandering around in an existential crisis would be no way to die. But then, wouldn't that just be my luck?

Speaking of those fires, how about the way we all just kind of ignore them now? How about that idea that they've become part of everyday life—a brand new rite of autumn in America? Here we're so wrapped up in our daily struggles and our civil war–level political dis-agreements that we've stopped even thinking about global warming. We're choking our oceans with plastic and depleting resources all over the planet as well. It's all just part of accepted life now. One of those things we can't do anything about, so we might as well just open our arms wide and embrace it.

Same with mass immigration and the displacement of refugees. The system is so imbalanced that even population growth is uneven, exploding in impoverished countries and declining in some of the world's wealthiest.

As this happens, the middle class is disappearing, work is becoming more autonomous and technology driven, and the global debt just keeps rising and rising and rising.

Anytime we feel like maybe we're catching a break—like maybe the new normal has finally set in and we can figure out what life is supposed to look like—we throw ourselves a nice riot or mass shooting or terrorist attack. Meanwhile, all across the country, people are dying from one of the other epidemics, like opioid abuse, suicide, cancer, diabetes, or any of the other reasons people are needlessly dying.

And even if we as a species can accept all these many forms of hell (and even if we're willing to accept them even though they're all solvable and preventable!), we had COVID to teach us that we hadn't seen anything yet.

You want hunger and poverty? COVID will show you hunger and poverty. All those millions of working poor are out of jobs, the poorest among us are being evicted quicker than we can catch up to the problem, and while most of us languish in confusion and stress about how to meet our day-to-day obligations, tens of millions of Americans and many times that number worldwide are pushed into hunger by the pandemic and our economic system's complete inability to adjust to that pandemic (or to anything, for that matter). When all of this shakes out, mark my words, more people will have died from hunger and poverty than from COVID-19.

Here we thought the Great Recession was the true test of what our economy can withstand! How about travel restrictions, government-mandated closures of businesses, crippled supply chains both domestically and internationally, and the isolation of refugees and/or poor people in areas where healthcare to fight the disease is lacking, famine is running rampant, and hunger was already a problem to begin with?

Everything about the economy we have wrought creates artificial shortages where shortages should not exist. So when you introduce a deadly, highly infectious disease, the whole thing collapses like a house of cards. A thousand people dying of COVID-19 every day in the United States? How about tens of thousands dying every day worldwide as a result of COVID-created food shortages? And we're not just talking about deaths in the Afghanistans and Syrias of the world, either (although they have been hit the hardest, to be certain)—this starvation has come for India and Brazil as well.

And we're only in the first year of this! Wait until all this mass unemployment starts turning into more evictions and foreclosures, which turns into more poverty, which turns into more hunger. The more people are laid off and can't make ends meet, the further crippled the world's capacity to create the goods and deliver the resources people need to survive. The more we shelter in place and reduce travel, the fewer people will be able to keep their businesses operational, which perpetuates the cycle of destruction.

What kind of economic system is totally unable to act in the face of global problems? The one we got! And what kind of economic system is this when a virus that infects less than .004 percent of the world's population can utterly destroy the economy, plunge tens of millions of people into poverty, and kill millions from starvation? The economy is worse than the disease. We aren't talking about a shaky system with a few flaws here. We're talking about a system that, when wounded slightly, prevents people from being able to meet their basic needs. If you have a system that can't at least ensure that everyone on this overabundant planet has enough to eat, that's no system at all.

So here we are, as I wander through the woods, all of us continuing to accept and live in a system that allows so many of us to starve to death, allows the planet's climate to spiral out of control unchecked, and utterly collapses in the face of trouble.

I'm honestly starting to question humanity's future. Even if we can get COVID-19 in check, what's next for us? If a world on the brink isn't enough to spark us into action and make genuine, lasting change, then what is?

Maybe, as a species, our ability to solve problems that will benefit the common good is too narrow. Or maybe the problems of our own making have become mountains too steep to climb. Maybe the world is too dark and too complex to find our way to a better path.

Speaking of which, there's Streisand again. So I guess I'm still wandering in circles just like the rest of it.

Maybe I should turn back. Give up. The sun has already set anyway, and the longer I stay out here, the more likely it is that I'll wind up having to find a way to sleep out here. Of course I didn't bring a flashlight—I'm a human; I don't prepare for problems until they're immediately threatening my life. I've got this light on my phone, but I spent so much time this afternoon playing Tetris to distract myself from depression that I don't know how long the battery will last.

It's getting too cold for these shorts. Definitely should've chosen some different shoes, because my feet hurt. Definitely should have used some sort of breadcrumb-based guidance system to tell me whether I was walking in circles.

Coulda shoulda. Isn't that how it is for all of us? Whether we're thinking about an individual day, a single choice we made, or a whole system we have been at least tacitly complicit in perpetuating, don't we all stress about what we could have done better? I mean, I'm not the only one, right? I'm not the only person who neurotically parses through the nature of daily existence, am I?

The rumble of thunder in the distance should be the tipping point for me. I'm unprepared enough as it is, and facing a downpour won't exactly improve my chances of lasting the night out here. But as the wind rustles the dense trees and that telltale smell of rain reaches me, I can't help but think about the time when, as a young Boy Scout, I found myself huddled in a cave with the rest of my troop as we waited out an unexpected howler of a thunderstorm off Lake Erie.

I should've been terrified that day. But our leader told us we would just have to change plans and make the best of it. So we built a fire, sang songs, told jokes, and shared the snacks we'd brought. After it was over and we got through it, we made our way back to the parking lot, where my parents, who'd heard about the storm on the radio and had worked themselves into a frenzy of worry, were waiting for me. I've never been hugged so hard in my life. That's one of my fondest childhood memories. That thing I should've feared—all it took was a reframing of my perspective on what that thing meant, and what would have been a traumatic experience became an overwhelmingly positive one.

Screw it. I've come too far to turn back. Time to start hacking and slashing. Time to wander off the path.

Beyond the Valley

Well, I'm about as scratched and bruised as I can ever remember being, and I'm 100 percent certain my lower extremities are crawling with ticks, but that was well worth it.

I could've given up. That storm still flickering along the horizon to the north says I probably should've. But here I sit, legs dangling over the rocky outcropping that serves as the scenic overlook for one of the better valley views I've ever seen.

When Ron brought me out here that first time, I remember being awed by the idea that I had accidentally come to own a piece of property with a view this awe inspiring. And back then, I'd only seen it during the day. Here at night, with a gray full moon carving through the clear half of the sky and the intermittent lightning giving light from the overcast half, I've never seen anything quite like it. The sight is humbling. It makes me realize that I don't own this at all. Sure, my name is on the land from which this outcropping juts, but like everyone else on this planet, I don't own it any more than the millions of generations that came before me.

Those people endured plenty. When you consider all the dark periods in human history, it's a wonder we made it this far. So maybe, by questioning whether we're just too innately destructive to survive, I was engaged in a bit of hubris. Maybe what humanity needs in order to change is an actual, tangible threat to its existence. Whether that threat is global warming, political gridlock, cultural upheaval, COVID-19, or the host of problems created by our accepted economy doesn't matter. What matters is that, now more than at any point in my lifetime, you can see, smell, and feel the storm.

Maybe I've been looking at this all wrong. Maybe I, too, have failed to see the forest for the trees.

What if convincing the public about the viability of the Big Solution isn't as complicated as I've made it out to be? What if it's just a matter of unraveling that one big lie at the center of it all?

That lie: the economy is too complicated to understand or predict, that we can never fully know where it's going, but only study where it has been and assume past is prologue. It's the lie that convinces people there is no up or down in this economy—no real predictability beyond the notion that everything is cyclical, that neither good times nor bad ever truly last. It's that lie that allows people to simultaneously believe that cutting taxes is good for the poor while raising minimum wage is somehow bad for the poor. It's this one big lie at the heart of it all, the lie that convinces people there is no way to fix this obviously broken system.

Just as I solved my problem of being lost in the woods by hacking off of the trail, maybe there is an equally simple way of showing the world a new and better path.

It has gotten properly cold out here now, but I'm not shivering from the chill. I'm shivering from the excitement.

Why should I worry about whether people can accept complexity? There are so many other things in this universe that are far, far more complicated than economics. The many ecosystems in this valley are more complicated and interdependent than bank loans. The trillions of star systems in the unfathomably large and volatile universe make the complexity of international trade agreements look quaint.

Yet these systems, for all their complexities, are perfect. Everything behaves as it should. Through careful study and observation, the behavior of nearly everything is predictable.

Imagine the sheer, outrageous complexity of the human circulatory system. Now imagine that every creature on Earth possesses similar internal systems. And all of them function with incredible efficiency, adaptability, and about as close to perfection as a system can function. Similar is our solar system, just one of billions of them in the universe. Here we see a system that exists in mass chaos and destruction, and still, perfect peace, tranquility, and predictability can and does exist just about everywhere.

Of course, human beings are not capable of creation on this scale, but there is no reason that this same sense of peace, stability, and predictability can't exist in the ecosystem of mankind. There are no outside forces controlling how we think about or flow the money into our economy—or at least, there doesn't have to be. We, human beings, are in control of our economic system, and so we, human beings, have the power to change it for the better.

There's just that one big lie at the center of it all to overcome. Here we are on this modern planet, and we have economists telling us that this kind of perfection we can witness in every other science just isn't possible within the economy that we create, foster, and run.

That. Is. Nonsense. Anybody and everybody should be able to see how completely that is nonsense. Anybody and everybody can understand how much control we should have over this economy, and anybody and everybody should be furious about how we are told that we do not have any control, that we have no idea where this thing is going, that it's too unpredictable for a mere mortal to understand.

> **We, human beings, are in control of our economic system, and so we, human beings, have the power to change it for the better.**

Mere mortals created this economy. We can recreate it. Just like the original internal combustion engines were loud, unreliable, gas-guzzling behemoths, we can alter the design and make things more streamlined, predictable, and just plain better. If scientists can predict the exact microsecond when the sun will rise five thousand years from now, then how are we supposed to believe that we are incapable as a species of predicting what the economy will do next month? One of these things is not like the other. We have the brainpower as a species to get this done.

But we have to take that first step. We have to accept that the economic system—the one we created—doesn't need to be this way. We have to recognize that if we're ever going to have a clear view of that perfect system to replace the one we have, we need to hack away the layers of unnecessary complexity and find that one lie, that one wrong belief at the center of it all. And the thing about a belief is that it is just a thought—a single thought.

There is an easy way to change thoughts, thinking patterns, and beliefs. Someone wise once said, "If you ask, you shall receive." We have to ask the ultimate question at the heart of it all.

As I get up off my ass and start wandering back to the path I created to get here, you might be asking, "What is that ultimate question?"

It's this: what is money?

If we're going to simplify a supposedly complex system so that anyone can understand it, everyone benefits from it, there is consistent stability and growth, and money quits being the source of all the world's problems, we first need to understand what money is.

Today, money is credit. Or rather, money is defined by the general ledgers of debt that banks keep. These ledgers give money value because they are the primary keepers of the information behind money. That information gives money permanence, so that it can seem like it is part of a consistent and controlled supply.

This is why it's so problematic. The ledger system is one dimensional and overly simplistic, but money needs to be multidimensional and able to deal with complexity. This means the ledger needs to be tracking more than just credit, debt, and loans.

The ledger system is also disturbingly powerful, as it brings this nasty tendency to create large liquidity events such as mergers and acquisitions that move massive amounts of money into circulation. This makes it very hard for the system to provide small amounts of money to many people. It is also the reason that millions of kids live with food insecurity, a state of mind that tends to snuff out a child's potential.

You may have heard of this concept of microloans, which in some ways is the right approach, but it still falls into this mindset that money must be credit. Think about it this way: banks make more money managing business deals and asset sales then all the small transactions combined, so why should they bother with the small once there is no money in it?

James Madison once said, "We base all our experiments on the capacity of mankind for self-government." Back in 1913, when banks took over the general ledger as a means of money creation as part of the Federal Reserve Act, a system like this one actually made sense. Back then, the banks were the most qualified people for the job of controlling what money is worth and how it flows.

But that's not the case today. Today, you don't even need a super-computer to manage and better coordinate the flow of money than the wildly outdated ledger system could ever hope to do; all you need is a simple laptop and a brilliant algorithm to coordinate an almost infinite amount of data.

Let's face it—back in 1913, the only way to crunch numbers for the banking system were the pencil pushers. Today, nobody is telling the banks that we can add a little complexity to the system and solve the world's problems because of this belief that money must be credit. Can it be that the world's problems can be traced back to J. P. Morgan's statement that "money is gold unless it's credit" because crafty old J. P. didn't want his bookkeepers to get overwhelmed? Nobody even uses pencil pushers or the term *bookkeepers* anymore.

J. P. Morgan's beliefs were entrenched in the idea that money was gold, but more importantly, the money in banks came from his customers' deposits and did not belong to him. When his banks loaned out money, he didn't own it. He needed it back. Money was credit. Put another way, money was CREDIT to banks. That may have been correct in 1913, and to banks, it's still true today. But to us, the nonbankers, money has never been credit; it has been work. To banks, money is their product. It's what they sell, and they don't owe it to anybody like they used to back when we were on the gold standard and loans were based on bank deposits.

Modern economics—in spite of all the tools available to us—continues to be based on an experiment from 1913 and a notion that only banks are capable of the diligence necessary to maintain the general ledger of money. Why are we still thinking this way? Why does the economy still run in this fashion?

Human beings are not like unto gods—I get that—but we're still an incredibly powerful species, and if we unleash that power, we are capable of remarkable things. We don't even have to create a circulatory system here! Economics is relatively simple compared to biology. The universe creates massive amounts of energy and power, and at least from an economics perspective, so could humanity.

To get us there, let us imagine a definition of money not as credit or as a ledger of information about debt, but as the definition of human work. In this way, the money ledger in essence represents the total tapestry of the work mankind does. If we replaced our ledger of credit with a ledger of human work, then that new ledger has the potential to unleash humanity's combined potential. The combined work of all mankind could be harnessed for a sustainable, peaceful, and enriching future for all.

It is not even that difficult to imagine this future!

If we reduce our examination to the perspective of money changing hands between two people, then it's easy to see how money is already fundamentally defined by human work. It is what we use to allow people to work for one another. Broadening the perspective slightly, it is also what allows work to happen smoothly in the economy. But neither of these perspectives have anything to do with credit—or at least they don't have to have anything to do with credit. When you ask someone to cut your lawn, you don't pay him or her with a bank loan. You pay him or her with money. In this sense, the money you give is defined by the value of that human work.

On top of this definition, we can also define money as information, but not in the same way the current ledger system defines it. You can wire money around the world in an instant. It is in this way no different from an email.

The nice thing about information is that it can be anything you choose to make it. Information is itself highly functional. By labeling money as credit (i.e., one type of information that only serves banks), our human potential is greatly restrained. As a result, all these problems we now face have manifested. If we simply release ourselves from these restraints, then we can start building the tools we need to eliminate all those problems.

It starts with accepting a simple truth: money does not have to be defined by credit. That's the big fallacy. That's the cause of all our strife. Money can instead be a tool to build a better world for us all. When you imagine it this way, it's easy to see that the government doesn't have to be a safety net for a dysfunctional economy. Instead, the economy should not need a safety net. And it's easy to see that producers should be rewarded with wealth for their contributions and not taxed into mediocrity because everyone is, well, forced into poverty. This in turn unleashes a whole new potential that humanity has never seen or experienced before. Forget about Making America Great Again. The world can level up to something so great it can't be recognized by us today.

I wandered into this wilderness lost, but now I am found. The future of humanity is not doom and suffering. The future is bright!

We are a powerful species, more than capable of creating the tools necessary to fix these complicated problems. We just have to be willing to see through all the bullshit. We have to believe in our ability to do these things. I believe in our ability.

I believe in our future. I believe in the Big Solution.

And I also believe that I can see the lights from my house through those trees up ahead. Here I come, Connie, Evan, and Laz. Give me a minute to pick these ticks off me, and then we'll get back down to the business of changing the world.

CHAPTER TWELVE

BLUESKIES, NEW GREENHOUSES

We hold these truths to be self-evident, that all men are created equal,
that they are endowed by their Creator with certain unalienable Rights,
that among these are Life, Liberty, and the pursuit of Happiness.

—DECLARATION OF INDEPENDENCE, 1776

Justin: I should start by thanking you all for joining me. It's been a long journey, and I know you're eager to hear about how I made it out of the woods.

    Laz: Yeah, I've been lost out there a bunch of times, so I for one would love to hear about how you navigated your way back. Especially since you made it back in the dark.

    Connie: I think he's talking metaphorically, Laz.

    Justin: I was talking metaphorically, but do remind me to tell you the actual escape-from-the-woods story at some point, buddy, because it was surprisingly epic.

Laz: Can't wait.

Justin: Definitely was a point where I swore I heard a bear. Had to run. There were brambles everywhere, and I was scared.

Evan: Guess that explains why your arms and legs are all scraped up.

Justin: I should not have worn shorts …

Laz: Well, I, for one, am on the edge of my seat.

Connie: Can we get a move on here, please? Some of us are wondering if we're going to be finishing this book anytime this century. Quickly, though; I'm totally digging the Declaration of Independence introduction.

Justin: Okay, fine. Gather around, kids. Sit down on your carpet squares.

Laz: Okay if we just stay on these nice couches, boss? They're super plush, and I finally managed to get my favorite reclining side that Connie's always taking.

Connie: It's another metaphor, Lazzie. And you're welcome to that spot any time you like it.

Laz: Aw, thanks.

Justin: I'm going to propose a new analogy to help accentuate the world we live in now compared to the world we're going to be creating with the Big Solution. It came to me just before I finally found my way back, so here we go.

Imagine a world where water is the currency. A group of savvy water companies manage to create a system of reservoirs that controls all the water in the world. This means that the water is tightly controlled by a small group of people. Whenever someone wants access to the water, the small group first requires that person/people to prove how they will replenish that water later. This leads to an odd sort of financial system where they only loan the water to people who have greenhouses, because people with greenhouses are the only ones who can ensure that, even after they use the water for their crops, it can be returned thanks to the condensation that naturally occurs in greenhouses. In exchange for this loan of water, the borrower also has to provide a piece of the product they're producing, which is how they cover interest payments.

Of course, everyone needs water, so in this strange world, there are greenhouses all over the place, every one of them making different, useful things with the water they borrow, and they are doing this very efficiently. Nothing is ever wasted.

Unfortunately, not everything in this world is perfectly efficient. There is also a Large Sprawling Complex (LSC) that keeps order of the system, but that complex is extremely wasteful. It uses water to keep all the people who don't have a greenhouse pacified and controlled. The water used for this purpose comes partially from the greenhouses and partially from the water companies, which qualifies as borrowed water. This means the LSC is also responsible for paying back the water it borrows, but it has no means of doing so. After all, it isn't producing anything; it's just trying to take care of all the people who don't have their own greenhouses.

This is not the only problem on this weird planet either. Running the greenhouses requires a great deal of energy, which pollutes the air and adversely impacts the natural habitats all around. Even with the help of the LSC, the very poorest people on this planet die of poverty and starvation at an alarming rate. Other similar LSCs often emerge to compete, and that competition only further reduces the water supply, especially to countries whose water companies don't have back big reservoirs.

Mostly, there just never seems to be enough water to make things work. The greenhouses can easily produce more, of course, but there's just not enough water to keep all those greenhouses going efficiently. All these greenhouses need water, but they also have to pay the competing LSCs to keep the peace and pacify the greenhouseless people. It's a system destined to fail.

This is, of course, how our own planet works. But in a new world, a world that runs on the Big Solution, things will work very differently. In this world, there are no owners of the water. In this world, it rains.

People do not have to hope and pray that they will receive water from the LSC in the form of welfare, unemployment, social security or some other safety net, and they won't have to fret about how they will repay the loans the government keeps taking, because water falls from the sky. In this world, the LSCs don't have to take care of people with no access to water, because those people no longer exist. Water is freely available to everyone, just like how nature provided for the woodsman.

Meanwhile, the greenhouses don't have to dedicate themselves exclusively to products that people with greenhouses can pay for. Greenhouses can now make products for everyone. Some of them can pivot to work that will improve the planet itself. They can dedicate themselves to repairing the damage the greenhouse system has done to natural habitats, employing huge numbers of people to help clean up the mess along the way. They can do this because they are no longer shackled to customers who have greenhouses; instead, they get paid with water supplied for the specific purpose of removal of pollution (or, for that matter, any other problem the world needs to solve). Essentially creating a *BlueSky* market for fixing things that could not be fixed before, like climate change, plastic pollution, and ocean acidification, which also means more jobs—a lot more useful jobs.

This world has a different challenge, however: too much water splashing around creating wasteful behavior. Fortunately, this world is technologically advanced. The greenhouses just keep their machines running a little longer to produce more of the products that are needed. This intelligent world also has controls that are able to remove water when it starts to muddy the fields.

This world has sunshine that evaporates the water wherever there is wasteful activity. If, for instance, two greenhouses are gushing water by creating sprawling headquarters, the sun heats it up a bit and some of it evaporates. Similarly, if some people start basking a little too much in their water supply—perhaps they bought a private jet for each of their kids, splashing water all over the place—the sun heats it up and it starts to evaporate.

This world is very efficient because it works like nature; wherever there is too much water and waste, the sun recycles the water, and the people clean up the waste by building a new type of waste-cleanup greenhouse. This world is not without owners of water, of course, but those owners own a small portion, and they do not control the rain. Instead, an intelligent council controls the rain and the sun.

The LSC (the government) still exists, though it is a much smaller complex. This is because it is no longer working to keep poor people alive and pacified; it only has to use its power to make sure everyone plays by the rules and no cheating takes place. It doesn't have to take care of anyone because everyone can take care of themselves.

It takes a system with only one genuine beneficiary and restructures it so that everyone benefits.

In all ways, this Big Solution optimizes a system that was already in place, but simply was upside down in terms of how it was run. It takes a system with only one genuine beneficiary and restructures it so that everyone benefits. Producers get to make the perfect amount of product because their customers at least have a minimum amount of money to spend.

These same producers can address pollution and the climate crisis directly rather than indirectly, as they will be incentivized to remove carbon from the air in exchange for money created specifically for that purpose. To anyone who produces CO_2, engineers can tack on the cost for its removal through deletion. And this same mechanism can be used for all the producers whose products create a cost to society.

People and corporations are further encouraged to use the fewest resources possible through savings accounts with high yields, where the money in the account isn't redeployed in the form of wasteful loans like today's banking system does. Even when wealthy people splurge on luxuries like private jets and megayachts, everyone wins, because high-cost transactions trigger a partial deletion of the funds used. The deletion of this money discourages wasteful use of resources while not preventing them from happening.

In its totality, the Big Solution creates a world where everyone has to work to succeed and make their dreams come true, but the system is different because it produces sustainable results, liberty for all, and prosperity for those who seek it. The way this world looks and operates is truly inspiring. And the best part? We don't need to change a single thing except that we must stop serving banks first and ourselves last.

There is another level to this as well. In engineering, we call it optimization. When water (a.k.a. money) is freed from the banking system, it allows for new inputs into the economic engine and new desirable outputs. In today's Bankism economy, there is only one input into the economy: it's called loans or debt (in the forms of treasury bills, municipal bonds, mortgages, student loans, leases, credit cards, and all the financial products the banking system has created over the years to increase their profits). These are all one dimensional in nature, and the only desired output is increasing GDP.

From an engineering perspective, this is like trying to control the performance of a combustion engine with only one variable, like controlling the fuel, and, even worse, by having only one desired output, like RPMs. In an engine, the RPMs can go super high, but that energy needs to translate to the tires so the car moves. It would be very frustrating as an engineer to not be allowed to tweak the amount of air allowed into the combustion engine, for instance. It would also be annoying to the customer, whose car would get very poor miles per gallon. Vibration and noise would be terrible, as well, because it's not an input into the design of the engine. Essentially, if engineers had to design the combustion engine by controlling only one variable, there would be no cars on the road.

If engineers could use money to create new inputs into the economy, the world's biggest problems would become instantly solvable—simultaneously. The concept of Optimizing America (reference to Book 1 of The Wolfe Trilogy) becomes possible. Heck, the idea of optimizing the world does too. What gets optimized? The sustainability of humanity! Doesn't that just make sense—that we all work toward making it possible to stay alive? And that's what happens in the Big Solution; whether you're flipping burgers or flying private jets to Davos, you're contributing to the sustainability of humanity. Even if you're just living on the rain, you're helping because you're using almost no resources to do it.

Everyone will have liberty in their lives. What could be fairer, then, to know that no matter what you choose to do, you are actually helping create a better world? Everyone gets equal treatment because everyone gets their piece of the rain. What you choose to do from there is up to you …

The other piece that is important is prosperity. It is important for us all to live in a world where we can make our dreams come true.

This means that opportunity and work are in abundance. The banking system will no longer throttle job opportunities with their interest rate hikes and limited options for financial products that actually yield too few opportunities for the working class.

The Big Solution world doesn't control inflation by limiting jobs; it checks inflation by deleting wasteful spending. If inflation sets in, the sun just burns a little hotter and evaporates more water. Yes, this means wages will skyrocket, but that does not mean inflation sets in, because wasteful spending will be more costly and therefore self-limiting. Savings will explode with high interest rates, which also means significantly less spending and therefore less inflation. This just leads us back to liberty and retiring with dignity. If wages go up and savings accounts offer bountiful interest rates, then planning for retirement becomes automatic.

Laz: Wow, boss! I think I get the problem with government safety nets. It's just a large, sprawling complex that's only necessary because the banks have screwed up the economy.

Connie: Laz finally coming to the dark side! Just kidding. There are no sides in the Big Solution world.

Justin: My existential crisis must have lasted longer than I realized, because I never thought I'd see the day you two got along this well.

Laz: Cats and dogs living together …

Evan: Could be that ultraliberals and ultraconservatives have more in common than they realize.

Connie: Yeah, we both like freedom, liberty, and happiness. Just about everybody likes those things.

Justin: Yeah, okay. So I wandered into the wilderness lost—both literally and metaphorically—but now I am found. The future of humanity is not hopeless. It turns out our Founding Fathers had the recipe figured out right from the start.

Connie: Hurrah.

Justin: We can do this …

Connie: Do what, exactly?

Justin: Save humanity.

Connie: Oh, is that all?

Laz: This is my favorite conversation yet.

Justin: Can I explain myself, please? Anyway, the problem appears to be that we were overcomplicating things—or at least I was over-complicating my consideration of the problems and obstacles standing before us. We don't need to systematically break down everyone's objections. All we need to do is present the tools—tools that bring our Founding Fathers' intentions back into reality in modern times.

Connie: I just got chills. Did anyone else get chills just now?

Justin: These are tools that we all know will work, because we've seen them work on the farm. And it just makes sense to apply these tools to save humanity and make life better. Why did they work on the farm? It helped that we had a captive audience of people willing to believe that the experiment would succeed, sure, but mostly it worked because all of this starts with a simple concept: money doesn't have to be defined by debt. On the farm, our money was based on the value of work. This is why we were seeing such organic, sustainable growth in economic activity—right up until someone burned down the Circus.

Laz: God, I miss the Circus. Did you guys ever have one of those bready donuts Muna used to make? I mean, before he went off to open that bakery downtown? Oh, man, I used to wake up early just to grab one of those and a coffee. Set me right all day.

Justin: Maybe we should institute a system where you have to raise your hand to speak.

Connie: Seconded.

Justin: I see you raising your hand, Laz, but if this is still about donuts, it'll have to wait. Okay, great. Let's talk about the tools we need to save humanity.

Tool #1: Direct Deposits (or Should We Call It Essential Liberty?)

Tuck in for this one, because it's the biggest tool in the box, and so it takes some explaining.

The fascinating thing about the laws of physics is that they are true in every corner of the universe—even in the makings of humanity. Just like all living things, we human beings are alive, and we need the same resources to survive and follow the same natural laws of the universe. In this way, it's equally fascinating that the Founding Fathers, in their brilliance, saw the fundamental ingredients for life in very human terms: "life, liberty, and the pursuit of happiness."

As it turns out, modern science has figured out the exact same thing, but from a biological perspective. And I quote from Adrian Bejan regarding the Constructal Law: "For a finite-size system to persist in time [to live], it must evolve in such a way that it provides easier access to the imposed currents that flow through it."[5]

Now, let's pass that same quote through a paraphrase that kind of layers it on top of that famous line from the Declaration of Independence: "For a finite-size system (life) to persist in time (to pursue happiness), it must evolve in such a way that it provides easier access to the resources (liberty) that it needs to live."

Am I right? I mean, the similarities are just too big to ignore. Also, I'm not alone here:

---

5   Adrian Bejan, *Advanced Engineering Thermodynamics*, 2nd edition, Wiley, New York, NY, 1997.

The similarity between Jefferson's claims of unalienable rights to the Constructal Law is a relationship we cannot ignore, a potential paradigm shift within the political and social sciences.[6]

—MICHAEL T. TAKAC, Scientific Proof of Our Unalienable Rights

One of the key words in the Declaration of Independence, and indeed, one of the key words related to the ability of life to even exist, is *liberty*. We're not talking about the liberty to do whatever you want; we're talking about the liberty to have what you need to survive. Liberty is, by definition, the ability to have what you need to survive. So for our economy to be a functional ecosystem for humanity, the economy must provide this very essential liberty.

In this way, the simplest, most easily appreciated component of the Big Solution is that it provides universal access to that very essential liberty in the form of the money a person needs to survive. The first and best tool at our disposal is the money that a new and better version of the Federal Reserve would deposit directly into the bank accounts of every single American of working age. This is not basic income. This is essential liberty.

> **Liberty is, by definition, the ability to have what you need to survive. So for our economy to be a functional ecosystem for humanity, the economy must provide this very essential liberty.**

Direct deposits are an easy concept for the average person to understand, because what's easier than the idea that the Fed wants to deposit "free" money directly into your bank account?

Now, don't get caught up on this word *free*, because it isn't free.

6   Michael T. Takac, *Scientific Proof of Our Unalienable Rights*, Robertson Publishing, Fremont, CA, 2012.

When someone does a favor for you without asking anything in return, it's free. Conversely, when the Federal Reserve puts a direct deposit into your account, it isn't really free because that direct deposit is just information. No one has worked for it at this point. Our minds have been indoctrinated into believing that money has value, and it does, but not at the point when the Federal Reserve issues it. The Federal Reserve has done nothing to give it value. What gives it value is the work it can be exchanged for.

So, in essence, direct deposits are future work. They represent future power to the people, the assurance that essential liberty, the ability to survive, is available to everyone. This ultimately means that in a very limited fashion, the economy is now providing a natural way for people to take care of themselves. It's the same way rain allows vegetation to take care of itself, or for a woodsman to build a life of genuine freedom, for that matter.

When the Federal Reserve prints money to give to banks, this empowers the borrower to get work done based on a one-sided transaction. The lender has done no work, but the repayment of that loan is with money that has been worked for. In essence, payments have the sweat and tears of the working class but borrowed money does not. In essence, this is why life doesn't get any easier. It is why there is more and more debt to be repaid, which has to be earned. This debt has to be refinanced with more debt that does not require work. This is an ugly road of indentured servitude.

The way out of this debt trap is direct deposits. Direct deposits create a new way for work to manifest and money to flow into the system. It also allows debts to be repaid the same way it came in, with money that has not been worked for.

Ask yourself why banks don't have to work for money but people do. Why can only banks issue money that has no work history? Why can't the people have this same type of money? Direct deposits put the people first. It forces the system to adjust to the needs of the people. And this is for the betterment of everyone. Think back to the Trickle-Around Mountain. People had no choice but to find a place to work on the mountain. The Big Solution is very different. It conforms to the needs of the people. It spontaneously reconfigures where the water trickles, how it trickles, and for specific, intelligent reasons like sustainability, liberty, and prosperity. The Big Solution conforms to society instead of society having to conform to the banking system.

Your first instinct might be to say that we're supposed to be talking about a natural system, but this sounds unnatural. But if you look at nature, human nature, and the requirements for sustaining life, there is no doubt that this is much more similar to the natural order of things than our existing financial system. Life needs a minimum amount of resources to sustain itself. Therefore, in order for the economy to function properly, it needs to provide this minimum amount of resources to every person.

What is unnatural is for banks to receive all the resources available and then dole them out with loans (which is unearned money) while the repayment (with interest) must happen with money that has been worked hard for. It is unnatural to have to earn the ability to live. The only time an animal brings piles of food to another animal is when it's for its baby, its offspring. The world is bringing piles of work to banks and getting nothing in return. It's like banks are a baby that we have to take care of. This is unnatural, of course. Nature doesn't work that way, and neither should humanity.

And now … drum roll, please … here is how direct deposits would work.

Each day, everyone—and I mean everyone, rich or poor—would receive the exact same amount of money in their bank accounts. These bank accounts would be set up and run by commercial banks; they would be open to every person regardless of credit history; and they would be easy to manage and access from anywhere over the internet. Put simply, the rules for these accounts would be special and controlled to ensure access for everyone.

The total amount of money that every man and woman of working age (maybe children too?) would receive is something that could be adjusted according to the signals we're receiving from the economy. If there's not enough growth, the size of the direct deposit would go up. If there's inflation, the number would go down. There would be other tools at the Fed's disposal to control inflation and growth and we will get to those later.

For now, the big message is that we're talking about money for everyone, not just the poor.

If this sounds good to you, then keep in mind that there's a big problem we must head off before it can become a reality: people who are more familiar with economic policy are always trying to make this very simple tool into something it's not. Sometimes they assume that it will only increase the national debt. This is incorrect, because that assumption is based on the wrongheaded thinking that money always has to be based on debt. It does not in any way need to be based on debt.

The money we're talking about for these direct deposits is money that the Fed simply creates out of thin air just like it does when it issues money for loans to banks. However, when it issues this money in the form of direct deposits, it is not creating a debt that has to be repaid. In this way, it does not grow the national deficit and it does not become a debt burden for the Americans who receive it. All the Fed has to do is ensure that the general ledger of money operates at a point where there is not too much of this money circulating. As long as that happens, we will avoid inflation.

And hey, Connie, here's a situation where the massive national debt is actually a benefit, because with almost $80 trillion of US debt and $300 trillion in debt existing globally, it's going to be a long, long time before we reach a point that there is too much money in circulation. This is true because if interest rates are raised, then people stop getting loans. Going back to the Jacuzzi pyramid metaphor, it means the banking system stops pumping water into the Jacuzzi and the task is simply to replace the jets with rain from the direct deposits.

The other way that people confuse direct deposits with other ideas is that it sounds like basic income. It is not basic income, for a reason that should be extremely easy to absorb: this money is not coming from the government and its tax revenue. I'll reiterate that in big letters: THIS MONEY IS NOT TAXPAYER MONEY. In addition, it is distributed equally to everyone, not just the poor. This might seem unproductive, but it is a defining aspect since everyone must have access to essential liberty at all times. Imagine ten people standing around a wild apple tree and they pick an apple each; rich or poor, it doesn't matter—all ten people can now eat an apple provided to them by nature. This is how direct deposits work; it's as if everyone gets an apple a day from a wild apple tree regardless of who they are, just simply because they are people. Notice that nobody paid for the apple; nature provided it, end of story.

By way of overexplanation so there is no doubt, we are talking about money that is not based on debt, does not grow the deficit, and is not subject to or originating from local, state, or federal taxes. Direct deposits are the depositing of newly created money with no strings attached, no regulation, just the essential liberty to survive, just like the fruit from a wild apple tree..

Why is this important? There are so many reasons, but let's just look at the basics.

First, direct deposits create a safety net for everyone. Where before every working American had the threat of losing their job hanging over their heads, this now frees them up to know that if they lose their job—or for that matter, if a pandemic comes in and disrupts everything, changing the way we think about how we work—they will always have access to that baseline of income they need to make their ends meet. Never again will a person have to worry about whether they will have enough food to eat, to house themselves, or to just survive.

The immediate benefits here are obvious. From a personal perspective, this eliminates the hunger problem in the US (and elsewhere … we'll get to the global stuff later). It drastically reduces poor people's housing insecurities. It defeats the homelessness problem from the ground up.

From an economic perspective, it ensures that every single working American has money to spend at all times and in all situations. For some people, this money will be used to buy necessities like food. Excellent! More people having the money to buy food means more demand for food, which grows the economy in an enormous number of ways.

For other people, this money will be used to buy things they don't need. Excellent! Growth in demand for luxury items also grows the economy in an enormous number of ways.

For *other* other people, this money will be deposited directly into a savings account or retirement fund. Excellent! People having money they can actually save will help raise the value of the dollar while also reducing stress on the economy in an enormous number of ways.

And for still other people, these direct deposits become a direct line to pursuing their dreams. Some people—many people, if the farm is any indication—will see all this demand for different products and services showing up all over the country thanks to the essential liberty money everyone has to spend, and they will work to meet that demand by establishing new businesses. Super excellent! This entrepreneurial activity grows the economy in more ways than any other, because new businesses mean new economic activity, new jobs, and more growth across the board. A whole new target demographic will be created that entrepreneurs can build businesses for, like housing, food, clothing and services that just could not be profitable before because there was no money in it. And this is important, because in a counterintuitive way, this causes the cost of living to come down because businesses now have to compete to serve the poorest. Today, housing is only built for wealthy people, which causes costs to go up. Meanwhile, housing for the poor requires government intervention, with devastating results with names like "the Projects" and "Skid Row" in Los Angeles.

My farm-building team and I have seen firsthand how there are so, so many people with the skills and dreams to become entrepreneurs. It's just that the existing economy, with all its stressors on holding a job so you can cover the rapidly increasing cost of living, prevents people from taking the leap. The combination of soaring demand and that safety net that comes from having these direct deposits can and will encourage a considerable number of these dreamers to become doers. It removes the shackles of the Trickle-Around Mountain …

Laz: Can I interject a question here?

Justin: Sure. I was getting tired up there on the soapbox anyway.

Laz: What does this do to big business?

Justin: Great question! Having the safety net of direct deposits will shift some of the power away from big business employers, who currently can do just about anything they want to their workers, because what else are those workers going to do, find another job? Not in a recession economy! And not in a reality where the vast majority of people don't have enough money in savings to cover even a single month's bills and debt payments.

With direct deposits, workers become more valuable, and big businesses suddenly have to try a little harder to retain their employees. Pay gets better, and benefits become more generous.

Connie: But what about international business competitiveness? How will business be able to compete if wages and benefits go up?

Justin: First, let's recognize that big businesses spend a fortune on benefits and safety nets for their employees. They also have to pay huge salaries for their management team all because the cost of living keeps going up. Direct deposits actually make it easier to humanely cut costs with technology and automation. It makes human work more valuable while making automation and technology a benefit to everyone. International competitiveness is only an issue because of the Jacuzzi pyramid, and we will get to that stuff later.

Connie: Sure, answer Laz's question … but you still have to explain how everyone having a little money lowers the cost of living. The math doesn't add up.

Justin: Simple. Take a look at San Francisco: it costs the city $25,000 a year for every homeless person in the city; that is a whopping $70 a day. Direct deposits of a fraction of that would allow these people to take care of themselves. This reduces the cost to the city and ultimately to the taxpayers. Efficiency winds up lowering the cost of living.

Evan: I've got one: what about the rich people who don't need this free money?

Justin: Doesn't matter because there just aren't that many of them. And anyway, it's money we're creating out of the ether and has to behave naturally. It's like air that everyone gets to breathe. It isn't based on debt. If rich people have no need for it and never use it, that makes exactly zero impact, good or bad, on this new economy. It's the same reason rain falls evenly from the sky. There are no forms or paperwork to fill out; everyone has access to the rain, every day. They can let it sit in their bank accounts. Who cares?

The bottom line is that direct deposits create a safety net for everyone. And hey, Connie, if direct deposits are creating that safety net, the massive side bonus is that government doesn't have to do that anymore. All those entitlement programs your side is always trying to eliminate? Eventually, they won't be necessary or relevant anymore. They'll be obsolete. We simply will not need them.

Connie: Sign me up for that.

Justin: Most importantly, as the Founding Fathers and Ronald Reagan warned us about, the government should never have been allowed to take care of people who can take care of themselves if given a minimum amount of liberty. In this context, we now see how government and its sidekick, the Federal Reserve, have taken our liberty, although the stealth-mode rollout has been downright devilish. But the jig is up!

Connie: You're couching this in patriotic terms, and I appreciate this, but there's something about it that still sounds kind of socialism y …

Justin: Not socialism. At all.

Direct deposit puts the power of spending and essential liberty into the hands of the people; it ensures our inalienable rights. It creates an economy that functions properly by providing for everyone just like a natural ecosystem. Here's the difference: socialism is the redistribution of people's work and their earned money to those who aren't working; essential liberty is simply keeping the Constitution relevant in modern times. Socialism forces one group of people to take care of another group of people through taxation. The Big Solution ensures that our inalienable rights are in place first and foremost without burdening anyone to make that happen.

It could not be less like socialism. Rather, it is more like nature—like the way a natural ecosystem is supposed to work: it provides people with exactly what they need to exist and survive, then leaves it up to those people to survive and thrive as they see fit. This is why it's called essential liberty.

Connie: But inflation could be a serious problem here.

Justin: Again, no. If I might overexplain why fear of inflation from money not based on credit is overblown ... If there's anything the pandemic has taught the world, it's that credit has nothing to do with the value of money. In 2020, people were essentially given $600 for weeks. Shouldn't this have led to massive inflation? It didn't. Prices went down.

There is nothing magical about credit. Money works just like everything else—supply and demand. In fact, we can take it a step further. It is very possible that the economy would grow a lot faster if it wasn't constrained by credit. It may not be possible for credit to keep up with demand and the potential for our supply chains to deliver to that demand. In fact, it is the most logical conclusion when you consider the ability of corporations to scale their production and the large number of people who are unproductive, unemployed, employed but not earning a living wage, or, worse, employed and doing frivolous work.

We are currently living under a camouflaged tyrannical rule by the banking class. Consider how easily the pandemic could have been managed. There literally wouldn't have been an economic issue. The direct deposit would have managed the whole thing autonomously, because guess what? If people are given the resources, they can take care of themselves. This exposes the system for what it is: a tyranny of resource deprivation but with no rhyme or reason, only to keep the banking system going.

Finally, Connie, the dagger in the heart is taxes. The purpose of government is no longer to create a sprawling safety net to take care of the people. The job of the government becomes to stay small and to get out of the way. This will lead to the biggest tax cuts in history. We're talking about a whopping 75 percent less in taxes by the time this is fully implemented. This leads to a fast reduction in the cost of living for the first time in a long time. In fact, the job of government should be to reduce the cost of living and not to take care of people. If they reduce the cost of living, then people can take care of themselves easily.

Connie: This is starting to get exciting. I have never twerked, but this might be the time.

Laz: You mean like this …

Tool #2: BlueSky Markets

A business is like a living, breathing organism. It is created with the intent to grow, and its driving motive is to survive. Like any living organism, an organization pulses with life and wants to flourish.

—JASON OLSEN, HUFFINGTON POST

Business is just like a living thing: it needs resources to survive. The fundamental resource for survival of a business is money and profit. The business, therefore, becomes whatever creates the most money and profits. It's as if it follows Darwin's evolutionary laws; in order for it to evolve, it has to increasingly become something that benefits everyone. There has to be money in it for them.

This serves as the foundation of Tool #2: BlueSky markets; it's money for businesses that pursue the common good. In this way, the Big Solution opens up the possibility of new markets that did not exist before. Let's define BlueSky markets as a new type of product or service that was not possible before and therefore completely new and different, which means people doing work that has never been done before and new opportunities for entrepreneurs.

We mentioned at the outset of this book that the country and the world at large have all these big problems that are entirely solvable, but there's just no money or political incentive to solve them. The BlueSky markets tool fixes all that by issuing money directly to fund commodity exchanges that effectively solve these big problems. Put another way, we take these big problems out of the government's hands and put them in the hands of all those entrepreneurs who will emerge as a result of these exchanges.

BlueSky market exchanges don't create money just to keep people surviving; they create money for the purpose of fixing what is broken and making a more sustainable, stable, and compelling future.

An example of a solvable problem that urgently needs solving is, of course, global warming. This becomes infinitely more fixable through BlueSky exchanges. In this case, businesses would bid on the exchange to remove CO_2 from the atmosphere. Money that is not debt based, taken directly from the Federal Reserve, would pay the lowest bidder to remove the CO_2. How much CO_2 to remove could now be controlled by entrepreneurs who figure out how to remove the most for the lowest cost. Competition for profits would compel entrepreneurs to figure out how to do it efficiently and effectively. The amount of money used to buy CO_2 in the exchange could slowly increase if prices are too high and quickly increase as prices come down. This kind of mechanism means global warming becomes solvable.

How does this happen, just to be clear? Through the creation of special commodities exchanges, where the buyer of the removal of pollutants is money from the general ledger of money at the Federal Reserve.

Imagine all that becomes possible in such a scenario. Now there is actual money and incentive to remove plastics from the oceans and nature, take acid out of the oceans, create fisheries in the middle of oceans (where there are no fish currently), save forests and plant trees, reverse the Sixth Great Extinction ... the possibilities are endless.

Laz: But climate change and saving the planet and our future isn't just an American thing. Other countries struggle with the same economic/climate issues.

Justin: Truth! As I've hinted, the Big Solution—once it takes hold and thrives in the US, of course—would eventually extend to the rest of the planet. We're trying to save humanity, after all, not just the United States. And we'll get into that in Tool #8. Yes, I recognize that fixing the climate calamity is not just an American issue.

Connie: I'm less concerned about the planet and more concerned about how this helps me.

Justin: Okay, fine. The tax cuts aren't enough for you? There will be BlueSky markets emerging for you too. Imagine, for instance, businesses established not just to manage disease—as our current and very broken healthcare system affords us—but to make extended healthy living achievable. These businesses, invested in health rather than illness management, can work on solutions to improve people's health and extend their lives.

Evan: People living longer could put a hell of a strain on the retirement savings problem we're experiencing ...

Justin: Solid softball pitch, buddy. Because people will have these direct deposits to save or spend in retirement, they will also have the means to remain happier for longer into their extended lives. How would this work? BlueSky markets can effectively flip the script on the insurance versus single-payer healthcare debacle. Instead of choosing between insurance plans or having no choice at all and just using what has been assigned, a BlueSky markets solution offers a choice of health preservation providers. These companies bid on providing you a service to keep you healthy.

Connie: Where's the money for this?

Justin: The money comes directly from the Federal Reserve. It is split between the business that provides the healthcare preservation services and the customer (that's you, if you're wondering). In other words, you get paid to stay healthy! Why? Because getting sick is so expensive. By incentivizing both companies and people to keep people healthy, the healthcare industrial complex will be shrunken down and dwarfed into a minor economic burden. But don't worry; all the doctors and nurses will not be out of work, because they will have plenty of opportunity in the business of keeping you healthy instead of treating your illnesses.

Think about how BlueSky health incentives would easily pay for themselves. If you work and you hit specific health markers, then you get paid, and your health provider gets paid too. This would reduce the need for hospitals, drugs, and even nursing homes. It would keep people working longer and staying healthy. In essence, just that fact alone—that people would work longer before retiring—would help the system pay for itself.

How much money could be used to keep you healthy? From a work perspective, about 20 percent of all work done today is used to treat sick people. That translates into a lot of money that could be used to keep you healthy. But on a daily basis, it won't take a lot of money to change outcomes. In fact, some insurance companies are already paying people to walk a certain number of steps every day. All this does is juice it up. Health insurance companies will quickly change their perspective when they can make BlueSky money by keeping their customers healthy.

Connie: That sounds incredibly false.

Justin: It isn't, and for a few reasons.

First of all, money isn't the only motivator for staying healthy. Second of all, the businesses that provide the health preservation services don't need a lot of money on a daily basis to scale up and make a killing.

Third, and most importantly, since our society is already spending $4 trillion on caring for the sick … well, flipping the script basically brings the $4 trillion into play for health preservation. And $4 trillion for the taking seems like a big enough incentive to me …

The potential for new markets that would emerge is limitless.

Tool #3: A New Kind of Savings Account

Today, any money you put in the bank immediately gets repurposed. It doesn't sit in your account; the bank uses it to invest, to loan out to other people or entities, and to create more debt. Depositing money in one of today's savings accounts is like parking your car in a parking lot and the attendant drives it across the street to Hertz to be rented out to other people.

But if, alongside these new direct deposits, the Big Solution created new high-interest bank accounts that are accessible to everyone (in fact, these are the accounts where all the direct deposits are made), then this keeps some of the money out of circulation. If leaving your direct deposits in a high-interest savings account is possible, then many, many people would choose to save the money and collect the interest. Where does the money come from to pay these higher interest rates? Directly from the Fed once again, and once again the benefits outweigh the downside.

Further, these accounts would be different because the money that goes in does not get repurposed; it effectively stays put. In this way, the high interest rates on the accounts help increase the value of the money that winds up in circulation. It also reduces the use of resources, which is something that should be rewarded with high interest rates. Most importantly, these savings accounts take money out of circulation, ensuring that inflation does not set in from all the direct deposits and BlueSky markets.

As a huge added bonus, this system makes planning for retirement a whole lot easier. If you know you always have access to those direct deposits and if you decide to save the funds in this high-interest-rate account, then you find yourself much more comfortable in retirement than you ever would have been otherwise.

The Big Solution could even improve the picture by making it so that the interest rate on these savings accounts is applied on a sliding scale. The smaller the amount of money in the account, the higher the interest rate. What would this do? It would encourage the poor to save for retirement. On the flip side, a lower interest rate for larger savings accounts would ensure that massive wealth doesn't collect the level of interest that would burden the balance of the money in circulation.

With that out of the way, I should say unequivocally that existing banks aren't all bad. Yes, they've screwed over the economy by insisting that everything must be based on debt, but some of their practices are beneficial and would still be useful in a direct deposit world. These savings accounts would effectively cut banks off from one of their profit centers, which is the repurposing of your hard-earned money.

But it's really irrelevant, since banks have huge reserves, and furthermore, even in this scenario, they can still borrow directly from the Federal Reserve.

Tool #4: Deletion

This may seem weird to say, but a huge benefit to information is that it can disappear. Debt can't disappear without someone getting screwed.

Why is it important to be able to make money disappear? I've described how we need to create a natural system. When it rains, our crops get water so that when the sun comes out, the crops yield a bountiful harvest. What also happens when the sun comes out is that the water evaporates. It disappears, in a sense, so that later it can rain again. This is the power of deletion … the ability to create a natural system.

We further the stability of the economy by recognizing that these direct deposits value money as information and not debt. The ability to delete information/money would have a miraculous effect on the economy. Take, for example, an-all-too common scenario where people spend too much and use too many resources; if a percentage of that money and overconsumption could simply be deleted, it would have a beneficial impact on the whole economy because making that money disappear reduces the money supply, which raises the overall value of the money in circulation.

However, the world is so deeply in debt and completely debt driven that it would take decades before deletion would even be necessary. There is so much debt to repay and quantitative easing to unease that deletion is really not even necessary for a very long time.

Connie: Sounds like a—

Justin: No, Connie, this is not a tax.

Connie: You know me so well …

Justin: Government, taxes, and so on. No. This isn't a tax. This is simply making money disappear. Whatever side of the political aisle you find yourself on, we can all agree that taxes tend to be wasted on government inefficiencies. Deletion, conversely, is hyperefficient because all it does is increase the value of money.

In today's world, a sales tax is considered evil because it impacts the poor the most and winds up being used on the poor anyway. So let's talk deletion. How would it work? Like so.

For any transaction larger than $100, the Fed simply deletes 1 percent of the money—or a nice round $1. The deletion rate is incrementally higher the larger the value of the transaction. In some transactions, the deletion rate is directly correlated to unaccounted-for costs, like CO_2 sequestration or removal of plastics from the ocean.

Laz: This sounds more like something that you and Evan should talk about on your own time.

Justin: Yes, it might at first sound like an econ-nerd thing to consider, but this is an important tool to control resources, the value of money, and the amount of money in circulation.

And it'll probably interest you more if we put it in real-world terms. First, because deletion only happens on large transactions, it doesn't hurt the poor. And because the deleted money doesn't go into the government, it isn't wasted on inefficiencies and, quite frankly, corruption.

Not to pat myself on the back here, but money deletion as opposed to taxation could be the best idea in the history of government when it comes to preventing corruption, government sprawl, and limiting the size of government to the basics.

Connie: That sounds lovely to me, but I'm still a little confused about why we actually need deletion to make the Big Solution work.

Justin: The purpose is to reduce the amount of currency in circulation, which increases the value of the currency that remains in circulation. Supply and demand, right? If we lower the amount of money available, the value of that money rises.

Evan: I'm going to play devil's advocate here. Why wouldn't I just create a criminal enterprise that sticks to microtransactions so deletion doesn't happen?

Justin: For the schemers out there, this deletion would work on an individual consumption total as well. So making many small transactions to avoid the deletion wouldn't work.

Connie: What about the noncriminals who can afford to make huge transactions? Doesn't this represent a huge burden on businesses and the wealthy?

Justin: No. Because of the way money circulates, it's likely that the top rate of deletion would be very small—in fact, it would be much smaller than current sales taxes.

The key is that this is an adjustable variable that allows the economy to be controlled, predictable, and optimized.

Tool #5: Increase the Reserves Banks Are Holding

There is currently $80 trillion of debt in the United States. This debt has to be repaid somehow. This can be a huge benefit in a world with direct deposits. Why? Because any inflation can be canceled out by increasing the banks' reserves.

Doing this effectively prevents banks from pumping money back into the Jacuzzi. The truth is that these reserves are not the banks' money; it is QE money that they did not earn.

It's interesting what this says about money: these reserves are simply money for the banks to sit on so they don't run out. The reserves used to come from people's savings; now it's just money that was printed from thin air.

Let this brew in your mind until it's very clear: once bankers decided to lend money out from savings over and over again, money stopped being gold and became something else entirely, since gold can only exist once and definitely not eighty times. In essence, banks have been issuing information from the very beginning. It was never credit or gold; it has always been information.

Laz: I just heard a big gong go off. I think it signifies a major dent or shift in the fabric of the universe.

Connie: The hell are you smoking, Laz?

Tool #6: Variable Interest Rates

Here we're getting so deep into the toolbox that we might not even need some of these tools! The way the Big Solution economy adapts might make variable interest rates unnecessary. But for now, let's imagine we will need them … because any engineer knows the more inputs you control in a process, the better the output. You know, quality in, quality out. Garbage in, garbage out.

As we shift the value of money to work instead of debt, I need to stress that we wouldn't be eliminating loans entirely. Debt can actually be a good thing, provided the work that gets done is beneficial to society. Hence variable interest rates.

If the Big Solution version of banks created low or negative interest rates for work that is beneficial, then everyone wins. Meanwhile, debt can be bad when it has negative consequences. Take pollution, for instance. Interest rates could be set very high for any debt that causes harm to society.

In general, loans in this Big Solution economy would have higher interest rates than we see currently because the goal is to reduce the use of debt as a means to grow the economy. As an added benefit, high-interest loans wind up indirectly funding direct deposits and BlueSky markets.

Before anyone objects to this, let me just say that the concept of variable interest rates is not about picking winners and losers. It's more like creating a sustainable future.

So … high-interest savings accounts, loans with interest rates based on whether the loan in question is going toward the betterment of society (or otherwise), and the ability to simply delete money from the ledger—this is a whole new kind of banking, a system designed not solely to benefit banks (although banks would still do quite well in this system), but to benefit people, whether they want to spend, save, or acquire a loan.

One great application would be to provide low interest rates for low-cost housing. In fact, a marketplace would be established to create competitive bidding to build housing with the lowest cost possible. This lowers the cost of living for everyone, because if lower-cost options are available, the price of higher-cost options comes down.

Tool #7: A New Federal Reserve

If you've been paying attention to this point, you had to know I'd be getting around to this one eventually.

The current Fed is an institution built by banks for banks. Its sole goal is to maintain the health and credibility of the banking system. This is obviously not legitimate anymore. The Federal Reserve needs a makeover.

It will be important to fill the board of this new institution with systems engineers, mathematicians, statisticians, scientists, commodity market makers—basically anyone smart who is not a banker. And most importantly! This is not an invitation to put politicians in charge of the Federal Reserve. They would do a worse job than the bankers.

The Federal Reserve and central banks around the world hold the future of humanity in their hands. It's time they started behaving accordingly.

The nature of how this institution works needs to change as well. No longer can the fate of humanity wait for a bunch of old Princeton economic graduates to make a decision about what is good for the banking system. Instead, algorithms will use real-time data to make adjustments to interest rates, savings rates, direct deposits, BlueSky markets, and all the tools available to it to ensure that humanity remains sustainable and prosperous.

The Federal Reserve will be driven by science, engineering, data, and math. It will need a new guidance document, which could initially just be a revamped monetary policy. And because the Federal Reserve is a private corporation, it might be possible to make these changes through presidential executive action.

In the long run, the Constitution needs to address what is essentially a fourth, equal but separate branch of government. Today, the Federal Reserve plays by its own rules called monetary policy. It is clear that monetary policy only serves the banks. The Founding Fathers created the Constitution to serve the people. The financial system that underpins society must in the same way follow the intent of the Constitution. And just like judges who are appointed to lifetime positions on the Supreme Court, so would engineers, scientists, data analysts, and people with other skill sets be appointed to optimize the financial system for the people.

Tool #8: A New International Currency

In today's economy, reserve currency and the currency of international trade is wasted. It serves no purpose other than making international trade into an "us versus them" dollar-dominance quagmire. The IMF, World Bank, and WTO are all complicit in the perpetuation of inequality and strife. The UN stands on the sidelines and watches, powerless, because it doesn't have any real tools to create liberty and peace.

Enter a globally accepted currency of trade and reserve. This currency would have a very high intrinsic value because countries would not be able to exchange it for another currency except for their own currency in order to stabilize it (which would be the case for some impoverished countries, at least in the early going of the Big Solution economy). The new currency would be in high demand because countries would use it to exchange goods and services. And it would have all the tools listed above to help it stabilize, persist, and be optimized.

Except in emergency situations—like natural disasters or a pandemic—this currency could not be issued for loans. Just like in the US, it would enter into existence in every country's economy by way of direct deposits to the citizens of all participating countries. This, in essence, ensures that the basic needs of all the people of the world can be met. We're talking about a direct deposit that is equal to two dollars a day, but this would be more than sufficient to completely wipe out extreme poverty worldwide. On the other hand, it is very likely that the direct deposits would be a lot more because it would drive business and efficiencies. And think about how this empowers people and makes governments look to serve their people to earn this currency! Pyongyang would no longer have the power to create famine and devastation. In essence, a Big Solution global currency (TBS) with direct deposit eliminates poverty, dictatorships, human trafficking, wasteful charities, most terrorism, and most war zones.

It would be easy to get countries to sign up. All they get is the benefit of their own people having money to spend. Why would a government not want that?

No more rich nations and poor. No more money flowing down a Jacuzzi pyramid. Everyone benefits from the same currency delivered in the same direct deposit fashion, with each country in control of the flow of its own currency and its own direct deposits so that they are never beholden to another richer country to control their economy.

And that's just the start! With an international direct deposit—based on this new, international, and independent reserve currency—every nation could do the real work necessary to fix the climate crisis and pursue any number of BlueSky markets of their own. BlueSky markets funded by this TBS currency would mean that countries would compete to remove CO_2 from the environment. Other BlueSky markets would emerge because the companies from that country would earn the TBS currency, making that country wealthier. Think about the implications of that …

On the individual level, there would be savings accounts with high interest rates. This would ensure that the currency would be in high demand, and that people could actually get ahead in life, no matter where they call home. Countries could also put this TBS money into savings to reduce spending and conserve the value of the currency.

As a massive added benefit, China could no longer manipulate its currency, because trade would not happen in dollars but in this new international TBS currency. Chinese companies could no longer pay slave wages to their workers. Chinese workers would have a choice to refuse to work in poor conditions. Child labor would disappear along with sweatshops.

It's also a well-known fact that countries that share resources also share peace. The more countries cooperate with each other, the more peaceful their relationship. This new TBS currency essentially makes the world cooperate and share resources on a level field. It means that when a man from China works ten hours a day, the German housewife in Munich benefits, because all work is now connected. A true global economy emerges, which will benefit everyone who receives the currency, works for it, and buys products and services with it. If you want world peace, this is how to get it.

But I'm getting a little ahead of myself here. This is what happens when I start to look ahead.

Connie: I like when you look ahead. It's sexy.

Laz: Right, then. Evan, that's our cue to get the hell out of here.

Evan: Right behind you …

Justin: Okay, so … So that's eight tools. All of them straightforward. All of them easy to understand. All of them easy to implement, as the only thing we need is motivation to make the change. It's all just about reimagining how we value money and restructuring how banks do business. This should be doable, everyone. Let me list the benefits:

World peace

The end of human trafficking

The end of poverty

The end of big issues like global warming, ocean acidification, plastic pollution …

The end of child labor and sweatshops

The end of terrorism

But before I start patting myself on the back, maybe we should kick around these ideas a bit by way of discussion.

Connie: Everyone left.

Justin: Oh. Right. Maybe you want to, like, go tell them to come back in? I'm not done with my list yet. You and I can catch up later.

Connie: Ugh! Where's the romance in this book?

CHAPTER THIRTEEN

THE BIG SOLUTION WORLD

God isn't coming back for the apocalypse. That's hell on Earth where the devil rules. God is coming back to the natural world that he built. God is coming back when we find a natural solution, the Big Solution.

—JUSTIN WOLFE

f I can start our big climactic chapter on a somewhat revolutionary tone, then I'd like to start our big climactic chapter on a somewhat revolutionary tone.

Connie: No arguments here. You're the one who asked for romance.

Justin: Wait, wasn't that you who asked for romance?

Connie: Fake news.

Justin: Fine, if I may begin …

J. P. Morgan's claim that money can only be credit is really just one example from history of how the manipulation of capital has been used to exploit the masses. It's no secret that the aristocracy and nobility classes have persisted through the generations because of familial wealth, a.k.a. money power. That wealth has ebbed and flowed over the centuries, but we're currently enduring a period where an enormous percentage of the wealth belongs to a small number of people. The twenty-first century, in fact, has ushered in the return of multigenerational wealth on a scale equal to that of the nineteenth century.

But here's the thing: money facilitates work between people. I do this if you do that. The beauty of the Trickle-Around Mountain analogy is that it shows two things: (1) how money is supposed to work, and (2) how J. P. Morgan's version of money causes money to actually work.

Here it is in a nutshell: money = human work. Credit ≠ human work. Credit is simply a notation in a ledger. It is information. This means banks wind up exchanging information for human work. The information is, in essence, worthless in terms of human work. Nobody has to do anything to make credit appear, except to keep the data.

This is a huge problem because banks looking out for their own interest will make loans for purposes that may very well not produce any value that anyone would actually want to work for. In other words, a bank will make a loan for the purpose of digging a big hole in the ground because they'll get the money back they loaned plus interest. The hole in the ground does nothing, but a rich person wanted to see thousands of workers slave away all day for next to nothing for his own entertainment.

None of the workers would dig a hole for the entertainment of this wealthy person, but they will do it for the money that was loaned to the wealthy person. You say, "Well, this is the rich person's prerogative. He got the bank to lend him money, so he can use it as he pleases."

There are several problems with this, though. First, if the rich person used his own cash or gold to pay people to dig holes, then that would be fine, but because he uses credit to do it, he's essentially exchanging nothing for the waste of limited resources. This is detrimental to everyone on the TAM.

Second, the TAM clearly shows that work done without the common good benefiting from it is in fact dangerous, because if everyone used all their efforts toward work that yielded no value, then everyone would suffer.

In the modern era, where interest rates are so low, the dynamic is even worse. The hole can be dug using negative interest rates. Negative interest rates mean that the wealthy person basically gets paid for his frivolous pursuit of entertainment through hole digging.

It should not be true that credit can be issued to simply anyone who can pay it back and issued for whatever purpose the borrower desires. Credit has a responsibility to society as a whole. Because banks control it, this means that banks also control the outcome and future for mankind. And since they are not taking responsibility for their power, that power must be taken away from them.

Laz: I'm ready for the revolution now, boss.

Connie: I get chills when you talk like this.

Justin: Keep your pants on, both of you, because I'm not done. Real estate is another element that gets bastardized here.

Asset holders buy properties because they go up in value faster than people can earn money. Many wealthy people just sit on assets and do nothing. They do this because assets are increasing in value faster than production can produce an equal amount of value. In other words, it's not worth working anymore when work has very little value compared to the rate of asset appreciation.

This is the same scenario that played out in the 1800s. The rich landowners wanting to protect and build their wealth controlled the money and laws. This forced people without land of their own to work the wealthy people's land, which in turn made the wealthy people wealthier.

The same thing is happening today, except instead of productive land, we're talking about housing. Rich people sit on those assets because they appreciate in value, which in turn leads young people and the working class to not be able to afford homes of their own. This forces them into rent situations, which only makes the wealthy wealthier.

Because the wealthy aren't working, and because the work that banks are causing to get done doesn't promote the common good, everyone suffers. The whole system isn't self-balancing, sustainable, or in the slightest bit fair.

So, why bring up our old friend J. P.? Because in this new age of aristocracy, credit is no different than inherited wealth. Just like familial wealth, credit is not worked for. It's just there for the taking.

For hundreds of years, money has been used to control the working man, and for that same period of time, the working man has been less educated than the aristocracy. Today, the picture is slightly different: money is still used to control people, but more people are educated than ever before, and the internet is there to explain anything.

Given this shift in dynamic, the time has come to end capital's control over people. The time has come for people to come first and banks, aristocratic capital, and the damned stock market to come last. It's time to flip the script, to make capital support people before it supports debt and capital assets like real estate, corporations, and asset appreciation. Now remember, this is beneficial to the producers, the entrepreneurs, a.k.a. the job creators, because

The time has come to end capital's control over people.

it opens up new markets of opportunity, it lowers tax rates, and it reduces the size of the government. This means capitalism for the purpose of production will be better than ever.

You want some motivation to get started on this bloodless little revolution?

Okay, fine. Here it is: money is still being used to make the rich richer and keep the poor poor. The system is such that if asset values don't go up, then banks won't be able maintain the money supply. Why does this matter? Because the working class needs the money supply the most, and when the supply is insufficient, it's the working class that gets hurt the most. Really, it should be banks that suffer the consequences of this, but they have that nice golden parachute at hand. Whenever the economy goes wrong, the Fed reacts by saving the banking system and the money supply through quantitative easing, which makes assets even more valuable.

Think about that garbage in simpler, bolder terms: we're being asked to believe that the only way to help the poor through economic collapse is to make the rich even richer. We are also accepting that the only way to grow the economy is to take on more debt. The last time I checked, the definition of an indentured servant is any person who is obligated by contract to perform work or make a payment of value. Is anyone really okay with the entirety of the human race being indentured to the banking system?

The results are predictable: as the debt mounts, the ability to maintain the money supply becomes more and more difficult, and working people ultimately suffer. Because there isn't enough money to go around, people have to work for less so that debt payments can be made.

Are you still not feeling the revolution? Okay, how about we compare the automation dynamic to slavery?

Slavery was tremendously beneficial to banks. A landowner could go into town and tell a banker he wanted a loan to buy some slaves. The bank knew the deal. The slaves would work the land, the land would yield crops and profit, and then the bank would get its money back plus interest.

Banks love automation in a similar way. A business owner can go to their megabank and say he would like a loan to buy some machines that could automate a portion of his company's work. The bank knows the deal. The machines work the assembly line, the business yields products and profit, and then the bank gets its money back plus interest.

This dynamic has led to a drastic drag on workers' wages. How else can the average worker compete with a machine, other than accepting barely above starvation rates? He's literally working against a machine that doesn't get paid. It's a modern slave but worse, because it doesn't eat, sleep, or require anything at all. In this way, using credit to pay workers who would starve or die without the wage they earn is really no different than slave labor or forced labor camps.

Laz: You're preaching to the choir with me on this subject, boss. But how do we end this dynamic?

Justin: Only when people have access to their essential liberty— enough money to ensure that they can live—can we end this modern version of slave labor or forced labor.

Evan: How would changing our thinking about money fix this?

Justin: When J. P. Morgan made the statement about credit and gold in the early 1900s, the role of capital in the manipulation of the masses was alive and well. What most people don't realize is that it is alive and well today. They just don't see it because they are told that what happens to their economy is their fault.

The Big Solution (TBS) is all about showing people how capital needs to work, not only to prevent human suffering, but also to solve the biggest challenges currently facing humanity. And most importantly, how to maximize prosperity, production, and the value of work while minimizing the cost of living and the size of government.

Connie: And we do all that by eliminating money as a function of debt?

Justin: In this new context we outlined in the previous chapter, capital no longer serves the purpose of the banking system. Capital becomes an engineering tool that now serves the purpose of society and humanity. It becomes a means of creating a better world. Engineered capital is not like communism or socialism. It's more like the freedom acquired from an engineered car compared to a car that is not engineered. In other words, all the problems a car has when it is poorly engineered are exactly like all the problems humanity is facing because the use of capital (human work) is not engineered. Rather, it is mindlessly deployed for the banking system.

Because capital wants to exploit labor, it should be no surprise that when the need for labor is reduced or removed by technology, that capital has no use for labor. Thanks to the advancement of technology, the postlabor world is here. If people do not wise up and use their education now, capital will return people to the living conditions of peasants from the 1800s. If the purpose of money and capital is not for all people, then the people who control it will give nothing to those who don't.

Connie: How about you break it down for us?

Justin: Great idea. The tools provided in chapter 12 offered a schematic of sorts, one that we can use to dismantle the Trickle-Around Mountain, the Jacuzzi pyramid, the banking system, and the Federal Reserve's role in the global banking system. I don't mean this in the sense that the tools will cause these things to disappear, but in the sense that their impact on our world and society will be drastically reduced.

In other words, the existing business system will remain—along with all the many companies and businesses in this country and the world at large. The difference is that none of these companies and businesses will be dependent on Trickle-Around Mountains any longer. There will be no need for the jets pumping the water into the Jacuzzi. There will no longer be any water sucked out of the Jacuzzi from bank payments and payments into savings accounts and so on.

Instead—and this is an important part—the water pumping into the Jacuzzi and flowing around the mountain will represent work rather than debt. We'll see the same amount of water flowing around; it'll just come from a different kind of jet.

This is the fundamental thesis of the Big Solution: we do not need banks to control the economy. In fact, we need banks to not control the economy so that we can have a stable economy, so that we are not dependent on banks for the water we all need to survive and thrive. We need to engineer the work that we do collectively through free market mechanisms and the deployment of capital in order to achieve sustainability, liberty, and prosperity.

> **This is the fundamental thesis of the Big Solution: we do not need banks to control the economy.**

A New Analogy

You know what? I'm kind of struggling with this whole water/jets thing. We've had poisoned ponds, Trickle-Around Mountains, and Jacuzzi pyramids to describe the existing economic system. So I think we need a new analogy to explain how the Big Solution economy would work.

Evan? You on that?

Evan: That's a tough row to hoe, Justin.

Justin: Did you just say a "tough row to hoe"?

Evan: Hey, I'm from farming country. What can I say?

Justin: Okay, Grandpa, it's a tough row to hoe. Too much for you to handle, then?

Evan: Now, I definitely didn't say that. I'm just going to need to think about it for a while, really. The Big Solution solves the TAM and the Jacuzzi pyramid, and it allows people to live naturally and have what they need to survive just like the frogs in that pond ecosystem or the woodsman of yesteryear.

Justin: That's right! I forgot about the woodsman. Man, we've got some analogies in this book.

Evan: And here you want another.

Justin: Lay it on me.

Evan: So the problem here is that we need to work with a new construct. The Big Solution essentially introduces a new way for money to move. Where before everyone was stuck on the mountain and in their place on the pyramid, these direct deposits, BlueSky markets, and all the other tools you introduced in the last chapter will essentially render the pyramid irrelevant and create a new self-adapting mountain that serves society and humanity.

You know what it's like? It's like we're now looking at money as energy. It's about looking at money as energy for the purpose of sustaining human life. If we think about money as behaving like energy, then we can begin to study and influence it in the same way that other sciences study and influence energy. We can borrow principles of thermodynamics, for instance, to predict how this new version of money will behave.

On the other hand, that's probably more complicated than it needs to be, because, as you point out, this new money is actually just plain old information. And information does not need to follow any sort of laws at all. It is completely free form in the sense that you can make it whatever you want it to be.

There are absolutely no limitations on information. Quantum mechanics allows it to span the universe instantaneously. Recent experiments have even suggested that information can be made to travel backward in time.

Justin: That sounds a bit more complicated than it needs to be too.

Evan: Okay, then what about starting with your original idea that money is work and then we walk that off into the whole money-as-information concept?

Justin: Show us how this would work.

Evan: Imagine an old lady who needs to dig a hole. Let's say this old lady hired a young man to do the digging. Now, if money was in fact work, then from a physics perspective, the fee would be equivalent to the amount of kilojoules the young man would require to take the dirt out and make a mound of dirt on one side next to the hole.

But money isn't that kind of work, because it's not about kilojoules or energy or anything. It's about this older woman who couldn't dig the hole herself because she's not strong enough. The man, who is strong enough and who wanted the money that the old woman was willing to pay him, agreed to perform the work. So in reality, the work is really this idea that the woman had a need for a hole.

Why does she need the hole to be dug? Well, she has this big shrub she wants to plant in the hole. And she has the man make a hole for the shrub, put that shrub in the hole, put the dirt back around it, and let the shrub take root. Basically, at the end of it, from a physics perspective, the energy required was really just moving a tree a couple of feet and moving some dirt a couple of feet. Let's imagine it took the worker an hour to dig the hole, half an hour to plant the shrub, and half an hour to finish the job, and so on. So he charges the old lady for two hours of labor. In this case, yes, the money changing hands could be defined by the energy it took to do the work, or by the hours it took to perform the labor, but it all started with information.

None of this work happens without the woman's idea, that information about how she wanted her yard to look. So her hiring of the young man was basically an exchange of information. It was an exchange of the value of money for the value of how her yard would look, both of which, from an energy and a physics of work perspective, added up to basically nothing. But the woman got what she wanted in terms of information and what she now gets to see in front of her house on a daily basis. And the man got what he wanted, which was an amount of money that he could spend on other things. So in essence, it was only information that these two people exchanged.

If you think of money just as information, then you don't have to lash that money to a system of global banking rules that limit its potential. You can do whatever you like with information. Just as the woman wanted her yard to look better, the Big Solution's money could be used to make life better for as many people as possible for as long as possible.

Justin: There is one more concept here that taps into my engineering education. This is wild, as it really destroys the status quo and drives home the need for change.

When money is understood as work and energy organizing it as information (kind of like a database), it allows engineering techniques and methods to be applied. This means we can move out of the dark ages where human suffering is necessary, global warming is a necessary evil, and so on. Why? Look what my fellow engineers did with the automobile. In one hundred years of applied science and engineering, the automobile went from the Model T to a Tesla, with hundreds of other finely tuned feats of automotive engineering along the way. Engineering on this level does not remove freedoms; it enhances them, cultivates them, and makes sure everyone has them.

Think about an engineered economy as transportation. Without engineering, you're stuck riding horses around or you're just walking. Engineering makes driving around in a car, or motorcycle, or even a simple bicycle possible. Each one of those engineered devices enhances freedom. An engineered economy is freedom engineered. It means peace can be engineered. Sustainability can be engineered.

Furthermore, the response to the pandemic does not have to come from the government. Instead, the mountain reshapes itself so that people can be productive from home. Besides the direct deposit ensuring that people can maintain their essential liberty right at home, the BlueSky money could reward people for strengthening their immune system so the virus could be beat without a vaccine. BlueSky money could also be used to construct large-scale, real-time data collection about why the virus spreads, what stops it from spreading, what stops it from making people sick, and what allows the body to recover quickly after showing symptoms.

How would this work? It's a bit geeky, but for a geek, it's awesome. It would start with a BlueSky-funded wiki, where data entry, supervision, and coding become freelance work perpetuated by BlueSky funds distributed via a commodity work exchange. This means infinite productive work that continuously expands the human knowledge base, and it can be applied to services for businesses and individuals, making work so easy to get done for those who need it done. It basically takes the wiki infrastructure that already exists and applies it to the exchange of work so that anything can be done by applying money to the wiki module. This idea of the economy conforming to the needs of the people instead of the people conforming to the needs of a banking

THE BIG SOLUTION WORLD

system (that has no purpose) is truly amazing. This is why the social science of economics is so dangerous, because blaming people for everything hides the culprit (the banking system) in the shadows.

Evan: Okay, you had to do it, didn't you? You had to go and make engineers look like superheroes and make economists look like Neanderthals. In order to save face, I'm going to have to one-up you with an analogy. What we have are car parts that don't fit together. We have advanced fuel injectors, turbo chargers, and high-octane gasoline, but we can't put them all together because we're not allowed to engineer the car. An engineered economy could easily mean that the combined value of the S&P, NASDAQ, and Dow would reach 1 million by 2030. Maybe we're writing this book for the Wall Street folks who are being deprived of massive valuation from BlueSky earnings, productivity gains, and a badass economy.

Justin: I think this resolves the Trickle-Around Mountain, but we're all still forgetting about the Jacuzzi pyramid. This new understanding of money as information could solve a number of problems, but we still have a hierarchy on this planet that will need to be reimagined as something more equitable. What does the Jacuzzi pyramid look like in this new world?

Evan: What does a direct deposit look like in the Jacuzzi? I think it looks like this.

We're no longer imagining money being injected into the American economy like water jets. Now it's like it's raining down from the sky in the form of direct deposits. In this way, the water distributes evenly to every country, rather than having to trickle down from one country to another. The pyramid construct would no longer exist. It would just be a collection of Jacuzzis standing side by side.

In America, with its massive economy, there would still be some spillover of water, but this just becomes more money and growth for other nations, rather than an overwhelming rush of cast-off water. This overflow doesn't hurt the US, and it doesn't harm other countries either. It only leads to faster growth for nations in need of growth. There are still massive amounts of US dollar debt in the world, debts that would continue to be paid. This will keep the demand for the dollar strong for a very long time.

On the other hand, when we were discussing the Jacuzzi pyramid earlier, we pointed out how impoverished countries suffered from water overflowing in their system because there was nowhere for the money to go. The hyperinflation experienced by these countries was what kept them in poverty in the first place. Wouldn't more money falling down like rain only exacerbate the problem?

No. In fact, it would help balance these economies and stave off hyperinflation. How?

The problem that these impoverished countries currently face is that there is no global demand for their currency. In their cases, the way out that the Big Solution provides is through every country's ability to adjust interest rates on savings accounts. If these poorer countries offer higher rates on their savings accounts—accounts that, again, are frozen in a way that prevents banks from reinvesting the money or issuing it as loans—then more people are compelled to take that money out of the Jacuzzi and stash it in a bank. This prevents the Jacuzzi from overflowing, raises the value of the country's currency, and incentivizes people to save more money. Slowly but surely, a formerly poor country sees its citizens getting wealthier and wealthier. Add to this idea that the international currency raining into their economy would provide a mechanism for wealth building and trade with other nations. These economies would quickly prosper because they could finally participate in the global economy. The international currency would allow them to prevent their own currency from hyperinflating as well.

Thinking of this new version of money as rainfall instead of jets also helps illustrate your BlueSky markets concept, in that rain doesn't just fall for citizens; it also rains for industries.

Some rain could go to CO_2 sequestration, as you pointed out. This is where a pound of carbon that a company puts underground could be worth, say, one dollar. So it rains one dollar for every pound of carbon put underground by these companies. Why would they not be incentivized to bury CO_2? This would all take place via an exchange that would make companies and countries compete to remove CO_2 from the air.

Okay, but where's this money coming from? Directly from the Fed, or in the case of the international currency, the World Bank. If money is just information, then it can be pulled from thin air. It can fall like rain.

If the rainfall starts in America, it doesn't matter how much money we pump into it because if the water overflows, it trickles over to other countries that need that water anyway. But if it does start becoming problematic inflation, then they still have controls over these jets. And they can also start creating higher-interest savings accounts that do not get recirculated.

So suddenly, you have this ability for countries to fix global problems by creating these BlueSky markets that didn't exist before.

In this case, it's like the Fed saying, "Well, if you clean up the CO_2 out of the air, then magically you will get paid for it." And where does the money come from? Either the American banks are loaning less money because of higher interest rates on savings accounts or just higher interest rates on loans. Or it is because the economies of other countries need the international currency anyway in order to pay their debts or keep their currency from devaluing.

The other way to control instability among the Jacuzzis would be to have variable interest rates. For instance, why should solar panels have the same interest rate loans as the oil and gas industry? It makes no sense to give a world-bettering technology the same rate as one that creates pollutants. So you can have discounted interest rates for certain industries that create a favorable, sustainable future.

There really is no end to the global problems we can solve just by dismantling the way we think about money and banking.

Connie Does Not Care for Thinking Globally

Connie: You can probably guess where I'm going with that last statement of yours.

Evan: How will we ever put America first in this new system?

Connie: Bingo, egghead.

Justin: That's the true beauty of this Big Solution. While America will certainly lead the way, there is no reason to think of things in terms of a Jacuzzi hierarchy anymore. If we establish an international currency that every country values in the same way, then there are no longer any such things as rich nations and poor nations. Every country's resources can be used to better their own economic standing. Genuine growth happens across the board, and shortages disappear.

Connie: How do we know those shortages don't just get redistributed to other countries—like ours, for instance?

Justin: The world is abundant in resources. Contrary to what you might have heard, there is plenty of food, materials, land, water, and energy—anything the human race needs. It's just that we've adhered to an economic system that creates false shortages.

There's something just shockingly wonderful about this concept, Connie: it renders the whole idea of putting one country first—or at the top of the Jacuzzi pyramid, as it were—unnecessary and completely irrelevant. And when there is no longer a hierarchy, and there are no longer have countries and have-not countries, nearly every kind of global conflict you can imagine simply disappears.

Trade wars? Why would we have trade wars any longer? Every country has what it needs to trade on a fair and equal level, using the same baseline currency to trade with, and that currency benefits every country that participates in the exact same way—power to the people.

Terrorism? If you have currency distributed in small amounts through direct deposits or essential liberty (just enough to ensure that every person on the planet has enough to live), then you drastically reduce and probably eventually eliminate terrorism. How? First, you no longer have one country wanting to fight another country for resources or because their resources were exploited by another country, which reduces the opportunity for propagandistic hatred between competing sects. Further, on an individual level, the motivation for terrorism is blunted because fewer desperate people means fewer people willing and able to submit to extremist reeducation. When your essential needs are being met, the concept that you're better off dying for a cause than continuing to live is a lot less compelling.

Connie: So, what? We're all just about to throw away our American dollars and start using this international currency of yours?

Justin: Not at all! The international currency would not replace or displace any country's own currency. It's just an additional, international currency. What that means is that shops throughout the world would take their own country's currency and this international currency. This allows each country to retain its sovereignty to control its own money.

Having these separate currencies furthers a country's ability to curtail trade wars, terrorism, and war over resources as well. If you have the stabilizing factor of the international currency, and you can control the value of your own currency (thereby controlling productivity), then all of a sudden every country is on the same plane. Very quickly, every country winds up benefiting from international trade and not falling victim to the American dollar serving as the almighty currency. That even playing field prevents any country from leveraging its currency to manipulate the resources of any another country.

Rather than having to worry about who is first and who is last, the international currency gets distributed to every single citizen on the planet, in every single country, and the global trading platform becomes fair.

The Dictatorship Problem

Justin: Laz? I see you've got your hand up. Thank you for playing by the rules, bud.

Laz: You're assuming every country would want to play by these rules. What about North Korea? What happens when you've got hermit-state dictators trying to use their share of the international currency to further their nuclear weapons program?

Justin: There's a simple answer to that, and it goes back to the ability to delete money from the ledger. "Listen, North Korea. You don't want to play along in our efforts to create a more peaceful, better world? Then you're no longer included in these payments. And in fact, the money you've already collected no longer exists."

Meanwhile, over time, direct deposits to individuals rather than nation-states ensures that the people of every nation are empowered to make their own lives what they want them to be. The government—even a totalitarian government—eventually becomes subservient to the spending power of the people. It completely flips the script. It's no longer about some dictator sitting high up in his palace, overwhelming his people with military might and forced starvation. People with

THE BIG SOLUTION WORLD

enough money to survive suddenly have the power to say what the government needs to do for them.

Sure, there would be hurdles to overcome, but in the long run, this disempowers dictators, Laz. And, Connie, there's something in this message for you to love, too: it reduces the role of government in everyone's lives. It grants people the freedom (the genuine, actual, unfettered freedom) to pursue happiness, no matter what country they call home. Ultimately, the Big Solution empowers people in a way that removes these costly conflicts between dictators and other countries, but also the trade wars between superpowers like China and the United States. There is no longer a need to worry about putting America first, because in this system, the people of the world come first in every country that participates.

And, Connie, how about that wall your boss never quite got around to building? If people have what they need everywhere, then the whole idea of claiming refugee status and seeking asylum is a nonissue. Because no matter where you are, your essential needs are covered. It's the end of the global refugee crises.

The China Problem

Evan: I know I've been doing this a lot lately, but if I can play devil's advocate again for a second ...

Justin: Advocate away. It's fun trying to poke holes in this thing.

Evan: What's to prevent China from continuing with its well-publicized currency manipulation and undermining the whole system?

Justin: That's a really fun question because it raises another: why has China been so successful in its trade war with the US, despite Connie's boss's blustery efforts to "win" that trade war?

The only reason—the one and only reason!—China is winning

this trade war is because it is able to manipulate its currency to devalue its own currency. But if there's an international currency of trade distributed with direct deposits, this completely prevents that same kind of manipulation from taking place.

If the whole world is basing its trade on an international currency that everyone values the same way, then it no longer matters what China does with its own money. China is forced onto a level playing field.

Meanwhile, the Chinese people are empowered by these direct deposits, which, as we just discussed, forces the government and the most powerful companies run by or alongside that government to stop all these human rights abuses. You can't force slave labor on a populace that has enough money to live without having to give in to big business's manipulative exploitation. These companies will be forced to increase wages if they want to keep people working.

Laz: If all that's true, then I can see this helping poor and oppressed people around the world.

Justin: Absolutely! With the right configuration, this international currency could be used to directly finance BlueSky markets throughout the world. This would in turn motivate nations to set up the exchanges as fast as possible.

It's this kind of thing that should allow all of us to take in a breath of fresh air, because with this kind of power at humanity's fingertips, the global climate disaster has a solution, and it's one that could be accomplished quickly.

The Wealth and Labor Problems

Connie: I've heard enough about global warming already. How does this help people on the ground?

Justin: Okay, fine. You want to be a right-winger and focus on money and work?

In the Bankism system, whenever goods or labor becomes too expensive, the answer is always, "We need to raise interest rates so people get fired and there's not enough money to buy goods and employ people." Obviously people suffer when that happens.

Especially the poor! Why? Because technology competes with labor, and the more competition labor has, the less pay workers get. With technology and low interest rates going on endlessly, there is almost never enough work to go around—and certainly not important, decent-paying work.

In order for wages really to substantially go up, there just isn't enough work, and whenever work is created, technology quickly comes in and replaces any inflationary pressure on wages.

In a Big Solution world, you no longer need this terrible "fix" that is raising interest rates to eliminate jobs because modern technology is a deflationary factor that keeps the cost of goods sold low on its own. Meanwhile, all these BlueSky markets that result from an increase in consumer demand creates more employment opportunities even in a world with more and more automation.

Put another way, now we have a situation where, even as automation continues to expand, full employment is possible.

Laz: Wait. Full employment? Like, everyone has a job?

Evan: It sounds like fiction, but this is an actual possibility, that you can have everybody who wants a job to have a job. And all without inflation, because once something costs too much, as long as there are enough companies competing with each other, automation will cause the price of things to either stay the same or come down. There's more. Just because people are earning more doesn't mean they're spending more. The high-interest savings accounts keep money out of circulation, preventing inflation while building wealth for the poor. Retiring in style will be all the rave.

Justin: In a Big Solution world, labor is no longer the driver of inflation or deflation. Technology and money supply are. And because we can optimize the economy by using engineering techniques, jobs can be the feature that is optimized both in terms of increased wages and the number of jobs available.

Laz: You mentioned the wealth gap, which is obviously one of the biggest problems of our time. How would the Big Solution narrow the divide between rich and poor?

Justin: Great question, Laz. How on earth do we narrow that gap without some kind of massive redistribution of wealth? People always say, "You can't stop poverty." But those people are thinking in Trickle-Around Mountain terms, where rich and poor are coded into the system. They aren't a bug; they're a feature.

The wealth gap is essentially the same thing. In order for banks to be able to circulate more money into the economy, you've got to have rich people paying a lot more for assets that are leveraged toward loans. So having wealthy people is a very important part of the system. The poor are just not really that important when it comes to this economy, except for in the sense that they provide cheap labor.

In a Big Solution system, we're not taking any money away from the rich; we're simply empowering everyone—rich, poor, and everyone between—with the means to take care of their most basic needs. The Big Solution allows poor people to acquire wealth, which means everyone becomes wealthier now. That's a win-win.

What About These Never-Ending Wars?

Justin: Evan, you look ready to jump out of your shoes.

Evan: I've just been waiting and waiting to get around to the less obvious fixes the Big Solution provides, but we keep getting wrapped up in money and work.

Justin: All right. What problem would you like to hear solved?

Evan: How does the Big Solution end all war?

Connie: You certainly do aim high, Ev.

Justin: He's right to. Because while I can't guarantee world peace, it is harder to imagine the level or frequency of international conflict in a Big Solution world.

That global currency we've been kicking around would effectively end wars—at least as we know them. Think about it: out of the Great Depression came Nazi Germany. Hitler told suffering Germans that he would make Germany Great Again.

Connie: Watch it …

Justin: Sorry to be flip, but the point is solid. WWII started in large part because Hitler gained power from people who felt desperate for help. WWI started because of a lack of capital and the competition for resources.

Obviously, the world wars are extreme examples. But name a conflict that didn't start because one side or the other (or both) had a desperate need.

With a global currency based on the Big Solution system, we eliminate desperate need. When people have what they need, then they are far less willing to be manipulated into fighting each other. Conversely, a global currency effectively makes everyone work for each other. Because when work is done for the purpose of earning the international currency, then it increases the value of that currency. And because debt is not allowed in this currency, any increase in its value (or work done to earn it) means that every single person on Earth benefits equally. It basically puts the whole world on the same team without having to have everyone in the same country or under the same government.

Okay, What About Corruption?

Evan: If I can go twice in a row, I have another one.

Justin: Shoot.

Evan: I was just reading an article recently that has me thinking about the Panama Papers.

Justin: Ah, tax havens! This should interest you, too, Connie.

Connie: You are correct.

Justin: Believe it or not, this does happen every once in a while.

Connie: Explain the tax haven thing, smartass.

Justin: Presently, countries compete for tax revenues by making laws that accommodate corporate profits without taxation. Enter Tool #4: Deletion.

The great thing about deletion is that it doesn't matter if we're deleting profit or not. If you move a large volume of money, a little bit of it disappears. Now all of a sudden, tax cheats and money laundering benefits everyone ...

Laz: Say what, now?

Justin: Money laundering is the largest industry in the world. Money deletion causes illegal activity, corrupt intentions, and tax avoidance to benefit everyone.

Stay with me on this. Because of the electronic nature of information, any large transaction in the Big Solution world has to be coordinated through the general ledger of money. The general ledger, when notified of a large movement of money, will automatically delete a small amount of that money. In essence, all the people of the world thereby benefit from all the corruption taking place in today's offshore accounts, tax havens, and money laundering.

Connie: But how can deleting money be a good thing? Don't we need it to pay down debt? You promised me this solution would eventually eliminate the debt …

Justin: The value of money is more important than getting rid of debt. The first task in getting rid of debt is to stop Bankism from forcing the economy to use loans to sustain the money supply. As soon as direct deposits are put in place, loans based on credit won't be necessary.

The second task is to reduce the size of government. When direct deposits are in place, the government can remove, piece by piece, its safety nets. This will reduce its costs and allow it to pay off its debts.

Third, the deletion of money prevents corruption, tax avoidance, and illegal activity to the benefit of all people.

How About the Most Broken of Broken Systems?

Laz: We're all ignoring the elephant in the room.

Justin: Solid tie-in to our opening analogy.

Laz: Thanks. But what about healthcare?

Justin: I should've seen that one coming!

If the TAM shows us that money, when exchanged between people, is human work, then it's clear that if a greater and greater amount of human work goes toward treating sick people, the best way to eliminate the healthcare issue is to keep more people healthy.

The American healthcare system will continue to look at anything—any chronic disease, any age-related disease, or any disease that occurs over time—as opportunity. We're not talking about acute care; we're talking about chronic care. The Bankism economy wants to develop a solution in pill form or in the form of a medical device.

Think about it! Dementia, heart disease, Alzheimer's—one of the fundamental problems or causes for all of these conditions is lifestyle, and we're all living on a TAM lifestyle.

Laz: You're saying that modern medicine can't build a pill for getting through the stressful life that Bankism causes.

Justin: So many of us are on pills of one type or another! And that's the point. Just like poverty, as long as Bankism and the Trickle-Around Mountain exist, we're stuck. Throw whatever political solution you want at it, but the healthcare system can't be fixed until we get rid of the TAM.

I mean, 70 percent of government spending is either poverty related or healthcare related. And of the total economy, around 20 percent is healthcare related. When you add all this up, it starts to look like the whole economy is basically working to fix the problems Bankism causes. It's like everybody is just chasing problems.

There is only a better life, an easier life, and an easier way to pay your bills. This lowers stress. This frees you up to take better care of yourself. This frees up money to help you eat better and get some exercise. Do these things eliminate chronic disease? No. But they cut down on their occurrence considerably. All of these illnesses have roots in lifestyle problems, and all these lifestyle problems are caused by the Trickle-Around Mountain.

In an advanced Big Solution world, BlueSky markets are created for longevity. Think about it. If you don't get sick, you won't die, and your quality of life will remain high. The reason scientists haven't figured out how to make people live longer is that they are looking for the solution in a pill instead of considering that the economy is causing all the illnesses.

What's It Gonna Take?

Connie: You say that last part as if it's easy. Just wave a magic wand and—poof!—the TAM is gone.

Justin: You're right, Connie. We've spent all this time discussing the problems with Bankism and the world in general. We've identified a three-headed monster that keeps people entrenched in their existing beliefs. But there's a bigger hurdle in front of us: people prefer to believe whatever makes them feel good about themselves.

In this day and age, the biggest challenge of all is bursting through the bubbles we have all created around ourselves—that comforting sphere that makes us feel right and justified and good.

And that's really all any of us wants—to feel good about ourselves. A person who gets to live off the money from his parents and has never worked a day in his life usually feels better than a poor person who has to work two jobs to survive. As disturbing as this is, it's exactly this formula for people's beliefs that perpetuates the acceptance of current systems and that slow return to aristocracy I mentioned at the start of this chapter.

People want to believe that it's the poor people who are at fault for their lot in life, all because it makes them feel better about themselves. This isn't conjecture; this has been proven time and time again in psychological studies.

Connie: So how do we break through?

Justin: Admittedly, that's the part I haven't quite worked out yet. I like to believe that it's all just a matter of showing people a more positive way to think.

When I think about the many ways the Big Solution can fix this country and the world at large, I like to imagine a future where technology always contributes to the common good, both for poor people and rich people (and hey, how about all the people in between?).

A future where politicians have more than just bad options/decisions to address.

A future where jobs are not precious, but instead ubiquitous and not thought of simply as a means to prevent inflation.

A future where supermarkets aren't throwing out 60 percent of their produce while people just up the street from the supermarket go hungry.

A future where five million children don't die a poverty-related death on an annual basis.

A future where the bottom 25 percent of the population no longer have absolutely nothing in their savings, and instead they have the means to continue saving as the years go by, build wealth, and retire in style.

A future where savings accounts yield a handsome return and not the insulting near-zero interest rates of modern times.

A future free of never-ending war and terrorism, one with drastically reduced rates of suicide, overdose, and mass shootings.

A future where the environment is no longer cast aside just so we can scrape to make the economy work.

A future where decisions are made for the sustainability of our well-being as a people.

But in the end, it's all still just imagination. For that future to become a reality, people have to embrace the idea. Then we have to act.

They say a good story should transform the main character from the beginning to the end. The main character must evolve into something more. The main character in this book is not me, Justin Wolfe. It's you, the reader. If this book is successful, you will have changed. You will have been freed from the rope that has been holding humanity down. You will be empowered and motivated to cut this rope that holds us down.

If this book is successful, you will have changed. You will have been freed from the rope that has been holding humanity down.

You now have this book as your guide, and hopefully you have cut your rope. Every friend of yours that you get to read this book is the equivalent of a pair of scissors snipping another rope. Freedom can only come when the majority of people have cut themselves free. So let's get to work. There are a lot of ropes to cut.

HOW DO WE ACT?

Alone we can do so little; together we can do so much.

—HELEN KELLER

Justin: Evan, you look like shit.

Evan: I've got to tell you, Justin, I haven't slept much since our last conversation.

Justin: Why the hell not? You should feel like celebrating, man. The book is done. We've solved all the world's problems.

Evan: It's like you said at the end of the last chapter, though. We haven't actually solved these problems. We've just presented a solution. It's going to be up to people to act. How do we get them to do that?

Justin: We can't make them act. We just have to hope they read the book and are motivated to act on their own.

Evan: I guess that's the real reason I'm not sleeping, then. What if nobody reads the book? What if nobody engages with the idea? Then what do we do?

Justin: You can be a real downer, you know that?

Evan: What can I say? I'm a trained economist.

Justin: Funny.

Evan: Justin, we've built a farm. We fought hard for it. The woman I love died for it. Now we've written this book. But we're still just hoping this book catches on. We can't just sit around and hope. We have to do something. What do we do?

Justin: Yeah, I've been thinking about that.

Evan: You could run for president.

Justin: Don't even joke about that.

Evan: Who's joking?

Justin: No. I watched Trump do it for long enough that I know being a rich guy is way more fun than being a rich guy in the White House. Just no. Never gonna happen. Not in a million years.

Evan: So what, then?

Justin: I've been thinking there are several approaches that will work. The first is to go on a book tour to promote *The Big Solution*. Who knows? Maybe that's all it'll take.

Evan: Are you kidding? People don't even bother leaving reviews. It's like it's too much to ask to save our world.

Justin: Maybe they don't know how much a five-star written review means to the success of the book.

Evan: It's amazing. If every reader who gets this Big Solution told three of their friends … the world would change in due course. Or how about if they send it to their representative? Eventually, they would have to read it.

Justin: So … know anyone who could help us market the book and build a movement through a book tour?

Evan: Maybe. But first, we'll need to find someone in power willing to help us. In fact, we need to build a following. We need to start a movement.

Justin: Yes, we need people to participate. We need to name this movement, this book tour. How about Optimizing America?

Evan: Now that sounds like a movement! And it's an engineering term as well, which ties everything together. What are we waiting for? I'll set up an email address for people who want to get engaged. How about connect@optimizingamerica.com? We'll add it to the end of the book so readers can just email us and let us know how they can help and we can let them know what we are up to.

Justin: Brilliant. Let's do this.